C000136894

Dylan Remembered

In memory of R. Selwyn Davies and J.V. Davies

Dylan Remembered

Volume One 1914-1934

Edited by David N. Thomas

Interviews by Colin Edwards
Transcriptions by Joan Miller

seren
in association with
The National Library of Wales

Seren is the book imprint of
Poetry Wales Press Ltd
Nolton Street, Bridgend, Wales
www.seren-books.com

Interviews © The Interviewees and
the National Library of Wales
Editorial, Introduction, Chapters 1-8 and
Appendices © David N. Thomas, 2003
Maps and family trees © Jacky Piqué

First published in 2003
ISBN 1-85411-342-9 hbk
ISBN 1-85411-348-8 pbk
A CIP record for this title is available
from the British Library

All rights reserved. No part of this publication may be
reproduced, stored in a retrieval system, or transmitted at
any time or by any means electronic, mechanical,
photocopying, recording or otherwise without the prior
permission of the copyright holder.

*The publisher works with the financial
assistance of the Welsh Books Council*

Cover image: Sketch by Oloff de Wet, 1951

Printed in Plantin by Bell & Bain, Glasgow

Contents

Maps, Family Trees and Photographs

Introduction

The two volumes of *Dylan Remembered*, of which this is the first, contain memories of Dylan Thomas, spoken on tape by his family, friends, teachers and colleagues. The recordings, which were largely made within fifteen years of Dylan's death, were carried out by Colin Edwards, a radio journalist and documentary film maker.

Edwards lived in California, but he returned to Wales almost every year. In July 1958, he paid a visit to one of his cousins, Mrs Tilly Roberts. Tilly had been friendly with Dylan when they were teenagers:

> He used to come here and we'd sit on the stairs and philosophise about life for hours. The man had more sense in his little finger than most people have in their whole bodies ... He was a very kind man I think, and he was very sincere ... talked about life, always about life, and the very ordinary people – and the more ordinary the better. I think he just wanted to be himself. And everybody else to be himself, and to live in peace. We used to talk about people being natural and to be one's self always ... I often think now, if there were more people like Dylan Thomas, the world would be much better ... Perhaps we were too serious. We talked about conditions in the world and how to improve them but he did not visualise the solution in political terms.[1]

Tilly knew Dylan's mother, Florence, and she asked if Edwards could come and talk with her. A few weeks later, he called on Florence, now living alone in the Boat House in Laugharne. They quickly established that there were already a number of connections between Edwards and the Thomas family. Edwards was also a cousin of Jackie Bassett, Dylan's boyhood friend: family members, wrote Edwards, recalled that Jackie and Dylan came "to visit my great-grandmother at our family home, a combined farm and mill in Pontybrenin [Kingsbridge]..." The two boys kept coming back to the mill, continued Edwards, "through most of their boyhood." The mill was Loughor Mill; Brinley Edwards, Colin's father, wrote to his son about it, describing Dylan's visits:

> I quite remember Dylan's visit to the mill ... Dylan was then, I
> imagine, about 5 or 6 years old. He was a delicate looking child
> with big brown eyes. May Bassett often visited Loughor Mill – a
> very ancient wheel water mill with a huge pond ... The garden
> (which my grandmother looked after) was well known for its fruit
> and flowers of every description. It was about an acre. That's
> where I saw Dylan among the flowers on a fine summer after-
> noon. We used to pick plums from the bedroom window.[2]

During their conversation, Florence and Edwards talked about
Dylan as a boy and young man. They thought it important that
someone should "bring out the Dylan known to his friends and
relatives in Wales, the Dylan of the years of growing up and maturing;
the 'real Dylan' ... before what happened towards the end." Florence
suggested that Edwards should do the interviewing.

He readily agreed and by 1968 he was able to write that "I have
interviewed one hundred and twenty-two other relations, close friends
and literary colleagues of Dylan during five extended visits home to
Britain, three trips to Czechoslovakia and two to Italy." By the mid-
seventies, he had interviewed more than one hundred and fifty
people, adding France, Switzerland and Iran to the list of countries
visited.

Florence's Missing Sisters

During the late 1960s, Brinley Edwards helped his son by researching
Dylan's family tree. His data are in Part Two, including his discovery
that Florence had another sister called Sarah Jane, who died at the age
of seven. Colin Edwards went one better, and found out that Florence
also had a half-sister – Florence's father, George Williams, had
fathered a child with his wife's younger sister, a family scandal that
probably precipitated George and family moving from
Carmarthenshire to Swansea in the 1860s – see Chapter 1 for details.
I have been able to use Brinley's notes to unearth further archival
material; this includes revealing information on Dylan's enterprising
relations and their property interests – particularly the rise of his
grandfather, George Williams, from amorous agricultural labourer to
God-fearing urban landlord, described in Chapter 4.

1. At the Boat House: Tilly Roberts, Florence Thomas, Colin and Mary Edwards

Squaring Florence's Family Circle

Edwards' focus on "the Welsh side of Dylan", as he once put it, helps us better to understand both Dylan's family relationships and the time he spent as a youngster in Carmarthenshire. The interviews with Tudor Price and May Bowen, for example, provide a flavour of the young Dylan at play in the countryside around Fernhill. The Edwards interviews make clear that Dylan's time with his Carmarthenshire relations falls into three clear, though overlapping, phases:

Llansteffan, c.1919-1922: Dylan and his parents stayed with his mother's half-sister, Anne Williams, and her daughter Doris, in Rose Cottage. These were bucket-and-spade holidays with excursions to Fernhill and the other family farms. The Llansteffan holidays probably came to an end when Anne died in 1922.

Fernhill, c.1922-c.1929: Jim and Annie Jones, Florence's sister, came to Fernhill about 1909. Whilst Fernhill was important in the young Dylan's life, it was only one of a cluster of Jones family farms that he came to know well. A few fields south, Jim's sister, Rachel, farmed Pentrewyman; a field or so to the north was Dolaumeinon, run by Jim's

11

2. Haulwen Morris, Dylan's second cousin, Llwyngwyn, 2002

half-brother, David, and Pwntan-bach, farmed by Jim's half-sister, Mary. And, of course, within easy walking distance of Fernhill were a number of other farms and cottages where lived the numerous Williamses – the aunts, uncles and cousins of Dylan's mother. The Fernhill phase ended when Jim and Annie moved out in about 1929.

Blaencwm, 1927-1934: Florence's siblings, Bob and Polly Williams, lived in 1, Blaencwm, having retired there from Swansea in 1927 and 1928 respectively. The ending of this phase coincided with the end of Dylan's teenage years, and his move to London, though he continued to visit Blaencwm, especially between 1941 and 1948 when his parents lived there.

The Williams family home was Waunfwlchan, a holding near Llangain whose 120 acres were farmed by Dylan's maternal great-grandparents, Thomas and Anne Williams, from 1841 to the 1890s. After their death, the farm went outside the family, but it was superceded as the centre of family affairs by Llwyngwyn, an even larger farm and farmhouse that lay on the opposite side of the lane to Waunfwlchan. Here lived Thomas and Anne's son, Evan, who was Dylan's great-uncle; he died before Dylan was born but his wife, Anne,

12

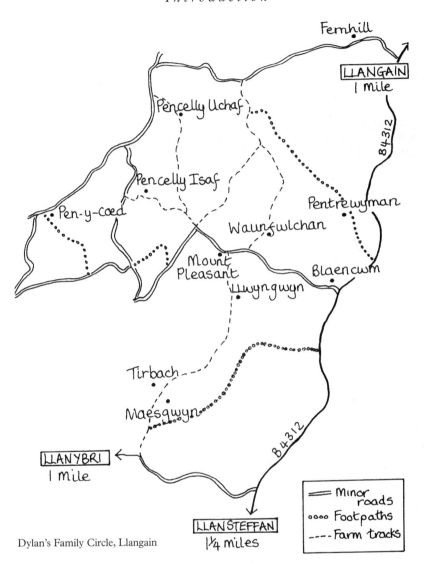

Dylan's Family Circle, Llangain

lived until 1924, and Dylan would certainly have visited her when he was holidaying at Llansteffan and Fernhill. Evan and Anne Williams were at Llwyngwyn from about 1886, and were succeeded there by their two sons, William in 1924 and Thomas John in 1942. Today, Evan and Anne's granddaughter, Haulwen, runs the farm, and neighbouring

Maesgwyn as well, with a little help from her children, the youngest of whom is called Dylan.

When Florence was a child, Llwyngwyn was full of young people of more or less her own age – her first cousins Anne, Anna, Jane and Thomas John. From 1895, as Florence started her teenage years, she would have walked from Llwyngwyn across the fields to see her eldest, and newly-married, first cousin Sarah, who was living in Maesgwyn – the two farms, which are a little over half a mile apart, have always been joined by a family track. Florence's eldest sister, Annie, who was married to Jim Jones, was living close by at Tirbach, the farm where most of the first cousins had been born. Playtime over, the teenage Florence might dutifully have walked back through the fields to visit her widowed grandmother, Anne Williams, in Waunfwlchan.

It is from within this concentration of Williams family farms – Waunfwlchan, Llwyngwyn, Maesgwyn and Tirbach – that we can best appreciate the significance of Dylan's Carmarthenshire background. From this genealogical epicentre – the "breeding-box" valley – emerged a wider circle that forms an historical route that can be walked on the ground today, complementing the familial roots charted on paper in Chapters 1 and 2. This family circle comprises the birth-places and/or homes of Florence's great-grandparents, grandparents, mother, her retired siblings, and her first cousins, most of whom were living here during Dylan's childhood and teenage years.

Dylan's poem, 'After the funeral', is about his aunt Annie, much of whose life revolved around the "cabbage valley" – she spent childhood holidays at Waunfwlchan, married a man from Pentrewyman, lived in Tirbach and Fernhill, and died at Mount Pleasant. As such, 'After the funeral', 'Fern Hill' and the second part of 'Poem in October' celebrate the Llangain family circle, the Williams square mile, as much as they mourn the loss of a particular person, place or phase of life. Pity, then, that Dylan seems not to have been at Annie's funeral, and wrote the first version of 'After the funeral' the day before – see Chapter 6 for details.

Young, Welsh and Dylan

The Edwards interviews tell us a good deal about Dylan's parents. Florence emerges as a jolly, sociable person, a good storyteller and one of the Kardomah girls:

> She wouldn't have been too literary because she was too – what

14

shall I say – hail-fellow-well-met to be a literary type, but she was very fond of meeting her friends in the Kardomah in Swansea at that time, and you could see her almost every Saturday morning with a little crowd of her friends ... she was very entertaining ... always delightful company ... she was very fond of company. (Harry Leyshon)

When Pamela Hansford Johnson came to visit Dylan in Swansea she found that Florence

...was very, very good fun and could tell very good jokes in a shaggy dog sort of way ... I know that she used to make her husband laugh inordinately.[3]

Gwyneth Edwards told Colin Edwards that she found Florence good company, and confounds FitzGibbon's portrayal of her as an irritating gossip: "I wouldn't say she was a gossipy type of woman. She was rather pleasant and interesting." Ralph Wishart thought she "was lovely, she was a charmer, proper old Welshy, and she was sad ... she was a lovely type of person. One you'd like for your mother yourself." There is much material in the Edwards interviews to confirm the picture of Dylan's father, D.J. Thomas, as a strict and sometimes violent schoolmaster, who nevertheless inspired many of his pupils to study and love English literature. This is captured quite strikingly in the interview with Charles McKelvie, who said that DJ was

a very distinguished teacher of English, and a man whom we held in high fear rather than regard ... we did pay him the tribute of regarding him, shall we say, of having the wisdom of a Solomon, but we soon realised we were under the discipline of a Centurion. He was a man of ferocious outbursts, but great scholarly attainments and a great ability to put over his own learning ... he encouraged us to read all the great English classics and he was particularly insistent on us boys reading the dictionary as if it were a novel. He said "Some of it will stick – and this is how you build up your vocabulary." And indeed, some of us took his advice and, even to this day, I still read the dictionary as a novel ...

Yet the interviews reveal many more aspects of D.J. Thomas. Gwilym Evans lodged in 5, Cwmdonkin Drive between 1919 and 1921 when he was a medical student. He told Colin Edwards that "Oh, it was a very pleasant house. Full of mirth ... I liked DJ very much. He was a scholarly type, very fond of music and was a fine piano player."

Mary Davies, who knew DJ and Florence from the 1900s, and who looked after Florence in her last years, told Colin Edwards that DJ "was what you could term a warm man. Yes. But you had to know him well, I think." DJ's first cousin, Rachel Evans, was interviewed by Brinley Edwards, and said: "What a happy family – David John was such a jolly sociable type, excellent personality. There was always a good welcome for all." May Bowen, the servant at Pentrewyman, thought DJ a

> smart man. Nice ... lovely ways, you know. Real gentleman ... always going up there for tea if I was doing a day's shopping in Swansea ... he was always home for tea from school, and Nancy and Dylan were there. We all used to have tea together there.

Barbara Treacher makes the same point in her interview with Edwards, and notes that one of the reasons for DJ retiring to his study was that, like all teachers, he had marking to do, as well as coaching.

Gwilym Price, who was taught by DJ and also visited him in retirement at Blaencwm, found DJ "a grand man altogether and a very likeable man and very human." Others, including Hansford Johnson, also found DJ warm and welcoming to visitors to the house in Cwmdonkin Drive. He wasn't just an English scholar and an accomplished pianist, but also a man who enjoyed football (see Chapter 1). In his school days, he was known as a good runner and rugby player.[4]

One of DJ's former students, Gilbert Bennett, remembered him "with great kindness and deep affection", recalling that he was known to pupils as '*le soldat*', a reference to his soldier-like bearing, and his very precise and "officer-like" speech. Bennett also noted the encouragement DJ would give to aspiring writers:

> ...at the same period that Dylan was writing, there were other people in the Grammar School who were trying their hand at verse and that period seems to me to be a very rich period, from the School's point of view. It may not have produced major people, major writers, but it certainly produced a number of people who made their life in journalism and letters generally. And largely, I think, because DJ encouraged them ... he was a very good corrector of other people's verse, and improver of it, and I think that his sensitiveness showed there ...

Undoubtedly, DJ was a disciplinarian, and sometimes an aloof and reserved man. But there is enough variety of material about him in the Edwards interviews to persuade us that there was a good deal more to him than that.

There is also material in the Edwards archive to make us cautious of Tremlett's judgement that Dylan's parents joined "in none of the town's activities" and invited few people into their home, besides relatives (1993, pp.28-29). Both were theatre-goers, for a start, and as Leslie Rees points out in his interview, "Mrs Thomas was a great chapel-worker, and she would therefore be closely connected with all sorts of organisations which, perhaps, are not so well known outside the chapel life." Florence, whose hospitality to Dylan's and Nancy's friends shines through many of the interviews, may have been the leading partner in the family's social life, but that is not an unusual role for a wife. It was certainly true, as Tremlett suggests, that the two worlds of the Grammar School and 5, Cwmdonkin Drive, seldom met, but that was the case for all families who had a father teaching in the Grammar School, as John Morgan Williams makes very clear in his interview.

Other Tremlett observations will also need revision. For example, it is hard to find anything in the Edwards archive to support Tremlett's view that Dylan "made hardly any friends outside his home until he had left school at 16", and that he had led "an almost reclusive life" to that point (p28). On the contrary, the Edwards interviews reveal that, in his pre- and early teens, Dylan had a variety of friends, with whom he engaged in a wide range of activities. Dylan's schoolboy escapades with "his gang", as Guido Heller puts it, on the Prom and in the Uplands cinema, are described in a number of interviews. Heller also talks about Dylan at play with his "close cronies" in the playground and the school dramatic society. Charles Fisher and Percy Smart mention visits, as schoolboys, to 5, Cwmdonkin Drive, as does R.M. Glynn Thomas, who also describes the camping trip to Mewslade. Dylan, says Smart, was also a boy (unlike Dan Jones) who mixed as much with the "roughs" as with the "academics". He was, too, a boy who played billiards in the YMCA and acted there whilst still at school. Much more could be said on this matter, including his schoolboy friendships with Vera Phillips, Hedley Auckland, Tudor Price and Jackie Bassett. Dylan was a shy boy, and a 'loner' in the sense that he sometimes preferred books and his own company, but friendless and reclusive he certainly was not.

The Edwards material also indicates that Dylan's wider family provided a positive cultural milieu in which Dylan grew up. Like his father, his aunt Polly was a pianist; she taught music and was the organist at Canaan chapel. His uncle Thomas "was a very cultured man and was very fond of poetry – especially Browning." Another uncle, David Rees who had married Dylan's aunt Theodosia, was a classical scholar, botanist and archaeologist. Thompson (1965) has helpfully noted the creative influences in the streets around Cwmdonkin Drive: the Crwys-Williams and Grant-Murray families, and the author Winifred Daniel, with whom the young Dylan discussed literature and writing.

It was this array of influences, including his father's own library and wide knowledge of literature and Classics, that gave the young Dylan an adequate preparation for the more heady cultural discussions that were held in a number of different venues, including the homes (and seaside bungalows) of Dan Jones, Bert Trick and Vera Phillips, as well as 5, Cwmdonkin Drive on Wednesday nights, and the Kardomah café, especially on Saturdays. Not to mention the Mackworth Hotel which was, as Leslie Rees describes, the meeting place for more informal political, often Fabianite, discussions.

The teenage Dylan was a cultural explorer in another sense. He was keen to understand, and enjoy, the world that lay outside the Uplands. He walked the Gower, and got to know the pubs and people of the docks area. His participation in the Little Theatre took him on journeys throughout the south Wales valleys. But, as some of the Edwards material shows, he also knew the pubs in the coal mining and tinplate making villages nearer home: Gorseinon, Loughor, Pontlliw and the Hendy, for example.[5] Hughes (1998) also notes Dylan's visits to Pontarddulais, when he was on his way to Carmarthenshire. All these places come to mind as "the industrial small towns" that Dylan passed through in the bus going to Blaencwm, "each town a festering sore on the body of a dead country, half a mile of main street with its Prudential, its Co-Op, its Star, its cinema and pub."[6]

Dylan's achievements as a schoolboy and teenager have been lost amongst the swell of fact and myth about Dylan the Reprobate – the failure at school, the truant, the drunkard, the petty thief, and the unsuccessful cub reporter. True, he excelled only at English but he left his mark on the school in other ways – his poems and articles in the magazine, of course, and his roles as sub-editor and editor. But there was also his participation in the Dramatic Society, and his secretary-ship of the Debating Society. He helped to found the Reading Circle, and was a successful athlete in the school sports.[7] From 1930 to 1934, he played a prominent part in the YMCA Junior Players and the Little Theatre, as actor, writer and producer. He wrote articles and reviews for the local newspapers. He was just eighteen when he had his first poem published in London (and was also a winner in *The Listener*'s poetry competition), nineteen when he won the *Sunday Referee*'s Book Prize, and barely twenty when his first collection of poetry was published. There is much here for a parent – and a country – to be proud of in a teenage son.

The Edwards Archive

Colin Edwards' tapes, diaries, papers and photographs were given to the National Library of Wales in 1996. Further papers and correspondence were made available to me by Mrs Edwards, used in the preparation of this book, and then deposited in the National Library.

The list of people interviewed by Edwards is given at the end of the book – it amounts to some one hundred and forty hours of interviews. They were made mainly on a reel-to-reel machine, but in February 1999, the National Library started to transfer them to mini-disc to make them more accessible to researchers. It also appointed Joan Miller to transcribe the tapes.

Edwards was assiduous in seeking out interviewees, but there are numbers of people he did not see, some of whom he may have approached but declined to be interviewed. He did not interview, for example, Daniel Jones, David Higham, Douglas Cleverdon, Helen and Bill McAlpine and Margaret Taylor, "who had been 'tied up' by FitzGibbon, like so many others."[8] Edwards interviewed only four people in America. There are but a handful of interviews from Dylan's Cardiganshire days, and, with the exception of Fred Janes, no interviews at all with any of the large number of painters that Dylan had been friendly with. Yet Edwards winkled out interviewees not seen by other writers – for example, two interviews in Iran, seven in Prague, five in Italy and a handful in South Leigh, Oxfordshire.

Edwards interviewed many people not approached by FitzGibbon, and some (for example, Vernon Watkins, Trevor Hughes and Oscar Williams) who had died by the time Ferris had started research on his biography. Ferris interviewed more people than Edwards, and talked with many of those not taped by Edwards. The two data sets of Ferris and Edwards are thus complementary: more than half of Edwards' interviewees come from Dylan's days in Swansea and his family roots in Carmarthenshire – the period up to 1934. Ferris, on the other hand, collected far more material from people in 'the second half' of Dylan's life. Edwards, therefore, has more interviews with the 'ordinary' people who knew Dylan and his family before he became a public figure.

Exploring the Archive

The Edwards archive is the most significant source of biographical material on Dylan to become available since the publication of *Collected Letters* in 1985. Yet its value goes wider than Dylan. The interview with Vernon Watkins, for instance, tells us as much about Watkins as Dylan. That with Ruth Witt Diamant is largely concerned with her life story, rather than her friendship with Dylan. The interviews with Leon Atkin and Bert Trick provide valuable information on the social conditions and political events of Swansea in the 1930s. The discussion with Zdenek Urbanek in Prague is largely about how writers and artists survived in a Stalinist state.

One of the advantages of tape recorded interviews is that they contain material, often small detail, that an interviewer using a note book may not have the time nor the patience to record. The Edwards archive contains a wide range of information on matters that help to set Dylan in context, but is often not about him. For example, some interviews go into great detail about life around Llangain. They offer little biographical material on Dylan, but they will prove valuable to Carmarthenshire historians.

Some of the Llangain and Fernhill interviews also contain interesting data on Robert Ricketts Evans, the eccentric gentleman farmer who lived in Fernhill before Jim and Annie Jones – there is more on this in Chapter 5, including Evans' friendship with Dr William Price of Llantrisant. Material from Ricketts Evans' obituary and his diaries tells us a good deal more about his activities as a hangman. I have also drawn upon his diaries to present a fuller account of his daughter's elopement and marriage.

The Llangain interviews are helpful, too, for the light they shed on several of the people that Dylan knew as a boy and teenager. His cousin, Idris of Fernhill, is a good example. Up to now, we have had to rely largely on the character of Gwilym in 'The Peaches' to make assumptions about the kind of person Idris was. Edwards' Llangain interviews reveal a good deal about Idris, and some of this is used in Chapter 3.

Edwards' interview with Superintendent Bill Francis of the Swansea Police tells us about Dylan's Swansea haunts when he was working at the *Evening Post*: pubs much used by the reporters were the Bovega, the Three Lamps, the Poseda and Archie Gustavus' Royal Hotel in the High Street.[9] There were also Frank Rabaiotti and Attilio Cascarini's cafés, and the Great Vitoski's barber shop in Salubrious Passage. Francis also provides interesting details about the more seedy areas of the Strand and the docks, and adds to the wealth of information on Swansea provided by James Davies (2000). Harry Leyshon provides further clues to Dylan's Swansea haunts:

> Dylan used to visit St. Thomas, very often – I think he was fond of St. Thomas as being a different type of place, and that adds to his experience. He loved, for instance, if he was down for a weekend, going to some distant pub where they wouldn't know who he was, where he could be quite free – an ordinary bloke ... there was an Arab café in Port Tennant road, and Dylan was very fond of visiting there, because he met all types of foreign sailors and foreign visitors to Swansea. They assembled in that café, and it was a very rare occurrence that you'd get any English or Welsh people in there at all, and Dylan seemed to revel going in there and weigh them all up, and try to get into conversation with them – this would be late in his life.

Richard Pelzer, one of Swansea's librarians, had only a brief interview with Edwards, but managed to evoke another Swansea haunt. During the 1940s, he often bumped into Dylan

> in Mrs Williams' the High Street, opposite the High Street station, the faggots and peas shop ... he used to lap it up, really lap it up! With plenty of gravy and the old bread. On his own. Always. On his own in a white mac ... that's the only place I ever met him. Faggots and peas shop. The old fourpenny struggle place ... you used to get so much there, they used to call it fourpenny or sixpenny struggle.

The Edwards archive lends itself best to focussed searches, and these will be far easier to carry out now that the interviews have been transcribed. The researcher interested in a specific theme (Dylan and his father; Dylan at school, for example) will certainly get more out of the archive than someone reading through the transcriptions out of general interest.

Yet occasionally, prospecting through the archive produces unexpected pieces of information. Leslie Rees, Chief Librarian at Swansea public libraries, recalls talking to Dr and Mrs Bronowski:

> Mrs Bronowski said that when they lived in Boston, Dylan was very fond of popping in and she found that he was happiest when Mrs Bronowski would be ironing or doing some household work or baking cakes, and he would then sit with her for a long time, talking about his mother. And she felt that he was escaping from the hectic rough and tumble of lionising life which he experienced there, and turning back to a memory of his mother as a sort of defence, or for some comfort.[10]

The Rees interview also tells us a good deal about Dylan's father. Some of this repeats information to be found in other interviews but then, quite unexpectedly:

> Oddly enough, Dylan's mother told me that his father would never write poetry, because he didn't quite approve, I think, of Dylan's method of writing or his style of writing, rather. But his mother told me something, that after the old man died, she had found a number of poems by him tucked away in a desk, which he had never brought to light and which she therefore would never show to anyone.

And then there's 'the drinking'. Edwards and his interviewees paid a good deal of attention to this. It's not difficult to understand why: it is partly to do with their reaction, not just to Brinnin's 1956 book, but also to FitzGibbon's biography, which was followed by a series of reviews and articles about 'the drunken poet', ranging from Philip Toynbee's 'Poetry and Alcohol' in the *Observer* (October 17 1965) to the *Reveille's* piece on 'The Pub-Crawl Poet' (October 14 1965). In my editing, I have had no alternative but fairly to reflect the interest of interviewer and interviewees in Dylan's drinking, even though at times the refrain may be a little overpowering. The picture that emerges from the interviews is of a social drinker who drank a good deal but was not, they say, an alcoholic – he seldom drank on his own, and never when he was writing. I shall return to this issue in Volume Two.

Dylan Remembered – by Others

Edwards was keen to collect memories of Dylan that had been published or collected by others, and these also form part of the archive at the National Library. Amongst the most interesting of these are transcribed discussions with Lady Snow (Pamela Hansford Johnson), Mervyn Levy, Robert Lowell, and actors Nancy Wickwire and Sada Thompson. The interview with Wickwire and Thompson contains a good deal of useful information about the first stage production of *Under Milk Wood* in New York. Levy's interview is full of interesting observations, such as his comment that Dylan's

> personality ... was curious in one respect, at least; that he seemed to have an obsession ... with dirty things. He liked ... talking about excrement and pissing and so on ... I remember that I have a lot of images of Dylan picking his nose ... I will tell you also that one of the things he did on one occasion with me, in the bathroom of my house in Swansea, was to dare me to drink a cup of my own urine, which I wouldn't do, but he did drink his...[11]

Of great interest, too, is an article published by the poet Allen Curnow in the *NZ Listener* in December 1982, describing a visit to London in 1949 when he met up with Dylan, drank a few beers and watched cricket at Lord's. Soon an invitation to Laugharne followed and Curnow went there in October. His article evokes the colourful town: Dylan is called 'Dyl' (rhyming with hill) by all and sundry; Curnow is taken to the writing shed and, from a chest of drawers, Dylan "fished out a draft to show me of the unfinished *Under Milk Wood*" that was titled *The Town That Was Mad*. This usefully adds to the evidence that Dylan had written most of the first half of *Under Milk Wood* at South Leigh, Oxfordshire, before coming to Laugharne in May 1949 – see Thomas (2001).

Curnow noted that Dylan was working on *Vanity Fair*, and was despondent about his poetry ("The craze for me is over. They won't like what I'm doing now.") He was also preparing himself, "very seriously" for the forthcoming first trip to America ("I'm not *reading* them poems. I'm giving them a *performance*.").

Curnow travelled ahead of Dylan to America. He met with John Malcolm Brinnin over lunch, who, says Curnow, "was a worried young man". He had already heard from English people in New York that he was "buying trouble". Curnow tried to reassure him but "I think that Brinnin's fears ... were already beginning to shape the distorted image of his *Dylan Thomas in America*, the ill-balanced, in places shockingly ill-informed book he was to write four years later." Curnow was with Dylan throughout his Harvard engagements, including the parties and receptions: "I was present at every one of them. Brinnin, who wasn't, has given in his book an account false in general, and constructively false in detail."

FitzGibbon Remembers Dylan but Forgets Edwards

In September 1963, Constantine FitzGibbon, who had not yet started to write his biography, heard that Edwards had interviewed Dylan's mother, who by now had died. FitzGibbon wrote to Edwards asking for a copy of the tape. Edwards readily agreed and sent him one, with the stipulation that FitzGibbon did not make any further copies – Edwards was worried that the tape would find its way to the BBC:

> I have very serious reservations about the approach that the BBC has taken to programs about Dylan.

Edwards' main concern was "to get out a fair and accurate picture of Dylan as a Poet and as a man." To achieve this end in the United States, he had already given his programmes on Dylan free to the educational radio stations.

Edwards generously offered copies of other interviews and suggested that he and FitzGibbon were not in competition and should work together. Curiously, they discovered that they were both also working on projects to do with the resistance to Hitler in wartime Germany – FitzGibbon had already written a book on the matter, and had made a short documentary film.

FitzGibbon wrote in November 1963 to propose a deal around their interests in Dylan: "I can put you in touch with people, and you can let me use your recordings." He then suggested a "little Dylan-tour in England and Wales with tape-recorder and then," he added as extra bait, "I could give you introductions etcetera for Germany." The idea of a tour was not without self-interest: one of FitzGibbon's difficulties as a biographer was that he could not drive. Many of his interviews were done in London, which he could reach easily by train, whilst others (Tom Warner and Fred Janes, for example) were done at his manor house near Dorchester. He was particularly anxious, he told Edwards, to get to north Wales to see Richard Hughes and Bert Trick. Edwards replied that he was "very happy, indeed excited ... I rush to accept your idea of a 'Dylan Tour' together." Generous as ever, he offered to pay for the petrol or the hire of a car. Edwards also offered to interview a group of people in San Francisco who had known Dylan, and to let FitzGibbon have the tapes. In his reply, FitzGibbon welcomed the chance to hear the San Francisco tapes "since I shan't be able to get out there myself." In February 1964, FitzGibbon acknowledged receipt of the tapes that Edwards had sent him. He wrote again to say "My position is that really the sooner we do our Dylan trip the better, as I have started to write, and am anxious to tie up the Welsh adolescence and early manhood part ..." He provided more information on the German project, and thanked Edwards for the tapes of his interviews with Glyn Jones, Ben Morse and Vernon Watkins "which are *excellent.*"

Edwards and FitzGibbon set off from Dorset in FitzGibbon's Jaguar on April 18 1964. They drove to Wrexham to see Bert Trick, and to Harlech to talk with Richard Hughes.[12] They then headed south, taking in New Quay, Laugharne, Swansea, Cardiff and Bristol. The tour was not a success: in all they interviewed just five people. They returned to Dorset, where Edwards interviewed FitzGibbon. He freely reminisces about Dylan, but does not match Edwards' generosity when it comes to what he himself has uncovered: "I'd rather talk to you now as to what my personal memories are, rather than what I have discovered as a biographer."

By the end of 1964, Edwards had carried out seventy interviews, with more than forty hours on tape. He had generously given FitzGibbon a quarter of the taped material before relations between the two became strained after "the 'unpleasantness' occurred":

> Part of my falling out with FitzGibbon during our seven day tour
> of Wales together in 1964 was due to his unconcealed attitude of
> contempt for the Welsh.[13]

A projected English tour together, to interview literary figures that Dylan had known, was called off. Edwards decided to see them on his own but, he complained, he found that FitzGibbon had blocked his access to them. Edwards also noted FitzGibbon's apparent

> deliberate disregard of various interesting leads about Dylan's
> connections and friendships in Wales. During our joint tour I

25

pointed some of these out, and also some inaccuracies in his note-taking, but all I got for me trouble was not thanks but a resentful dismissal of my observations.[14]

When FitzGibbbon published his biography of Dylan, he did not mention the access he had been given to some of Edwards' tapes, nor their Welsh tour together. Neither did he include Edwards in his list of Acknowledgements.[15]

Edwards continued to be generous in responding to other Dylan researchers, notably Ralph Maud, to whom he sent some transcriptions and the addresses of many of Dylan's friends. Edwards, wrote Maud, "was a wonderful soul who did an awful lot of work and didn't get the proper recognition."[16]

The Editing

The transcriptions of Edwards' tapes amount to just over a million words, reduced to some 120,000 words across this volume and the next.

In choosing material for publication, I have tried to convey something of people's own experience of Dylan. I have not simply included information that is startling or 'new'; on the contrary, many of the interviewees cover points of Dylan's life that have been dealt with already in biographies, but I hope that here they have an original freshness and vitality. In making choices, I've rarely had the Dylan expert or aficionado in mind: they may well remember every point that has come up in the stack of books written about Dylan since his death. But most of us certainly will not, so I've had no hesitation in choosing material that I think many will be happy to be reminded of.

There is indeed new data in the Edwards archive but I have not included anything simply on the grounds of its newness; for example, the archive contains much of interest regarding *Under Milk Wood* and other works, but this is not included here because it is not directly about Dylan.

Taped interviews inevitably contain a good deal of small talk and repetition, as well as the flotsam and jetsam of everyday speech ('er', 'you know', 'you see', 'um'). Joan Miller's excellent transcripts also include every cough, chuckle, gasp and sharp intake of breath in an interview. All these I have mostly removed, and I've also done much silent editing. I have sometimes shunted passages together that are about the same topic but occur at different stages in an interviewee's train of thought. For example, an interviewee may talk about Dylan and his girlfriends at the beginning of an interview and then at the end. Where this occurs, I have brought the passages together. I have tried to keep interviews intact but sometimes it made better sense to split up an interview, e.g. those with Eynon Smart and Hedley Auckland in the 1914-1930 section, and that with Bert Trick, which is divided between Volumes One and Two.

If you are interested in a particular point in these edited versions, you should go back to the original transcripts, particularly to see how the interviewee may have taken the matter further. You may also want go to the National Library to listen to the interview: the accent or tone of voice of an interviewee may be as informative as the printed version of his or her words.

I have avoided, where possible, including biographical notes on each person interviewed, and have tried to use material in the interview to explain who the interviewee is, and what their relationship to Dylan was.

The presentation of the interviews in both volumes is broadly and flexibly chronological, beginning with Dylan's birth and school days, much in the way that Edwards himself ordered the material and his own unpublished manuscript. But this does not mean that inter-viewees' comments relate just to the chronological period in which they appear. For example, one or two of the interviewees in the first section talk about Dylan as he was later in life. Others make general comments about his poetry or lifestyle.

In brief, what has been assembled in the Edwards archive, and, I trust, faithfully represented in this book, is a gallery of portraits of Dylan made in different times and circumstances, by different people and from many points of view. Yet there are some common, and often prominent, features in these portraits: tenacity and determination; a love of ordinary life and the company of ordinary people; a joy in the bizarre, the eccentric and the unexpected; warmth of friendship; generosity; shyness and reserve; an absence of self-importance; profes-sional dedication and reliability and, when a piece of writing demanded, the capacity for hard work.

The 'truth' about Dylan – the defining portrait – remains always elusive. For any five of his friends, there are six opinions, particularly about his health and drinking. The American Dylan is not the Swansea Dylan nor the London Dylan, and none are close to the New Quay, South Leigh and Laugharne Dylans. And, as some interviewees point out, the midday Dylan was nothing at all like the evening one.

3. Colin Edwards

Colin Edwards was very aware that there never was a single Dylan – indeed, the original title for his biography was *Dylans We Remember*. It's a useful waymark for the paths ahead.

Colin Edwards: A Biography

Besides radio journalism, Colin Edwards was also an author, university lecturer, Plaid Cymru activist and founder of the American CADW – the Committee to Aid the Defence of Wales. He was an acknowledged expert on Middle Eastern affairs, and was often called upon for advice by the United Nations and policy think-tanks. But Edwards was also interested in the arts, anthropology and science: his broadcasts included the Irish theatre, European witchcraft, Congo tribal customs, chemical pesticides, the Abominable Snowman and Vernon Watkins.

Edwards was born in 1924; his father, Brinley, who worked in the meat trade, was a member of the Welsh Cob Society, a dog breeder, show judge, and an amateur historian. Doris Edwards, Colin's mother, won a scholarship to the Sorbonne, but did not take it up and went into teaching. She was a member of the Swansea Writers' Circle, now remembered as Doris Williams after her second marriage. As Doris Seys Pryce, she published poetry in *The Welsh Review* and many other periodicals. After Brinley and Doris parted, Brinley married Olwen Morse.

Much of Colin Edwards' early life was spent at the Kingsbridge Inn,

Gorseinon, a village just outside Swansea. After attending local schools, he went to the Royal Naval College, Greenwich, and in 1942 joined the Fleet Air Arm. He flew as an observer on the Russian convoy route, was shot down over the Atlantic and later rescued. After the war, he studied at St Catherine's College, Oxford, but left within a year to take up journalism at the UN headquarters in New York.

In 1949, Edwards became a combat correspondent with the British army in Malaya, and then covered the wars in Burma, Indochina and Korea. Over the next thirty years, he broadcast radio documentaries from around the world, the majority on Middle Eastern affairs. He also produced commentaries on the wars in Biafra, Northern Ireland and Vietnam. More than two hundred of Edwards' documentaries and interviews were made available for distribution to universities and schools by the University of California at Berkeley.

From the 1970s, Edwards virtually gave up radio reporting to concentrate on lecturing and writing, including working with Moshe Menuhin (Yehudi's father) on his autobiography – *The Menuhin Saga*, published by Sidgwick and Jackson in 1982, and translated into four languages.

Edwards wrote an unpublished biography of Dylan based on his interviews. The first chapters, dealing with boyhood, grammar school and the Little Theatre, are in the National Library of Wales. He made three documentaries for the Canadian Broadcasting Company called *The Real Dylan, Dylan as a Youth* and *My Son Dylan*.

Colin Edwards died on July 11 1994 in Oakland, California, where he and his wife, Mary, had lived for some thirty years. His ashes were brought to Wales, and interred in Oystermouth Cemetery, Swansea.

David Thomas
Ciliau Aeron

Volume Two: 1935-1953 will be published in 2004, the ninetieth anniversary of Dylan's birth. It will include interviews with Fred Janes, Mably Owen, Vernon Watkins, Glyn Jones, Rayner Heppenstall, Bert Trick, Constantine FitzGibbon, Laurence Gilliam, Robert Pocock, Enid Starkie, Phillip Burton, Aneirin Talfan Davies, Harry Locke, John Laurie and the villagers of New Quay, South Leigh and Laugharne.

Part One: The Memories

1914-1930
"A sweet baby, a precocious child, a rebellious boy, and a morbid youth"

Dylan is born on October 27 1914 to Florence and D.J. Thomas. He is a fretful child who is soothed by the birds of Cwmdonkin Park, and his father's reading of Shakespeare and the Bible. He goes to the local dame school and then Swansea Grammar, where he edits the magazine, acts in school plays, plays moochins, tramples the Headmaster's rhubarb, succeeds as an athlete, walks the Gower and avoids excelling in any subject but English. He spends his school holidays in Carmarthenshire on his family's 'insanitary' farms – he rides horses, cuts mangolds, slurps *cawl* and goes to chapel.

Gillian Williams (née Jones)

You are probably the first person in the world to see Dylan Thomas – even before his mother, because you delivered Dylan.
Yes, that's it – and Dr Alban Evans was the doctor.
And was it a difficult birth?
Oh, no. Quite normal ... he was born about two days after the date I'd given them ... in the front bedroom ... oh, a lovely little boy he was, dear little chap – he was about seven pound – he was a lovely baby. Florrie, his mother, and I, were big pals. I didn't used to go quite so far out of the district to work, but being it was Florrie, I stretched the point.

Addie Elliott (née Drew)

I was with Mrs Thomas in the same room assisting the midwife – I think Mr Thomas was home from school in the evening ... Nancy was ill ... she was in bed in the middle bedroom with the measles, and Mrs

4. Addie Elliott

Thomas was in bed in the front room ... upstairs, between six and seven o'clock ...[17]

...no, just a normal birth – when he was born, he had rather dark hair, but within a short time it got very fair. Everybody admired him when he was a baby – he had such nice hair. Oh, he had beautiful hair – fair, very, very fair and very curly ... he was a very good-looking little boy.

...he wasn't very big, and I'm afraid he was a very cross boy. He cried quite a lot, and caused a lot of anxiety because they couldn't find out why he cried. But evidently his food wasn't satisfying him, but eventually he got better ... his mother and father were very fond of an evening out on Friday – they liked the Empire variety show, and somehow or other that Friday evening was a nightmare to me. He cried from the time they went out until they came back ... both of us were crying when they'd get back – because whether he missed his mother, I don't know, but he was a naughty baby – and he didn't grow very quickly.

Did you see anything of what some people call petit mal *in Dylan's early years, that is, blackouts and fainting?*

Oh, not when he was very small. No – he was quite an ordinary little boy, with little children's illnesses, but I never thought there was anything wrong with him, with his health, then.

What kind of children's illnesses did he have?

Well, the measles and whooping cough and all those little illnesses ... he was a bit chesty from early days ... if he had a cold, it always affected his chest.

His mother referred to lung haemorrhages when he was a boy. Do you recall any sign of that?

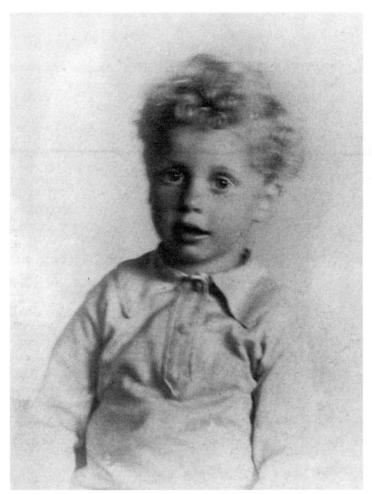

5. Dylan as a young child

He must have been about ten or eleven when those started. It may have been before he went to grammar school ... he was delicate when he was small. He didn't attend school regularly, but his father taught him quite a lot at home ... and he was intelligent, was easy to teach ... as a child, you know, about three or four year old, he'd have a book and draw different things, and tell you what they were, just like an ordinary boy. I didn't see anything outstanding in those days ... he used to draw beautiful pictures in his little way.

You used to read stories to him, didn't you?
Yes. Always read stories, from about ten or twelve months old ... [until]
I left there when he was just about two, or soon after two. But I met
him several times after that ... you could get him spellbound, read him
a story and the comic papers, you know, he used to like those.[18]

Was he full of questions?
Yes, he always wanted to know ... you had to tell him the right story,
and if you tried to make up a story, he'd say "Well, that's not what you
told me yesterday!" You had to be correct. His greatest delight was to
go to Cwmdonkin Park and he'd look at the birds in the trees, and you
could always get him, if he was a bit cross, to look up at the trees and
birds, and he'd be quite pleased and excited. Yes, that was his delight to
go to the Park – when he was a baby – when he was about six or eight
months old right up until he was quite a big boy – I took him out every
day in the pram. I took him out when he was only a few days old.

...they had a dog, but it was after I left there. He was very fond of
this little dog; I can't tell you what breed it was, but he was very fond
of his little dog. ...he had a little friend – I think his name was Peter
Jones. He'd only be about two or three year old, and he used to go out
to Peter's house, or Peter'd come down to their house to play ... his
father was, at that time, the minister of the Unitarian church, Mr
Simon Jones ...

...oh, Nancy was the most charming child I ever met. She was really
a lovely girl ... she was *very* fond of her baby brother – *very* fond of
him. Some little girls would be jealous, you know, getting to that age
and a new baby coming, but she wasn't. She loved her brother –
although she was so many years older, she was always ready to play
with him and have a game with him ... she was very motherly to him
... and her friends were his friends, you know. They'd all get together,
and they could take anybody home. They always had a welcome there
... she was very artistic, Nancy was, she liked to draw and paint.

...and you know, if Dylan did anything his father disapproved of, he
was punished – he had to go to bed, and he had to stay there ... he
didn't believe in caning him or anything – but he had his punishment.
His pocket money was stopped ... oh, Mr Thomas was ... very strict,
with him ... no, his father never beat him at all.

...Mr Thomas was a very studious man – they were of two different
kinds, Mr and Mrs Thomas. Mrs Thomas loved being at home but Mr
Thomas liked the country and would go for walks for miles and miles
in his spare time – on his own, yes. On a Saturday, of course, there was

6. Florence Thomas as a young woman

school in the morning. He'd finish school at twelve, we'd have lunch ready by the time he came home. And then he would go for a walk; he'd go right down to Gower – Parkmill was one of his favourite places and he'd call in a farmhouse and have high tea – ham and eggs – he'd have a good feed and then go walking further on – and he'd call in a pub and have a drink, and if we were still up, Mrs Thomas and I, well, it'd be one or two o'clock before we'd get to bed!

Did he ever take Dylan on these walks with him?
No. No, never. No. ... he was a man that read his Bible a lot. He could quote any part of the Bible to you ... when he was very young, he always liked to read the Bible to Dylan ... well, quite young when he would read him a Bible story. And tried his best to get him to read.

Mrs Thomas was a very natural person.
Oh, very homely, very nice person. Very kind person ... she had her

troubles, yes, and I wouldn't like to tell you – I knew a lot of them ... children seem to sense when there is trouble and, of course, Mr Thomas was a master in the grammar school but, you know, the wages of a teacher aren't too big, and they've got a certain standard to live up to, haven't they, so of course, money wasn't very plentiful.

...Mrs Thomas was gay ... she was always happy, you know, always bright and cheerful ... a very good looking woman ... very popular ... she'd go in the Market, and do a bit of shopping. In those days, a lot of Welsh people came from Carmarthen to the Market. Well, she knew a lot of Carmarthen people ... oh yes, they visited each other very often. And so did Mr Thomas' mother. I met Mr Thomas' mother many times. On a Saturday ... a little old woman, a dear old woman she was.

...they all spoke Welsh ... Mr Thomas' mother, she rarely spoke in English ... Mrs Thomas' family were Welsh ... they didn't speak to each other in Welsh, it's only when one of the relatives would come by ... everybody that went there spoke English, it was a habit to speak in English, you see.

It wasn't that they wanted Dylan to grow up speaking English only?
Oh no, no. I think they would have been delighted if he could speak Welsh.

But they didn't make an effort to teach him?
Not at that age ...

Barbara Treacher (née Auckland)

I'm Dylan's cousin – my grandmother [Annie Righton] and Dylan's father were first cousins ... I'm a month older than Dylan.

... I was living in Sketty ... my mother and my grandmother used to take me up as a child, also my sister, and we used to play with Dylan and Nancy as children, and go up every Friday, and ransack Uncle Jack's study and get into trouble. Auntie Florrie used to make us lovely home-made cakes ... tea was always laid when we arrived. Then we used to go into the study – Uncle Jack used to go and talk to my family – we used to go into the study, have our pens and pencils with Dylan and he used to do little poetries, and we didn't realise then what he was doing, but we always had a little poem, as I say, in our pockets.

...we used to go to the bug-house, as we used to call it, the Uplands Cinema ... we were a little older then, I should think about eight, nine maybe, and we'd go on Saturday morning, used to wear our blazers,

7. Barbara Treacher

and often I'd come home and find just a simple little poem ... we'd go in our pockets, there'd be a little poem ... just the simplest little poem – we'd come home, pick it up, "Oh look, he's been at it again!"

...we always used to go up on a Saturday morning, either to the bughouse, or to Cwmdonkin Park, and we used to let rip up there, and always go back to Auntie Florrie's for lunch on the Saturday ... she was a loveable person, very joyful, always happy, always pleased to see you. Always a cup of tea when you went in.

...[Uncle Jack] was tall, he was a very aristocratic-looking man; you know, a real gentleman. Very quiet. Would come in, would lecture Dylan, sitting down in his study and lecture him – whether Dylan took any notice or not, I don't know – but he was a charming gentleman, and his voice was absolutely beautiful to listen to ... he was a perfect gentleman.

...I always remember him bringing his work home from school and doing the markings and all things like that. He used to have tea with us, and he'd always wanted to be excused to go into his study after.

So he wasn't reclusive about his study?
Oh no, no ... we all played in there – when he wasn't there. But once he came home, he'd always have tea, and then he'd be excused and go into his study, which was the middle room ... he didn't keep people out, and when we all went, he always used to come out, and he was very, very ...

Sociable?
Very, very sociable, yes. He had to retire to his study, because I mean, being a schoolmaster, he had to bring his work home, didn't he, and do a lot of marking ... Uncle Jack used to coach at nights ... they all did.

They had to, didn't they, to make the money?

We were talking about DJ, and talking about poetry at home.
Yes, I've often heard him discussing poetry and also reciting little bits of poetry there to us, you know, as kids ... not only to Dylan, no, because I had a sister who was only fifteen months older than myself, and she was always with us as children you see, with my family. He used often to say a little poem to us, and talk to us.

And when DJ was talking about poetry, would Mrs Thomas join in?
She'd really laugh ... not make him look ridiculous at all – "Oh, there he goes!" Just like that – she was a jovial person, she used to go "Oh, just hark at him." And he used to laugh ... took it all in good fun.

Do you think Florence spoiled Dylan a bit?
Yes. Definitely ... more so than she did her daughter. She loved him, absolutely loved Dylan ... everybody mothered Dylan. Everybody, even my family mothered Dylan ... he played up to it.

Do you remember anything about Mrs Hole's school?
Dylan was there with me ... Mrs Hole was gorgeous ... she was a very kindly person ... Mrs Hole was fantastic – like Auntie Florrie.

Do you recall Dylan and Nancy in Llansteffan?
Yes, I recall them in Llansteffan; but I can't remember very much about it ... they used to often go and stay with my grandmother when she had relatives in Carmarthen.

DJ didn't speak Welsh in the school – but at home he did, didn't he?
Both Auntie Florrie and Uncle Jack always spoke Welsh. And my grandmother. They all spoke Welsh together. But we couldn't – nor my mother.

So Dylan grew up at home hearing Welsh?
Oh yes, he grew up hearing Welsh.

But he didn't speak any Welsh?
No, but he heard it, but he may not speak it. I heard it, but I don't speak it.

Esther James

With me is Miss Esther James, sister of Miss Gwen James, who taught Dylan elocution and speech.[19]
I think he had private lessons, as far as I can remember ... he was so lively, very lively.

How old was he when he came here?
Oh, I should think he'd be in elementary school ... a couple of terms, I should imagine ... once a week it would be ... and that would have to be in the evenings ... for half an hour at a time ...
And he did this as a boy, and not when he was at the Evening Post?
Oh no. No, no. No, no. No, no. When he was quite a small boy, in elementary school ... I remember her saying that it was a big voice for a small boy ... I think Dylan had a little Welsh sort of intonation, because you can't really get absolutely rid of an accent, and in excitement, it would come out a little bit.
...if he was on the air, or anything like that, we used to listen to him always, because of his voice ... it was a naturally good voice, you see. She couldn't claim credit for the voice, because it was a gift, wasn't it?

Ocky Owen

He used to come here [Llansteffan] every summer, and father and mother – and his sister ... Dylan used to come every day, with his little curly hair, pale little face, for an ounce of tobacco and a box of matches ... a box of Swan, and I think it was Westward Ho tobacco.[20]
...rather delicate ... puny little fellow, sallow complexion and didn't look very strong. But a very delightful little chap ... everybody liked him ... his sister was a delicate-looking little girl, too ... his father was a nice man, you know.

8. Ocky Owen

They stayed with some relation in a house called – I'm not sure it was called – Ty Gwyn or something. Mrs Anne Williams – she was a relation, and they always came there to stay ...

This was when he was visiting at Fernhill in the summers?

Yeah, probably visiting from here then, but his holiday was fixed here ... they stayed here – for about three weeks or a month ... he came here, as I say, for many years, probably visiting Fernhill and places *from* here ... Dylan didn't live on the farm, he lived here ... he was fixed here – the holiday was spent here ... buckets and spades on the sands. Spent the day as every other child spent it ... didn't seem to possess any special gifts beyond the ordinary child, you know.

As years passed on, Keidrych Rhys came to me one day, and he asked me if I knew Dylan Thomas. I said "Yes, I know him well." "Do you know," he said, "he's a great man." "Well, that I don't know," I said."I haven't got the intelligence perhaps or the brain to recognise a great man when I see one." "He's a future Shakespeare," he said to me. "Well, I don't know about that. The only answer I can give you to that," I said, "God help poor Shakespeare."

...to those who had got eyes to see, probably a great man. But to those who haven't got the eyes to see, they don't recognise greatness when they see it ... and it was such a sad thing that one that could contribute so much to life, that he didn't pull himself together ... he had such a lot to render.

Doris and Randolph Fulleylove

DF: I used to stay at Fernhill a lot with Nancy, you see. Nancy and I used to stay there together, and then during the summer holiday, Auntie Florrie and Uncle Jack and Dylan would come down ... they stayed with us in Rose Cottage, Llansteffan ... Dylan was my cousin, mother and Dylan's mother, Auntie Florrie, being sisters ... he was quite a little boy when he came to stay with us at Llansteffan ...

...he was very fond of rice pudding, I remember that! He had to have that, every meal he had rice pudding! And I'm trying to think of the other thing – he had a panama hat on ... a little boy, a little panama hat, you see. And somebody asked him in the village "Ooh, you do look smart in that hat." And he said "Oh, a guinea – Sydney Heath's."

He was always having accidents, his mother told me.

RF: And yet I don't think he ever realised fear, did he? What about that

9. Dylan as a boy

occasion when we were going round Cray Waterworks? ... snow and ice were on the ground – and I lost control of the car – you get to the bottom of the hill and there was a right-hand turn – sharp right-hand turn, a sharp left – and anyhow I negotiated it – somehow – but when I got round, I pulled the car up and I bathed my face – I was sweating like a bull. And Dylan calmly turned round and said "Lovely, uncle – go and do it again!"

Was he showing the promise then of interest in English and the use of words?
DF: Yes. He used to get the dictionary and find a very long word, and he used to make crossword puzzles up – as a little kid – he'd just write them and bring them to us to read.

How did his father react to this, because his early poems are quite extraordinary for a young child?
RF: I don't think he approved very much – not his dad.
DF: Because he didn't excel in any other subject in school, did he, only English ... and that used to hurt Uncle, because he was the English master, wasn't he?

What do you remember of DJ?
DF: Oh, he was the most *charming* man

10. Randolph and Doris Fulleylove

RF: Commanding ...
DF: I idolised him. Well, he was a brilliant pianist, you know, Uncle Jack was ... marvellous. And I was the only one that he'd play for. Auntie would say to me "Knock the study door, and ask Uncle to play." And it doesn't matter what he'd be doing – he'd drop it and he'd play for me. Classical music, of course – brilliant pianist.

How close were Dylan and Nancy?
DF: If I remember rightly, she used to call him 'Baby' when he was little.
RF: Because they corresponded, if they were parted, there was always some method of communication ...
DF: I think she was quite thrilled about [Dylan's writing].
RF: She was.
DF: Oh, yes she was very proud of him, although once she was rather upset – she went to some literary do in London and Dylan came in rather late, and he arrived with sort of green trousers and orange shirt and a yellow tie and all this and that, and she wished the earth would have swallowed her up ... she was rather disappointed. Because she was so perfect herself. In her dress ...
...she was charming. She was my bridesmaid. She's my son's godmother ... although she was rather artificial. I mean, when we'd stay there we'd go out somewhere to tea. And on the way there – "Now, for

44

God's sake Doris, don't eat more than *one* little sandwich and one little cake. It isn't correct to eat any more." And we'd leave there, you know, at about quarter to five, dash home, get in the house – "Mother, for God's sake give us something to eat, we're starving!"

...she married a Bristolian [Haydn Taylor] ... he was the manager of brick works outside London, and they lived in Ellen Terry's cottage, at Wisteria Cottage, Laleham on Thames ... she got a bit bored with life – she joined the ATS.

RF: Mechanized section of the ATS, I think.

DF:Yes – because she thought it [the War] would only last a short time ... when she left that she used to drive some brigadier about, didn't she? And then when that was over, she took a course in cookery in London, flower decoration. Then she divorced Haydn and Haydn married his secretary, and Nancy went back to her old home and prepared their wedding breakfast.

Mr Fulleylove, you got to know Dylan ...

RF: Oh, during our courting days – that's at Cwmdonkin Drive ... 1927, actually.

He was thirteen then. In the Grammar School.

RF: That's right. And I found him very, very good company.

DF:You got on well with him ...

RF: Maybe because I was more or less interested in the boy and I satisfied him by answering questions. He would go to his dad or his mother and say "What can I write about?" and they hadn't got the time or didn't want to tell him anything. He'd turn round and say "What can I write about, Uncle?" I'd say "Oh, so-and-so" – it may be just the headline of a daily paper – and he'd immediately write about it. I think by satisfying him that way ... we became real pals ... they had a form of dinner wagon, with two cupboards absolutely packed with his writings.

DF: Oh, everywhere there was, and his little bedroom was very small.

RF: Packed.

DF: Bits of paper everywhere, and he was always writing.

RF: His bedroom was plastered with them.

Pictures as well as poems?

RF:Yes, yes ... mostly of bird life. Now the heron – I don't know what it was that the heron had got, but Dylan always brought that bird into his arguments or into his conversation. Why, I don't know.

...I remember an occasion we went to a little pub between Laugharne and St Clears, and it was an oil-lit, little public house. And they'd got these boxes of stuffed birds around the little bar. And Dylan called for a pint as usual – "and a bottle for my friend that can't drink" he said – that was myself you see – and just as he was about to start this pint drinking, he spotted this one bird in a cage, in this box, stuffed, and simply flung this pint mug at this box – smashed the glass to smithereens. Well, I expected a rough house – I expected the landlord to come and get the police ... but nothing happened – apart from the landlord apologising to Mr Thomas. He said "Don't you ever let me see you keep a bird like that up there again". That was a heron.

...I remember going into another house in St Clears, where they'd got a china model of a heron dipping into a sort of ashtray ... he destroyed that himself by smashing it on to the fireplace.

DF: Oh, to me he was the most wonderful chap. I'm very honoured to be related to him, you know.

RF: He was a God-fearing fellow. And his principles were good.

May Bowen (née Edwards)

Mrs Bowen, you knew Dylan as a very small boy. You were living in with Rachel Jones, his aunt?

Yes – at Pentrewyman ... about two or three fields away ... Dylan and Nancy used to come over to us to play in the summer ... every afternoon, and in the morning do some riding ... the cart horse. Every summer, from the time he was about eight or nine ... to about fifteen or sixteen, something like that.

What age were you then?

About twelve to fourteen ... he was staying at Fernhill. And sometimes he'd sleep over in Pentrewyman with us ... if he felt like staying overnight, he'd stay. If not, well ...

Was there room there?

He used to sleep with me.

What was he like in those days?

Oh, he was very, very pretty ... rather thin, curly-hair mass, and freckles all over his face ... he had a lot of freckles ... no, he wasn't sick, but to me he didn't look so robust as what he was when he grew up ... I don't remember him coughing. No.

He didn't have any blackouts when he was a boy, fainting spells, did he?

No ... unless he had it in Fernhill. He didn't have it over with us ... and

11. May Bowen

he had a hearty appetite because we used to bake bread in there, and he used to love the homemade bread and things ... he was fond of the stew, they call it *cawl* ... I wouldn't say he was mischievous, but he used to like riding and all, you know – he was on the go all the time ... never was quiet for a minute.

The horse was definitely at Pentrewyman?
Yes it was, then, at the time. And they had one in Fernhill, as well ... he rode the both ... he liked horses, yes. I didn't see him feeding the horses but he was very interested in horses, always.

He was also fond of the dog on the farm, wasn't he?
Yes – Fan ... a sheepdog. Sometimes Fan would go over to Fernhill and back with him, and romp about with him ... he was always out of doors. He was always romping about, and down the river, and, you know, with the pheasants ... he wasn't shooting pheasants, but he was going to the fields after them and looking ... I remember he was very fond of going round the trees to get the apples ... he was always after the fruit and things ... he'd get the apples whatever'd happen ... he always had something in his pocket ... he was always chewing something.

...in the very hot weather, if they came on a very hot summer, we'd be all out together. We'd go down to the sea to fish and look for trout.

...when we used to cut the mangolds down for the cattle, he used to always be there, during that time, you know ... enjoying hisself, he was! Romping about and enjoying himself. Well, it was a holiday time.

...I remember once there was a very boggy place down by the old stream, where we used to fish ... we had a cow got right up till here in mud, and they had ropes to take her out then. To pull her out. And he was the one pulling more than anybody else! Helping the men ...

...there's a blacksmith down the bottom – Blacksmith Evans – Daniel Evans his name was ... we all used to go there when they used to shoe the horses. Yes ... in Llangain. Down the bottom of Pentrewyman field, in the village. Yes, Brook, they called it. Brook, Llangain. And we used to go down there after dinner sometimes and have a lot of fun with this old gentleman that was shoeing the horses ... Dylan used to be mischievous and always poking into what he – trying to find out what this was for, and taking the irons, and trying to ...

...he was very wiry when he was with me. I never seen him reading.

...oh yes, he was bringing books down, but I didn't see him reading when he used to come over to us. Didn't see him doing any writing, either.

Did he like telling stories in those early days?
Oh yes. He was quite witty in a way, you know. He always had some little finishing touch to something, always ... he'd finish it off with something witty. Always very witty in his ways ... a deep voice he had you know, very nice voice. He was talking very fast, quick. He was a quick speaker ...

Did he ever try to speak any Welsh, because you were Welsh-speaking, and his Auntie Rach was Welsh-speaking, wasn't she?
Oh yes, but we were speaking English to him, though. At the time. English we were talking to Nancy, and we never heard Nancy talking Welsh. No ... Mrs Thomas was talking English to them ... I never heard them speaking Welsh to them ...

Dylan's Auntie Anne died, and Dylan wrote a beautiful poem about her ... 'After the funeral', it's called. He was very fond of his Auntie Annie, was he?
Yes, he was very fond, yes ... whenever she was walking, she'd always do this with him. This, I can remember her doing this. Say we'd go over of a night, now. She'd always put her arm around him, and pull him to her side, yes ... this type of thing, you know ... "Dylan bach", say like that ...

William Phillips and Tudor Price

Both Bill and Tudor spent time at Fernhill, as boys, with Dylan.
TP: That's right, yes ... at this farm called Pentrewyman where Rachel

Jones, his aunt, resided ... Fernhill was the next farm more or less, just over the hilltop ...

My mother's people kept the Factory, which was an adjoining farm on the other side of Pentrewyman, which was the meeting point between the three farms, in effect – the Factory was a woollen factory which also had a smallholding of about eight or ten acres – Dylan, of course, was in school, and came down from Swansea to stay at Fernhill. I was at school, and came down to the Factory to stay at the same time, so we also knew each other in Swansea. We both lived in the Uplands.[21]

...I would say from 1920, when I was five years of age, up until the time I was sixteen or seventeen I would say we saw quite a lot of each other – every summer – from the time school broke up until it started again, which was a matter of about six weeks, usually ... we more or less parted our ways when he went to the *Evening Post* as a local reporter...

WP: We played around the Factory. The water that came down along the side of the road to turn the wheel of the Factory was very deep and if it was a warm day Tudor and I, and Gwilym too, would bathe in the water. And then we'd go across and up to Pentrewyman and we'd have dinner of *cawl* ... brought out of the saucepan where the grease of it hung from the cabbages to your plate, nearly ... it was the real food in those days, and people all enjoyed it. And when it was served up, you ate it with wooden spoons. In wooden soup dishes. Never in china, or never in a silver spoon, but just a wooden spoon ...

...my stepfather's brother, Watt, worked for Miss Jones at Pentrewyman, and he was a grand fellow with Tudor and any boys that came along, and so we always went up there then to play or to help, as we say, with the harvest and doing some little jobs. I quite remember Tudor riding the front horse, which was Prince, and me riding on the binder, which was cutting the corn on the top field.

What kind of a rider was Dylan?
WP: Well, he had to be a good rider to sit in front of Tudor, you see.

When you rode Prince, you were riding bareback, were you?
WP: Oh yes, bareback. All the harness was thrown off and we just had the bridle that he'd been working in.

TP: The three of us were installed on this horse, Dylan in the front, myself in the middle and a cousin of mine behind, and somebody gave this horse such a whack with a stick, we went tearing away down this field and the horse's front foot stumbled and, of course, over the top we went, and Dylan landed on the pit of his stomach on a stone. We thought that he surely must have died because he was as white as a sheet and we were trying to smack his face to revive him and so on, and a handful of water from the brook ... I would say he would be round about ten years of age at the time ...

Watt Davies said that he often observed Dylan sitting in the hedge reading when other children would be playing around.

WP: No, we wouldn't be there when Watt would see those things, because Watt was working there regularly. As I say, we only went at certain times of the year, and Dylan was going there constantly, because his aunt Rachel was there and she was very nice to everyone, wasn't she?

TP: Oh yes – she was a very good type of person, you know. I was going up there to Pentrewyman ten o'clock in the morning, come home at night when it got dark, and we used to have these samples of *cawl* regularly – and so did everybody who called there in effect, didn't they? It was an open house as such.

What were they harvesting?

WP: Hay mainly, because it's milk-producing country, but there was a certain amount of corn, in those days – not so much today, but there was a certain amount then, and Pentrewyman used to always have top fields in corn.

Dylan had, as a child, suffered a great deal with his chest. Were you aware of this when he ...

TP: Oh yes, I was aware of that. Yes, of the chest business ... I think he was considered a weakling really, alongside both of us.

WP: Yes – quiet, sulky type.

TP: Never a robust child.

WP: No ... not our type, was he?

TP: No, no.

Did he ever talk about it?

TP: No, he never talked about it ...

WP: He talked very little, Tudor.

TP: Yes – he was quite a quiet child, but I do recall well that he was certainly not a robust child ... I would say that we were far more rough and tumble than he ever was ... I should say he had quite a sheltered upbringing, for the simple reason that he was delicate.

What kind of farm was Fernhill? Was it a prosperous farm? Was it good land?

WP: Oh no. Fernhill was a small farm, with a lot of rush land behind it on the one side, and then a couple of hilly fields on the other side ... it was gorse and fern and fir-trees ... there was quite a lot of gorse round those hills ... quite close to Fernhill.

TP: Fernhill was surrounded by pine trees ... Fernhill has always been a rather dark and dismal house, solely for the reason that it was surrounded by this cluster of trees. In fact, I can remember the days when, you know, a nice bright, sunny afternoon, it was already very cool at Fernhill in that the sun never struck it.

...I would say that Llangain wasn't a village, in effect. I would say that the centre of Llangain parish would be the Smyrna Congregational Church plus the church itself, the Church in Wales, those were the two focal points of all the surrounding farms. These were the two centres ... of culture and meeting places of the young and old in the parish.[22]

WP: If you had an *eisteddfod*, it was always in Smyrna. It wasn't in any schoolroom or anything. And there used to be a little sweet shop just up the road, and we could go on Sunday afternoon, and perhaps she'd let us have some sweets.

I'm interested in knowing to which chapel or church Dylan went, or was taken, when he was at Fernhill during the summer-times that you spent with him there. Because his mother was a Congregationalist, his father was Church of England. Did he go to Smyrna, the Capel Annibynnwr?

TP: Oh yes, yes ... that's where I recall him. I recall him going to Sunday School there.

Regularly?

TP: Oh, I couldn't say that.

WP: Nearly everyone went to Smyrna ... especially on a Sunday night, 'cause that's where most of the girls were congregated – so nearly everyone went there – it was the popular place ... you had no other places of attraction, no other interests, only to come to Smyrna and hang around by the old stable, when people were putting their horses in their traps to go home and then you all walked down past Fernhill road and down past the Factory ... and very often you could hear them singing, as they were coming down along ... Oh yes, they coupled up, girls and boys from everywhere. Of course, it's often been said, you never asked anybody down there who their parents were. You only asked them if they had any relations, because there's quite a lot of ...

TP: Treacherous ground! Of course, at this Smyrna chapel they all had *eisteddfodau*, which were very interesting affairs in as much as they started at ten o'clock in the morning and they carried on until about three or four in the following morning ...

The services in Smyrna – were they in Welsh?

TP: Oh yes, completely in Welsh.

So Dylan therefore heard Welsh sermons?

TP: Oh yes, yes ... the preacher was a Mr John, who'd been there for many years. I wouldn't say he was a great preacher, but he was a very fine pastor ... and he was a fine type of man who would have known Dylan undoubtedly very well, through the family connections.[23]

You went to Sunday School with Dylan then, did you?

TP: Yes. Yes.

Did Dylan go to the church down in Llangain, too? Perhaps when his father was visiting?

TP: I wouldn't know it in as much as I never went there. I always went to Smyrna.

WP: But old Jones Fernhill, used to try to cut a dash far above what he really should have done. And you could quite understand James Jones taking Dylan along to church on a Sunday morning. You know he was a little bit above *Capel Annibynnwr* ... he liked everyone to think that he was Gentleman Jim ... he wanted to cut a dash always ... he was that trim type – how can I say? He'd wear his bowler hat different to everyone else ... he had a big moustache – the old farmer type of those days.

Did they conduct services in Welsh?

TP: Always.

WP: Yes. All in Welsh – when we used to go down to Watt's mother, my sister and I being English-speaking people, we'd go down to see them, we'd arrive at the little place, and she'd say "Good bye." "Good bye." That was the only two words she knew ... she knew no more English at all, and very few people spoke English.[24]

TP: It was all Welsh – and the children played in Welsh and that's why I say that Dylan must have had a smattering of Welsh in as much as he couldn't speak English when he stopped at Fernhill. I should say that in all his surroundings, everybody else spoke Welsh ... as a child, you're bound to pick that up much, much quicker than when you are grown up.

What were the pursuits of young boys in farms like that?

TP: Well, you know snaring and ferreting – we used to do quite a lot of trout fishing in this river which ran the mill in effect. There was a fair abundance of trout there and sometimes some sewin coming up, depending on the tides and the season, and we used to do a fair amount of that. But I can't recall Dylan ever accompanying us on any of these missions.

The furthest he got with you was haymaking?

TP: That's right. Where our connection came along was at Pentrewyman, where he was visiting his aunt, and it happened to be the next farm to the Factory and I spent a lot of time there because of the animals and the horses and, particularly these horse rides attracted us to Pentrewyman farm – it was a very easy-going sort of place, and you could do what you liked, couldn't you?

WP: Yes. You don't hear anything about Albert ...

TP: Well, Albert, of course, was the son of Miss Jones at Pentrewyman, who arrived under the Queensberry Rules ...

WP: Albert was never in the harvest field. It was Watt and Tudor, and Dylan and myself. We'd be there and perhaps a man from another farm, perhaps Idris would be there from Fernhill ... there was no work in James Jones, Idris, nor Albert. The one that was the worker of the ones that I knew was Miss Jones – Rachel. She was the worker at Pentrewyman.

'Percy' Eynon Smart

I first met Dylan at the dame school which we both attended before the Grammar School – we didn't know it as Mirador School. We called it Mrs Hole's. Mrs Hole was the proprietress and Dylan came to this school two years behind me ... I remember that he was then a perfectly normal small boy. Mischievous, as we were, and there was nothing particular about him ... Mrs Hole was a delightful woman. I believe she was English; she showed no trace of Welsh in her speech. She was a very cultivated woman, and it really was, in my view looking back, one of the best kind of dame school. She was assisted by her daughter, who was married, and by Miss Sadler ... the three of them ran this school of about fifty pupils, ranging from, I suppose, seven to eleven. Boys and girls, mixed ...

...the basic sorts of subjects. We were brought up to the standard that we could go on to the Grammar School. We got as far as doing elementary algebra, for instance, in the top form there – we were taken as far as our capabilities would allow us. She was quite ready to go as far as we could go ...

...I've no idea what the fees were, but it certainly wasn't expensive.

There was nothing of the prep school element about it ... there was certainly nothing lush about the place at all ... very gentle. We were kept in order, but no more. Quite definitely nothing savage about it.

Hedley Auckland

I really picked up with Dylan at the age of about eight, when we met first of all in Cwmdonkin Park, and played games of cricket on the grass there ... at that time Dylan was in a small private school in the Uplands – Mirador, that's quite right. He was a cherubic young boy that all mums used to stop and smile, and say "Isn't he sweet?" If only they really knew what was underneath that Dylan. Even in those days, at the age of eight or nine, he was quite a wild boy – in the nicest sense – a boy who would get into all sorts of trouble, but people would say "This can't be true. This angelic little boy – he couldn't possibly do these things that he's doing."

...rather more than normal mischief. Nothing really wicked but if there was trouble, Dylan was in the front of it. Anything that was agin the government, that was agin the accepted convention of the time, Dylan was there to do anything that he shouldn't do. It wasn't really naughty, it was just wickedness.

John Morgan Williams

I came to the Grammar School in 1924, and Dylan started as a boy in 1925. They came in quite young at that time, because there was an entrance exam for a scholarship, which I think was only given to about thirty boys. There was also an examination for the fee-paying students. I would gauge myself that Dylan was a fee-paying student. The scholarship boys were not put into one form. The headmaster at that time had his idea was that these scholarship boys should be spread over the forms.

...we started in the Grammar School in the first year with the Thirds. The second years were known as the Removes. Then you become a Fourth form, and then, of course, the Fifth form. You sat your matriculation in the Fifth form in those days.

...I taught him Latin in the first year. I thought that Dylan had quite average ability, myself. Good average ability. Point was that at a very early age he decided that he wasn't going to work, and I'll quote you a personal experience of mine. I had set homework for the form, and

12. John Morgan Williams

Dylan hadn't done his homework, so I let him off the first time. It happened the second time. I may have let him off the second, I don't know, but the third time I boxed his ears for not doing his homework.

Of course, you've got to remember that his father, the senior English master, was at that particular time a very forbidding figure in the staff room. He wasn't a very approachable man, he had a rather choleric and a short temper. So when I came out and mentioned this to a colleague of mine, he was appalled that I had dared to strike Dylan. "I don't care about his father," I said. "If he doesn't do his homework, he gets it." And I was expecting to be approached by D.J. Thomas. Well, nothing happened. But about two terms later he said to me "I see Dylan's getting on very well with his Latin." – because I had no trouble afterwards with Dylan. I said "Yes." He said "He told me that you had been rather severe with him." I said "Yes, I was. He hadn't done his homework." And I was surprised when he said "I'm very glad. I wish that other masters had done the same." Because at that early age, Dylan traded on his father. And he traded on his father right through the school. And therefore, of course, when you lose, say, the trend in mathematics or Latin or French, you become a poor scholar. Not necessarily because of your ability.

When you say 'boxed his ears' –

Just bringing a little clip across the head. Just a little touch – I scared him and from that moment his homework came in with regularity. And well done, I must say.

I still believe that Dylan would have done well, quite well, if he had knuckled down to it. But it became quite ingrained in him not to work, and the whole time he was there he cultivated the art then of absenting himself during examinations – he got away with it because the other masters were not prepared to trample on D.J. Thomas' toes.

...it's hypothetical I know, but interesting, what Dylan would have made like if his father wasn't on the staff. There is that undoubted effect that he did take advantage of it. There's no doubt about that.

You only taught him in the first year, the Thirds?
Oh yes – then he was out of my hands. I met him during the course of the school year. I knew all about him; we would discuss boys in the staff room, and everybody mentioned "Oh, Dylan Thomas", and they simply washed their hands of him – the point was that in the Grammar School if you wanted to work, you could, if you didn't want to work, you needn't work.

...the fee-payers didn't come so very much from working-class families. They were the middle class of Swansea. Fathers in the Docks and their sons had jobs already made for them, if they wished to, on leaving school. Either into business with their fathers or this and that, so there was a very free and easy atmosphere so far as that was concerned.

No great pressure, you see. If you wanted to work, you could. Of course, there was always a very good Sixth Form, especially on the Classics side, English side with D.J. Thomas, and Mathematics side, so the scholarships could be won for the school. But most boys had a good time, and yet they worked if they wanted to.

The relaxed atmosphere was largely due to the personality or policy of Trevor Owen, 'Gaish', the Headmaster, wasn't it?
Yes, yes, quite true. He was a gentleman in the real sense of the word. Great respect for him ... he never interfered, and the boys loved him ... he was a north Walian, coming from Caernarfon. He went up to Cambridge to read Mathematics, and after teaching, as he told me, in either Somerset or Devon, became the first Headmaster of the first grammar school formed in Wales – or county school, as called then. At a very, very young age. And then, 1900 I should think, around that time, he became the Headmaster of Swansea Grammar School.

Nothing nasty at all about him – he was a wonderful character ... very distinguished – very strong, powerful physique, grey hair, whiteish hair which he combed back and a nice radiant colour face ...

there was a kindliness in his face ... I mean, he would shout at the boys and make more noise if they were making noise themselves in the examinations. The boys felt that here was a man you wouldn't do anything really bad to in class or anything underhanded, because you felt an affection for the Head. And you never, never saw him snooping around at all. He'd be about, but never looking for trouble. The result was that you had to keep your own discipline.

Did you discuss Dylan at all with DJ?

Yes, I did ... DJ was very satisfied when Dylan began to contribute to the magazine, his poems. He often showed them to me before they went into print, and asked what I thought of them – he seemed satisfied that Dylan was able to compose poetry. And, of course, Dylan was losing so much school because of, supposed to be, ill-health. Well, if it was ill-health, naturally his father wasn't a man who would pressurise him in any way, and wouldn't pressurise him in any case, because he was a typical master of what I've said at the beginning: if you wanted to work you could, and if you didn't, well, he simply washed his hands of you.

...we've all had sons in school, many masters. There's no need for you to be talking to your son in school but you do make enquiries from other masters in the Staff Room how your son is getting on – and if there's any trouble, they come and tell you that your son wants watching. We did that, naturally. But DJ never asked anyone how Dylan was getting on.

...I don't think that DJ would in any way, say if Dylan was in difficulties with his algebra or geometry, be able to show him or take an interest in that respect. DJ gave one the impression that teaching was beneath his dignity ... and, therefore, I can't imagine DJ sitting down and helping Dylan over his homework or anything like that.

...now, I must make this clear, too. To my mind, there were two D.J. Thomases ... the man I've been talking about, the choleric, irritable, vain, very vain, man I've been talking about, is a D.J. Thomas of the first years, until he had the serious illness ... he was away for a very long time. And he was very, very ill. And it mellowed him ... he became then a man that was entirely different ... there was none of this irritability about him ... quietened down, he talked – I realised now he was a very good raconteur, and if there was a story with any kind of Welsh embellishment, then he would bring the Welsh accent out.

...we talked books, and then he would relate some episode in his life, because he used to thoroughly enjoy himself over the weekend, because he used to imbibe pretty heavily, and he'd be very good company. Very good company.

...we discussed books by American authors ... all those novels of Dreiser and Sinclair Lewis ... I introduced him to the American authors but we were both reading D.H. Lawrence at that time ... I was very interested in his explanations on *Sons and Lovers* ... the most interesting speaker when you had him to talk. There's no doubt that his appreciation of literature was of a very, very high standard ... I'll say this, that if he'd got the Chair, he would have been a worthy person in that Chair.

...the *Observer*, that was his paper on Sunday ... it was good on books...[25]

...I don't think he had any interest at all in politics ...

...he was a man who was very secretive about his background. Never discussed it ... he never even gave a semblance of the fact that he could speak Welsh. Never heard it. Never gave any idea about his relations with Gwilym Marles, the Welsh poet and preacher ... never did he touch Carmarthenshire with me.

...very, very, very, very punctilious about his dress. Well, on the Saturday morning he'd come to school, he'd look then the real country gentleman – loud tweeds. Oh yes, loud tweeds. And very careful with his dress. Everything matched, you know. Rather inclined to dress loudly, as it were. Light clothes ... the county type of dress – the country squire ...

...radio started to come out ... the headmaster, Trevor Owen, was one of the pioneers of the radio. He made one himself ... one of the first in Swansea ... it was much bigger than that fireplace ... D.J. Thomas was fancying getting one, and he was telling me he had to put an aerial up. Well, he told me that he wouldn't be able to do it. And it wasn't a question that he wasn't able to do it, but it would be something beneath him to do it! He said "I wouldn't know, Williams, how to put it up, and I don't see why I should." I said "You can always get someone to put it up for you." "Oh, can you?" You see, he was entirely ... he didn't know ...

He called you Williams all the time? He never called you John?
We called ourselves by our surnames ... then after 1929, there was a fair amount of retirement and youngsters [came in], and that was the time when we called ourselves by our first names ...

Did Mrs Thomas come up to the school at all?
I never met her.

Was this unusual? Did other wives occasionally come to school?
No, no. They never came to school. No ... there was no cause you see ... the building didn't allow for any sort of social activity.

But weren't there occasional tea parties where the masters had parents in?
Only one I remember ... I think after some prize day ... yes, he [DJ] was
there, but, of course, the school was such a rambling place, they must
have walked around and I never met Mrs Thomas.

*Dylan, in 'Return Journey', gives the impression that the Grammar School
boys considered themselves a cut above the other boys in the town, and that
the working class children, on Sundays for instance, promenading, would
make fun of this, of their accents and so forth.*
Yes, that's true, because the majority of the fee-paying boys came from
the Uplands and Sketty area. And there was an accent, known as the
Uplands accent, and the Sketty accent – there were working class
pupils, of course, because if their fathers were working in the steel
works or the tin works, they could afford to pay. Oh yes, we had quite
a cross-section – you must remember that Fforestfach and Llansamlet
and Morriston were more or less Welsh areas, but they were wealthy
Welsh areas. Morriston particularly, with its two tin works, the Forest
and the Dyffryn – there was money to be made there, and they could
send their boys to school.

Did you take Dylan in other subjects?
No, but I came in touch with him later on in the school; we formed a
dramatic society. Of course, Dylan was in his oils on this – there were
only three of us who were in charge – D.J. Davies, the junior history
master, who produced, myself who was stage-manager and treasurer,
and Mr Lavender the art master, who did the scenery. Well now, we
started from scratch. Oh, it was really pathetic. With the scenery we
did, we had to tie it up and hold it – we started off with plays like
Abraham Lincoln, and Dylan was in that. And I remember *Strife* partic-
ularly, John Galsworthy, where he had the part of Roberts. It's easily
nearly forty years ago. I can remember it to this day.

Dylan was the strike leader – it's an emotional part, but he has to
arouse these workers and then, on the other hand, as Galsworthy shows,
the poverty he has to suffer as a result of leading the workers, his wife
having to suffer – we had no facilities at school, we had no stage or
anything, we just learned the parts in the classroom and made them
walk round the art room a bit, so when it came to the final rehearsals,
because we produced in the Llewellyn Hall, YMCA, we would go for
about half a dozen rehearsals just before the play, in the evening.

I can remember quite well it was typical of Dylan, when his cue was
required, he wasn't there, and I asked "Where is Thomas?" and they

said "He's in the Billiard Room." So I sent down a boy to fetch him. He didn't come, he hadn't finished his game, so I went down myself and simply pushed him out of the Billiard Room and remonstrated with him on the way that we were waiting for him, and he got on the stage, I remember the old box there, he got on that, and within seconds he was at the height of his emotional ... I was afraid he'd never last out the rehearsal, because it was belying his physique, you see, he didn't look very strong but all these rehearsals and a big part, and on the night, three nights. It was remarkable. He was undoubtedly a good actor, wonderful actor.

A resonant voice. Plenty of volume. He gave the impression to us, of course, that he was straining at the bit because he was only fifteen or sixteen, but he obviously wasn't, because the voice lasted throughout his life – oh, he made a wonderful impression in those plays.

What was Dylan like at games?
Oh no, nothing at all. No use at all.

But he claimed to be a good bowler.
No, he never played. I was in charge of cricket. He never appeared anywhere, he never – nothing at all. If he did bowl, he bowled in Cwmdonkin Park. Oh, no, no, no, no, oh no. I knew all the boys who could play cricket in the school.

...you asked me about the fact that he did very well in cross-country running – he held the School Mile for two years, but now you've got to take that in its proper perspective. It didn't make him a miler ... the master in charge was Mr Gwynne ... he handicapped the boys according to age. Well, Dylan was very young – he would probably have a start of about two hundred yards in a mile. But nevertheless, it was an achievement in respect of his tenacity, that here he was grinding himself along with these Sixth Formers and everybody. It wasn't a Junior Mile, it was a Mile ... he was there, right to the very end, there was this tenacity – which comes out in his poetry, of course. It's credited that he would take a day or more, or days, over a line. Trim it this way and trim it that way. There was that tenacity. My argument about Dylan is if he could learn all these lines that he could in plays, if he'd only put that effort into his work, he could have done his school work.

Mr & Mrs John Morys Williams

Mr JMW: It was quite a unique school I would say, in the sense that the headmaster was many years ahead of his time, in that the boys ran the school rather than anybody else, and Dylan was particularly free in every way. He came to my classes for a short time, at his own request, and then disappeared to edit the school magazine. Nobody worried whether he came or not, and I think that was typical of his school career.

...I was teaching Latin there then, and he asked if he should come to some of the Virgil lessons. He came for about a term and seemed to enjoy it, but it wasn't really for exams or anything like that. He just came to enjoy himself – I don't think he made very much progress. He wasn't taking Latin really as a subject. He just came to listen.

He had no ambitions to go to university, did he?
Mr JMW: Oh no. I don't think his father ever had ambitions in that way for him because he really wasn't – we must be quite clear on this – he wasn't a model schoolboy at all. And he didn't seem to have the urge to work at purely scholastic stuff. Because there were a lot of very able chaps there then – whom he was very friendly with – but he just didn't seem to join in the race, as it were. And was quite happy as he was.

...Mr Lavender was, you might say, a conventional art master, and Dylan was a young, far-out sort of poet, and it was suggested to Mr Lavender that there was more in the newer, modern art than there was in the old. Mr Lavender was not exactly pleased with this, but later on seemed to have thought it over and had a shot himself at these abstract paintings. One especially seems to have been done to show Dylan that he could do them if he wanted to.

Mrs Williams, did you talk to Mr Lavender or Mrs Lavender about this?
Mrs JMW: Yes, later. After Mr Lavender had died, Mrs Lavender had an exhibition of his paintings and etchings and I was particularly interested in one ... and she said that it was the abstract that Mr Lavender actually did. She didn't mention his annoyance with Dylan at all at the time ... it was called *Tannhauser* ...
Mr JMW: His father was a wonderful reader. He taught me; I was a boy there myself, and that's one of the things I do remember ... I should say that he had a better voice than Dylan himself. I never heard him acting or anything like that; I don't think he did anything like that, but he had a very wonderful speaking voice ... he spoke beautiful English and Welsh.

...there was something very, very nice about DJ. I don't know whether I should say this, but he was bit aloof in the mornings, first thing, but after lunch he was very, very different. Of course, he liked his pint of beer, you know, and when he'd had just that – he was not a man who drank in the sense he over-indulged, but he certainly seemed to free himself ... DJ on Wednesdays, as far as I can remember, used to go down town and have his lunch in the Mackworth, I think it was. And I used to meet him quite often on his way back when I was going up to the school field, and he was then at his most charming ... not as abrupt as he might have been first thing in the morning.

...the Swansea Grammar School in those days was the only school in the town which had Wednesday afternoon holiday and Saturday morning school ... it had tremendous advantages. I think you see that in Dylan's knowledge of Gower. That was one of the things that one could do. Wednesday afternoon, nobody else was about on holiday so we had the run of the sands, and Mumbles and Gower all to ourselves ... we had bikes and the whole peninsula was open to us. Caswell Bay, for example, was a great favourite. It was out of reach to any but small boys on bikes because you had to walk from Mumbles to it if you wanted to go there. Nowadays, the bus runs right down into the beach and I suppose it's the most populated of the beaches. There's been a complete change in that way.

Do you recall the time Dylan won a race?
Mr JMW: Oh yes, I can remember that well. His father was there at the end. The famous race when Dylan came in with blood on his vest ... his father was delighted ... I can quite well remember him going to his father after the race was over, and they sort of just disappeared off.

Charles McKelvie

I actually saw that race, when he won it with a great gang flurry in the end, because he had been rapidly overhauled by the powerful, the really powerful, runners of the school ... he'd been given quite a reasonable handicap start, but his general physique wasn't comparable with the most senior boys. It was just sheer determination and courage in the end that got him to the tape ... he might have had a spot of blood on his singlet, but it wasn't from a lung haemorrhage or anything which he might romanticise about, because he had stumbled and fallen just before he got to the tape, and picked himself up, so he could have had a spot of blood that way quite easily.

Ronald Cour

I was an exact contemporary of Dylan's. I was born in 1914, as he was. My clearest memory is when we were together in what was then known as the Fifth at the Grammar School ... this, incidentally, was the first year that Dylan's father taught us.

...one of the things that is most outstanding in my memory is the fact that when I went there from the other school, I found that the impact of this school was immense, enormous, because the whole climate of the place seemed to me to be centred around one big idea, and that was to stop the masters from putting a lesson on. And I found this quite incredible. Ragging, as we called it, was prevalent in the very first year that I went there. I, as a timid youngster, was introduced to a core of hard-boiled people who'd been kept down for the first year. A lot of people had been put into the Grammar School by parents who could afford to do it, but the boys themselves were never cut out for the job, and they spent most of their time in doing all sorts of things, like breaking open the master's locks, not exactly breaking it open because they were expert locksmiths. Nobody could ever produce a lock that they couldn't open. They would easily undo the lock on the master's desk, introduce little cones of incense and light them, and the smoke would come filtering up through underneath the inkwell aperture when the lesson was on.

Everything was destined to bring the lesson to an abrupt halt. To embarrass the staff, to embarrass that master in some way or other. Singing when the geography master would bring in a piece of mechanism illustrating the way in which the earth went round the sun, and the moon went round the earth. This was a man called Mr Benfield, and he would turn the little handle and then gradually, very gradually through the whole of the form this rising crescendo of "When Benny turns the handle the world goes round." And this would reach chorus proportions, and the whole thing would become quite a farce. And then a boy would jump up and say "Is that right you played for Surrey, sir?"

...I can remember the ragging and pranks that went on in the Fifth particularly – R.M. Lewis the French master, a man from the Rhondda Valley, who was nicknamed 'Lulu'. There were many incidents in the Fifth when he was subjected to all kinds of ill-treatment. In a boyish, prankish way. There was nothing insidious about it, but he was the subject of a lot of this sort of thing. The tying up of a large map-like photograph which consisted of a village scene, this was rolled up at the

13. Ronald Cour

back on the blackboard, and we were asked to speak in French about it. It was rolled up and ties with a piece of cotton and then drawing pins were attached to the room all the way round so the boy in front only had to cut the cotton and down would come this thing in the middle of the French lesson. 'Lulu' was known to have not a very strong heart and he would then be in a state of collapse, and there would be great sympathy from the boys who would then rush out and ask if they could get water and put him to sit down quietly and so forth. And this sort of thing went on right through. It was quite incredible.

...this rather curious business of ragging was in many ways a legacy from the days, perhaps, when it was a public school ... it had that tradition about it, because there were dormitories there, there was a chapel there ... they weren't used as dormitories, they were used as laboratories when I went there.

...another thing one had to be very careful of was one's pen. In those days, of course, pens were the ordinary steel-nibbed ones. There were a few who sported fountain pens, but in the main we used these steel-nibbed pens. And in the Hall, which was a very high-roofed building, high ceiling, with a hammer-beam roof, if you happened to have a class which was in the Hall, you'd suddenly find a boy walk past your desk, pick up your pen and with a very deft movement cut two slits down the handle with his penknife, and insert a home-made dart flight. Then your pen would be flighted up like a dart into the ceiling, and the whole ceiling was plastered with hundreds of boys' pens, almost impossible to recover ...

The great thing about the Grammar School was that the calibre of the staff was excellent. There were these people like Dylan's father DJ, who was a great teacher, a superb master of his subject. And there were others: W.S. Davies who we called 'Soapy'. He was a man who was unable to keep control over a class, and this I think was one of the real troubles with the place, the fact that the men – brilliant men in their own field – were unable to keep order ...

...Jimmy Gott left or died in the year that we went there and then we had a very short period without an art master and then we had Mr Lavender ... I am greatly indebted to Mr Lavender because he was responsible for my going to the School of Art here, as it was then in Swansea, and he was the person who I have to thank for giving me the right kind of guidance and influence in my early days.

Do you know of anything of Dylan's work in the art class?
Yes. I do know that Dylan was very interested in the Modern movement, not only in art but, of course, as we know in his writings and in many other spheres as well – there was another very interesting article he wrote about films, about the introduction of what was going on then, well before his time. I know that he was interested in abstract art ... this was why so many people didn't understand Dylan. This was why he was looked upon as something which was quite different. It's only comparatively recently that people are even beginning to understand, shall we say, the true significance of Dylan's writings. When he wrote them, it was looked upon as rubbish, because it didn't conform, it wasn't the kind of work that people understood readily or easily. This, of course, has been much more easily understood than in art, which is my business, and the same thing applies here. People want to see that which they know, they want to see that which they understand and anything which is being done which has, for example, what we call imagery, isn't easily understood ... Dylan was able to understand these things at an early age and this, I think, is something that set him apart.

Was he a controversial editor of the magazine?
Not a controversial editor, by any means. He became a very interesting editor; perhaps one of the most interesting that they've ever had, because of his ability artistically; and I must say, that although I have made what might be called criticisms of the school, they're not really intended in that way at all, because, by and large, I enjoyed my Grammar School days. I think it was a wonderful school. It did an awful lot for me; I was thrilled, excited, a little petrified by the circumstance

of it possibly, but it was of tremendous and lasting value to know the boys and the staff who were there at that time and the way of life and everything. But I have got to say this, that unfortunately the climate – the atmosphere – of the school then was one which was a little bit anti-art. And when I say anti-art, I don't just mean art in the accepted sense of the word. I mean it in its broader sense – the arts were looked upon as something which were just that little bit beyond the pale. The two things that you had to go for were the sciences – in which it was a very good school, excellent school; and the other was, of course, the ancient subjects like ancient languages, Greek and Roman history and that sort of thing. You either did one or other of these two. If you did anything which savoured of the modern, you were automatically looked upon as being in a class which was consisting mainly of people who couldn't make the grade in either of these other two things.

... it is a curious thing that there were these people like Mervyn Levy, Fred Janes, Daniel Jones, Dylan Thomas and many other people who one would have thought would probably have come from a different place than the Grammar School. The Grammar School, as I said earlier, was not the sort of place where the arts were promoted.

...there's another point that occurs here, and that is this: that because Dylan – I think it was probably his second year in the school – was introduced to this idea of being the sub-editor of the school magazine, he was automatically given a lot of free time to go and do this particular job, so that he was missing – very conveniently I presume – on many, many occasions when he probably would have been involved with some of these other subjects which he didn't like ... when he was involved with the production of the school magazine, he was allowed legitimately to be away from these classes, with disastrous effect, I'm afraid.

But he had no ambitions to go on to university, so he wasn't worried.

No ambitions at all. No ambitions at all in that direction. And one of the things I think about him was the fact that he was so complete in this way. He knew exactly where he was going – where he wanted to go. And it was no good these other members of staff who didn't understand him or his ideas abusing him in this way and saying all sorts of unkind things, because they really didn't understand.

Guido Heller

I met Dylan first at school because we were both involved in the school dramatic society. Dylan was a peculiar character; he was always, with his deep-throated, gurgling laughter, laughing most of the time at one thing or another. He sort of created verbal situations which he and one or two of his close cronies would think hilariously funny.

The lower playground ... was surrounded completely by trees and bushes, and it had been the custom that all new boys when they first arrived at the school, had to be initiated by being thrown down into the bushes. Dylan had apparently been initiated when he arrived and he was determined that in his turn he would also take a main part in doing the same for all other arrivals, and this I know gave him considerable pleasure because I have heard him discussing the fact that they'd thrown half-a-dozen of these boys down into the bushes to initiate them, but he was certainly quite a ringleader in this style. There was nothing of the sort of stand-off, cultured, literary, poet attitude about him. He was just as robust as any of the lads that arrived in the school, and you certainly wouldn't single him out.

...Dylan was always pretty rough-and-tumble. There was nothing frail about Dylan at all. In fact, Dylan had quite a remarkable amount of strength. I've seen him tussling with other boys and although one always had the impression that Dylan was never very keen on exerting himself physically too far, he nevertheless showed an extraordinary strength and fitness for one who wasn't prepared to do too much in the physical line.

...there certainly was no question about Dylan that he was too namby-pamby or too delicate to play games. There was no question about this at all. Dylan, to the best of my knowledge, was as fit as a fiddle at school and it is difficult, of course, to definitely say, but I can never remember during any periods when we – and we obviously rehearsed school plays for long spells – I can never remember him being absent from any of these due to illness or ill-health or anything of that sort at all.

His mother told me that he was always breaking an arm or a leg, both when he was a child, and when he was a man.

If this were the case, then surely I would have seen him with his arm in a sling or something, and to the best of my knowledge I certainly have never seen him in any way incapacitated. If he had [asthma] as a boy,

14. Guido Heller

he certainly didn't have it while he was at school – this, I believe, was part of the old Dylan try-on. Let's face it, anybody that way minded can put on a very fine wheezing act, and there was nothing in Dylan that suggested that he couldn't do this quite easily when it so suited him ...

...we had a Prefects' Room which was obviously considered, like the Headmaster's study, as quite one of the holy of holies, but Dylan, if he wanted to get out of a class, he tried to come up there because he knew very well that that'd be the last place anybody would look for him. On this particular occasion, I was up there on my own and Dylan came in. And so we started chatting, and in the course of his chatting he picked up the poker and while he was talking he put it into the fire until it got red-hot, and then he started boring holes in the floor. So then I said to him "What on earth are you doing?" He said "As a matter of fact, the staff room is down below. I want to see if I can get this poker through the ceiling of the staff room." Well, clouds of smoke were coming up from the burned wood – in the end I had to make him stop, because the situation was getting a little bit out of hand.

...we had a Debating Society at school, and Dylan took part in that – on a variety of subjects. I was only looking through the school magazine the other day, and noticed that on one night there were debates and Dylan took the lead on one subject ... I was involved in the debate myself, and it varied through capital punishment to all sorts of subjects. And it was a very, very lively evening always. He was, strangely enough, quite serious in a lot of his debating. He could also introduce quite a lot of humour ... but Dylan was quite a fervent orator when it came to it – his diction was good, but it was Welsh. The intonation was definitely Welsh ... you'd never have Dylan in a company or in a crowd and not immediately recognise him as being anything other than Welsh.

...during the course of our chats, I said to Dylan "Why on earth don't you spend the weekend like the rest of us, playing rugby or cricket?" "Oh, no," he said, "I spend my weekends down the Strand." – which, of course, was a very shady area in those days ... and he was always down in the very sleazy pubs at the bottom of Wind Street ... whether Dylan went down there merely to feel that he was mixing with prostitutes – which he did – but whether he went quite as far as then having any associations with them other than just sort of joking and exchanging bawdiness there, it would be difficult to substantiate.

Then again there was the Prom, which in those days was a very famous meeting place. I used to go down there with fellows of my own age and Dylan was there with his own gang, and many occasions he'd pull on an old hat of his father's rather than have his school cap on, obviously, and he'd be slouching about there trying to make out that he was a lot older than he really was, with his cigarettes. He used to smoke as well as drink in those days, although he hadn't reached the age of sixteen, and you'd see him and his gang surround three or four girls, and subsequently always see them walk down off the Prom onto the sands. And you then drew your own conclusions ...

...I can remember at nights around Cwmdonkin Park and the houses there on one particular occasion, I don't know why, but I was with Dylan this particular night, and there were several of us, and Dylan had the grand idea, he'd got reels of black cotton in his pocket, and the thing was then, to tie this cotton to the knockers and then run round the corner, you see, and then start bashing the knockers as hard as he could on the end of the string. And this we did half-a-dozen times, and he thought this a terrific evening's entertainment. I mean, he was like that. A lot of the things he did were quite puerile and childish. Other things he did, such as writing for the school magazine, he was possibly years ahead of his age.

...he told me on one occasion that he was experimenting to see how long he could keep his head in a gas oven before he lost consciousness. So I said to him "Don't you think you could sort of pursue more profitable pursuits at weekends than doing this?" "Oh no," he said, "it's all great fun to find out what exactly you can do and what you can't do." But this was Dylan all over.

...in the Uplands in Swansea there was a cinema, which was called by all of us the Flea Pit. Now, it was a recognised thing that, on a Saturday night particularly, everybody used to go to the Flea Pit with our girls. Dylan used to go there, usually with a boy friend, but when they got there they usually used to sit up at the front of the cinema, and I can remember that he was nearly always slung out for misbehaviour. He was either sort of creating a situation by being noisy and generally disturbing the other patrons in the place, or else he'd get up there in the front rows and there'd be girls up there and then there'd be such a carry-on generally, up in the front, that the manager had to come and chuck him out.[26]

After he left the Grammar School, he went into the Evening Post. *You were then still in the Grammar School, were you?*
Yes, I was there for about a year possibly – perhaps not quite so long – and then I left Swansea and I went abroad; so there was then a considerable gap ... my next [meeting], to my great surprise, was at Twickenham, when England was playing Wales at rugby, and I happened to be there on one of the terraces and who should walk in front ... but Dylan in a rakish cap with a beard ... it was, as I remember it, a rather long, fair, lightish brown beard ... I thought that particular day seeing him, that he quite looked the part at Twickenham.[27]

...my next association with Dylan – and this involves subsequently Caitlin as well – came when I had returned to Swansea and I had come down here to Rhossili, and one day I happened to be in Swansea in the Uplands, and who should I bump in to but Dylan and Danny Jones together. It was after the War, yes – Dylan immediately said "Right, we have to celebrate this meeting, we must go into the pub and have one."

...while we were standing up at the bar drinking, a dog walked across the bar, you see, a little brown terrier. So Dylan turned to me and said "You know, I do like a dog. But this particular dog has got to have a really nice brown arse." And he said "There, look at that one, it's got it." And this was Dylan.

George Guy

Gaish was quite soft-hearted; very erratic. Very brilliant mathematician but hopeless in trying to teach anybody maths ... but he was a quite a nice Head. The only thing about it was that he was the one that gave the tannings ... across the seat. He used to have a cupboard in his room, twenty or thirty canes, so when you went into the room, you had to bend over his desk, and then you could hear him go and rustle among them, and select which cane he was going to hit you with. And he was an expert with it. He'd put half-a-dozen on within half-an-inch of each other.

...the Deputy Head was the reverse. He'd put one at the back of your neck and one down by your ankles. He wasn't so particular.

...Sergeant Bird [nicknamed Oiseau/Wazzo] ... he was an artist with a fencing cane. He used to take us in Punishment Drill as well as the games ... there were three types of punishment in those days. There was the Punishment Drill which the Prefects could give you; there was the Detention, which they could also give, and the masters gave you; and there was also a tanning by the Head.

Punishment Drills took place on a Wednesday afternoon, which was our half-day. ...whoever was there had to drill under Wazzo ... the drill really involved trotting. Trotting round, but your hands had to be at the back of your neck with the tips of the fingers just touching, and you had to jog round and round for perhaps an hour-and-a-half, something like that ... Wazzer used to have rather a big fencing stick and a stone, and he'd be beating time with this fencing stick on the stone ... he'd change time on this thing, and if you were out of step, you felt the fencing stick, of course. Back of your seat.

Charles Fisher

It was in school I met him. I think we were in the same form; certainly in 4A and afterwards in 5A – he was one who I came to know gradually. I know that soon after we met I went to his home and we spent many evenings then, mostly reading to each other. We used to read from the Bible, from Isaiah. Dylan especially liked Isaiah, he liked the thunderous roll of its phrases. I think the words of the scripture had a very deep meaning for him, quite apart from anything they might have been trying to say.

Did Dylan ever talk to you about his ideas about religion?
Yes, I remember when he said "In religion I am not a pantheist but I think in a pantheistic way." That was his idea then on that particular evening. I've no idea whether that was his feeling generally or consistently. I should doubt that it was, but it might be possible he thought in a pantheistic way. Some of his later poems seem to confirm that ...

71

we were very interested in words at the time. Now, pantheism is a fine word, one would immediately find out what it meant and how it was to be applied, and it might even lead to thinking in a pantheistic way, which is no bad thing.

D.J. Thomas was a master in the school. Can you recall something of him as a teacher?

Yes, I recall him very well, and I think of him often. I am obliged to him for his part in my education, and but for him I should have had little education indeed. His were the only classes at which I paid any attention. He had a character which demanded attention. Other classes resembled a kind of a rough-house, very often a consistent rough-house from beginning to end, but his were always perfectly conducted. There was utter quiet, complete discipline and most often he taught rigorously but well. I can only think of one or two occasions when he lost his temper. It was a frightening sight, but he did have a very hot temper on those few occasions, once or twice a year when – nothing in the class itself, the class was very well-behaved – when something provoked him; a boy dropping a book perhaps, purely accidentally. I owe a great deal to his meticulousness, to his own undoubted feeling for the language and for poetry and for English. And to his careful use of words and to his own way of speaking, which was one of the first I copied. When the local accent was fearful, I thought.

...D.J. Thomas' way of talking was meticulous and precise, almost dry, but one would say gentlemanly, perhaps. Whereas Dylan's was flamboyant and rotund and almost baroque in the use of his voice, in the manner which his father might well have believed was – oh, how shall I say – an unwarranted display of ability.

...father and son were necessarily close at that time. I don't think it was a warm relationship, whatever that means precisely. It wasn't, I think, sentimental at that time or there was undue affection. I think that Dylan's father was understandably perturbed at times by the course Dylan and Dylan's education seemed to be taking. It did, in fact, disturb Dylan's father greatly and there was a great deal of tension, I think, between Dylan and his father on many occasions.

Did Dylan discuss the writing of poetry with you?

Oh, yes, interminably, and often. I remember very little of these discussions, as might be expected. I can remember some of the poems he was writing at that time ... beautiful sprung rhythms, with that great sense of rhythm which he always retained. I remember little in particular of

15. Charles Fisher

general discussions about poetry at that time. It was a time of enormous increase of interest in words and material of the language itself. It was a time when he was interested in sounds; "metrical biscuitry", he often used to mutter, "metrical biscuitry".

...collecting words, they were rare butterflies, and pleased him. He had an idea at that time that poetry came from words and that he had a notebook there and he would put down fine words, word combinations and this was a process of finding out how things worked. I think he was conscious that he would be writing, needed to write, and that part of his mind was going the same way as the tape recorder is ticking away, and he was then able to use recollection in order to write more poems ...

I remember the time when he was writing *The Map of Love*, and reading bits of that and then I heard many things for the first time – the one which most impressed me on the first hearing was 'Ballad of the Long-legged Bait'. Read in a fine rumble, deep-belly voice, all-stops-out, at the Langland Bay Hotel. He had been telling me for some time he was engaged on a long and important poem, and he came and read it to me.

What about Dylan's health?
I thought he had the physique of a bull and he must have had, you know, to have stood the pace he did. Dylan must have had extraordinary physical stamina of one kind and another, simply to have gone on being Dylan for so long ... I suppose ultimately it would have a

cumulative or possibly medical effect, but certainly he could drink far more than I could at that time, and far more consistently.

...he was mainly a drinker of mild beer. It was a discovery that there were such things as treble whiskies, about which he told me about in an awed voice one day ... he asked me once when we were probably just out of school "Do you like beer?" and I said, no, I don't. But he said "Well, I *like* it, that's the trouble. I like it." He really liked the taste of the stuff.

I wouldn't say that he never drank while he was at the grammar school, but it was unlikely that he did; I never saw him drunk. It is extraordinary, that I remember knowing him for a long time so clearly before he drank anything at all except tea or ginger ale. He must have started drinking on the *Evening Post* because he was a gregarious man and got on very well with all kinds of people on the staff. And in the evening, I didn't see him at any of what we did. We went dancing; but not Dylan, we went to balls, but Dylan was around pubs in Swansea and there he got the tale for many stories

What was he shaping up like as a reporter?
The slick, old-fashioned idiom, which you were expected to write, didn't suit him. It was like a too-cramped shoe; it was a form utterly unsuitable for his gifts, as if some world-famous *coloratura* had been asked to sing 'Roll Out the Barrel'. He found it extremely limiting, and those limitations produced some oddities. It was a case of the idiom of reporting not suiting him and he soon left when he realised that. He had a very good capacity for withdrawing from untenable situations which didn't suit his gifts.

While he was at the Post, *Dylan indulged in theatrical activity in the Little Theatre, but he'd started acting while he was at grammar school.*
I do recall Dylan's contributions to the Little Theatre and being amazed at the time at his capacity as an actor. I had no doubt that he could have become an extremely celebrated actor had he chosen. The vibrancy of voice and the passion of his performance and complete identification between himself and his role were something which I could remember. It was astonishing to me that Dylan – who I'd thought of as being primarily a writer – could have succeeded so completely as an actor.

Swansea and the parts of Swansea that Dylan came from, the Uplands area; this is very much Anglo-Welsh or English-speaking Welsh people.
We know about Welsh, and we know, of course, that we are cut off in a

sense from our natural-born language which one presumes would have been Welsh, since we were all, I think, romantic to a certain degree and would have thought about Wales. We often read Welsh stories and Welsh magical and mystical stories of the past – in translation. Now what we were left with was a culture, if one can call it that, that was not completely viable; when ultimately Dylan would have to go to London, that was fairly clear.

...Dylan was able to over-awe even those who were most accustomed to over-awing other people. He did it by his fine acting sense, and partly by his natural gifts, but his fine voice, which could be South Wales by turns, or Kensington, or even a completely upper-class voice full of *hauteur* and rudeness which couldn't be rooted in any part of London. He'd switch these mannerisms and voices around, mocking, sarcastic and indulgent by turns, and had an enormous success. I think this was equipment, more or less, deliberately acquired because the equipment one had, merely being an Anglo-Welshman from the Uplands, wasn't sufficient.

You must consider the transition which is being made from a circle in Castle Street in the Kardomah to Chelsea and Kensington. One is still finding out in what areas one is deficient, and the first glimpse of the rich and the successful and the highly educated is always a somewhat astonishing one. They reveal remarkable changes of pace and adroitness hardly suspected. You find that there are other ways of doing things – rudeness, for example – which we can scarcely achieve in a local circle. But Dylan was a very swift learner and later on he could equal any of them at their own game, quite easily.

Dylan always had a common touch. He was received as an honoured guest by Labour Members of Parliament, for which I give him credit; he had dinner with a group of Socialist MPs. I was working at Westminster then and I saw him as he left, and I said "What did you talk about?" He said "Mostly we talked about diseases. They were all telling me they had the arthritis in their arm, and the other one said his lumbago; then I had some diseases of my own to talk about." And I said didn't you find that rather disappointing to spend the evening talking about diseases. And he said "Good God, no ... much better to be sitting there happily talking about our diseases than discussing strong-arm tactics about the world." He got on perfectly well with Labour, talking in the most homely way about their various afflictions.

Did he ever say anything to you about his feelings about Wales and the Welsh, and the fact that he couldn't speak Welsh?

It's rather a sentimental thing to regret not speaking Welsh. That occurs, I think, later and I can't remember Dylan, who was so supremely fortunate in his use of English, he never regretted another language. He had immense sympathy with Wales. We used to meet occasionally, having drunk a certain amount of beer, and we would all weep for Wales. We would say "Let us weep for Wales", and real or simulated tears would quickly flow as we would think of all the woes that Wales had suffered. It was deeply appreciated that something might have been different in our environment.

...the Slump carefully skirted the Uplands – at least, the children of the Uplands, I don't think it reached them at those years. The Slump had become an environment of which we were used; we were well used to the difficulty of raising thruppence for a coffee, and were well used to walking to school and back during the lunchtime in order to have dinner at home. That means three and half miles, four miles, part of it uphill – walking there and back made no difference. Fred Janes would accomplish the walk up Walter Road so rapidly that he told me he was afraid only of "taxiing off". The material elements of a child's life are not immensely important if he has boots and clothes and food, as I think we all had. Dylan preferred, for the reason of his type of writing, to think of Swansea as it sometimes was: crowded and rollocking and shopping and colourful.

I might say a word now about the tolerance and kindness of Dylan. It seems to me that towards myself and towards so many of his friends there was an attitude which he didn't maintain to everybody but rightly in London I found him easy-going, easy to get along with. I never felt that Dylan was the same as the other people that I knew at that time, and the others could even talk better than Dylan – that was surprising, there were people that could out-talk him, there were people who were more amusing. I was very, very sure that in Dylan we had a great, major lyric poet and it does inhibit one in dealing even with an eighteen-year-old who one believes to be that, even if that view was still to be shared by the majority of people, it does inhibit and I think my own dealings with Dylan, our talks, were always less successful. I was always conscious of that. He was one of the very few people I was always to some extent trying to impress at that point. It handicaps one. With everyone else it wasn't the same. I think one got along a good deal better; but taking into account that relationship that was established at that time by my regard for him, my regard for his writings, I always think of his great good humour, and the warmth of his friendship.

Many things which I would probably find very difficult to say on this tape ... I never for a moment forget him. Always think of him. Many a glass I raise to him.

'Percy' Eynon Smart

Dylan followed me into the Grammar School. I knew he was in the school; I used to say 'hello' to him, that's all. But we came into contact when I was in the Sixth and I collected the job of editing the school magazine, with Dylan. And my knowledge of him is almost entirely confined to the one year in which we edited the magazine together.

...One of the outstanding things about him was the fact that through his schooldays he was writing enormously. He was turning out great sheaves of material and I remember well when I was visiting his home – had tea there or something or other one day – being shown a pile of manuscript in the corner of the room, quarto manuscript, standing, I suppose, about four foot high from the floor, Dylan's productions, which his mother was a little impatient with because it was a great pile of paper, but his father insisted on keeping because he thought it might be interesting one day. And I've often wondered what happened to that pile, which undoubtedly got bigger before it was dispersed.

...on the magazine, the interesting thing about Dylan was the magnificent – no, that's the wrong word – the quite remarkable good light verse, very often of the Austin Dobbs style, that he was turning out that was way above the school magazine standard. Perfectly conventional, rhyming and scanning; of course, as we all know now, he was at the same time writing the much more advanced poetry that we couldn't have printed in the magazine; no-one would have understood it. And I remember asking him why he wanted to write poems that I couldn't understand and a lot of other people couldn't, and his answer, of course, was typical of him and many, many others in that situation. "I'm not writing for you or for anybody else. I'm writing for myself." Which again, is the correct kind of arrogance of the genius. Arrogance in the nicest sense of the word. One doesn't think of Dylan as being arrogant, but in this instance he was. He didn't care whether we understood it or not – if we were swine and we had pearls in front of us, then this was our misfortune. The interesting thing though, as I say, was the perfection of the conventional verse that he was writing – I was only talking here of the form – the form being conventional – but his sense of humour was obviously highly developed already, and equally obviously, his depth was appearing – he had astonishingly varied ability. This again obviously became much more apparent as he became a public figure.

...this is not the wisdom of hindsight. I think I did see that I was working with a genius. I remember my parents didn't know the Thomases at all well. My mother knew Mrs Thomas very slightly, but I can remember mother saying more than once how she sympathised with Mrs Thomas in having Dylan, rather a scamp, as a son. I can remember telling her repeatedly that whether he was a scamp or not, that he was, in fact, a genius ... a scamp in a very mild sense at that time – I remember my mother and myself going to the cinema one afternoon and seeing Dylan in the back row with one or two other chaps, smoking. And of course this was an appalling ... dreadful crime.

Dylan as co-editor with you had the job of taking part in the decisions on what would be included in each issue. Was he very aggressive in having his own work in, or was he rather shy about it?

No, I think he was rather relaxed about it. He was certainly not aggressive; he wasn't in the least shy. He was very willing to fill space, if there was space to fill and there was nothing else to put in, he would write something, it was just as simple as that. He took no particular pride in what he was doing, he was a craftsman as far as this was concerned, turning out good work to the best of his ability and wonderful it was. But there was no aggression and there was no diffidence. He was quite relaxed about it.

The school magazine had a sort of board of masters over it, didn't it? Wasn't Dylan's father and Tom James involved in that?

It was Dylan's father only, as far as I was concerned, he was a sort of editor-in-chief one could say, or the censor ... Dylan's father, as everybody who sat under him knows, was a lover of English, and he had a profound knowledge and understanding and love of English literature, and it was quite a surprise coming up into the Sixth and taking this job, to see that he didn't write with any facility at all. He didn't find writing easy ... what he wrote, of course, was impeccable, but words didn't come easily. In marked contrast, of course, to Dylan. But he was a very relaxed censor. We ran this very easily, and comfortably.

...switching away from the magazine, one of the most startling signs in my view of the developing genius was the fact that he went through school, as has been frequently recorded, almost completely idle. He did no work – I think that this is a quite remarkable demonstration of a boy deliberately excluding from his experience everything that he knew already didn't really concern him. Because he was an intelligent boy – we all know this – and for an intelligent boy to fail all the subjects one needs concentration of some kind, even if it was only subconscious concentration. In the one subject in which he passed, his father told me afterwards he had ninety-eight per cent, which is now, as it was then, a quite remarkable mark, and this in spite of the fact that on the day he sat his English paper, I met him coming away from the examination room, and I asked him how he'd got on, and he said "Oh well, I've failed that, too." He said "What can you expect? One of the set books was *Pilgrim's Progress* and I spent a large part of the morning telling them what I thought of *Pilgrim's Progress*, so I've failed."

...he seemed to be a tough youngster ... one of the remarkable things about him was that he was not in school in any way an academic ... he was one of the roughs ... he mixed outside the school with Danny Jones, for instance, and this was one kind of social life, but another kind of social life in school was with some of the rougher elements. He was skylarking in the lower playground and he was definitely one of the roughs. Now Danny Jones never was. He was ostentatiously an intellectual in school – quite definitely. And in school, he and Dylan hardly mixed at all.

R.M. Glyn Thomas

He was just that bit junior to me in school, but later he caught up ... I stood back for some terms to play rugby, and he caught up with me. That's really when we first became friends, and we went down on the old bus, the Vanguard bus, riding half-price on the flat roof to camp in Mewslade ... most of our parents allowed us a grandiloquent sum of fifteen shillings a week on which to live ... this would be at the end of 1929, when we were leaving school ... it was the sort of final school leave that we joined up in this camp, and had this great time down there. It was rather hard work living actually because, as I say, on fifteen bob a week you couldn't put a lot of stores in. You sort of scrounged your food from everywhere.

We were down there for a couple of months, probably nearer three months. Dylan probably wasn't the best of campers. I can remember on one occasion, getting very, very cross with him because his bed had not been aired for about ten days and had got mildew. When I threw it out he became very, very cross and then came up to me a few minutes later and said, "You're quite right, Glyn. I'd probably catch pneumonia sleeping in that flipping thing." Or words to that effect.

...ordinary bell-tents, pitched in a field just at Pitton Green, or Pitton, which is the head of the little valley running up from Mewslade Bay. There's a house built there now ... several other people in tents around in other fields nearby ... hired these from the tent-maker in Swansea, who was a Ralph James, I think.

...I can remember Dylan, on one occasion, starting a minor revolution. I was the cook. Whether I was a good cook or not didn't matter very much, but I was the best of a bad bunch; but I cooked on condition that I did no other carrying and fetching, and Dylan objected very strongly to carrying water and getting firewood and decided that I was going to be sacked from my post as cook. And this resulted one evening in a lovely picture of Dylan sitting over a roaring log fire, in an open field with a frying pan that was black as the back of a grate, in which he'd put some fat and some chipped potatoes, and the lot had caught fire, and he ended up with these chipped potatoes looking like bits of charcoal but he insisted on eating them, and even insisted that they were delicious!

He was as stubborn as that in some ways, and a determined little figure. I can remember another occasion when he fell out, over some minor thing, with Bob Rees. Now Bob was a fellow standing about six foot two and a very big lad and, in those days, a very strong fellow. Dylan insisted on taking him on and, of course, all Bob need do was hold him off, you see. It looked exactly like a little terrier going for a mastiff. And Dylan got so infuriated that he couldn't hit Bob that he stood back and he ran at him, and he tried to run up his body to hit him! I always remember this – and he fell flat on his back and that finished the fight! The things I remember of Dylan were many little incidents when we were down camping, such things, perhaps, we'd better not say, like crawling down the potato rows on a cold, misty morning to pinch potatoes to eke out our meagre living, and fishing.

...no, they fished from the surf. Some of the lads were quite good at it and they used to bring the fish back and I'd cook it, and some very good meals we had, indeed. Dylan wasn't very adept an anything like this. But the other source of eking out your livelihood was to 'stook' ... which means that you go haymaking and you put the hay into bundles. And some of the lads were very good at this, and I on occasion went along and put my hand at it. But it meant that you had a very good ham and egg supper for this, and some bread and cheese during the day. But Dylan, again, was not particularly interested in the laborious side of life.

...another thing I remember very distinctly and very clearly about Dylan, was one night we had a terrific party around the campfire. It consisted of several ladies who were camping and staying in the near vicinity, and chaps from other parts of Gower who had come over ... this fire was sort of dying down and Dylan started talking in that sort of round sound he had then. His voice wasn't quite as plummy, if I may use the word, as it became later, but he still had that sort of fullness. And he started talking about infinity. We was lying out around this fire under the stars and he took us down and down and down, and fleas on the lesser fleas' backs and all the way down, until we felt like giants; and then he took us up, and we went up from start to stars, to bigger ones to bigger ones until we were afraid to leave the light of the fire to go back into the tent! He had this ability then of expression, use of words, I suppose. Very wicked in some ways but a great character.

How many boys lived in each of these bell tents?
Well, we sort of split up as one does. We were at times fourteen, I remember, on a weekend. And that meant seven or eight in one, and six in another ... but we had two of these big bell tents, apart from store tents ... and I remember the normal split was that the Davies brothers were in one, and I think Bob Rees, Dylan and I in another during the week, and then whoever came down to join us, of course, they came in, mucked in with whoever, whichever party they liked to be with. I don't think there was any sort of serious difference of opinion between the two tents; it was just a difference of ideas on how to enjoy yourself. The one side liked to go off working, and the other side didn't. And I was included in the side that didn't particularly like working, and there we are!

Did Dylan talk about what he was going to do?
Never very seriously. He was always sort of interested in words. At the time when I can remember him he had a terrific vocabulary as a young man, even when I first met him, a comparatively young lad – I don't know that he had any particular ambitions. The only thing that he did come out with at one time, he did let out to me – we were on the way up Cwmdonkin Drive to his mother's for tea, and he came out with a secret which I was sworn not to divulge to anyone, and that he'd just had a book of poems published. I think this must have been his first ... he was still in school at that time. But I never saw this book of poems, I must say. But I remember him saying that, whatever you say, you

must never let this out.

Did he like going off on his own and sitting in the sand reading?
Yes. Dylan was inclined to be, I think, a little bit of a lone wolf. He liked company in a sense, but he liked to choose company at a time he wanted it. During the day, we were all fairly busy, either with one thing or the other, in the way of sort of fetching, carrying, cleaning up and so on. Afternoons were usually free; it was a question of down to the beach for a bathe. Most of us went down for a bathe before breakfast. Dylan would quite often join us, but if there was any sort of a party going off at night, Dylan was always there. He enjoyed this. He liked to have people round him, but he liked to choose his own time to have people round him.

What kind of parties would these be?
Open fire in the field, where we'd be doing our cooking normally. We'd build this fire up and anyone who was sort of available would come along and yarn and sing – they were quite innocent sort of parties. And, of course, there was always interest in some lass from somewhere or other that we'd found and brought over ... there was another encampment. I think there were six girls camping there ...

...I remember one other little funny incident. Going across from Middleton, which is the little village just above where we were camped, across to Llangennith, there is a so-called Roman road. This is a heavy stone road in among the bog that's there; there's a rather bad, boggy area, and I'd got very familiar with this and could do it in the dark. I remember coming back one night – and again, Dylan would resent the fact that somebody else was leading. As the person who knew it rather better than most, I used to lead, you see. And he resented this one night, and I said "All right – you lead". And we all ended up to our knees in the bog, and Dylan was so excited about this, he said "That'll teach you to lead in the future."

Was he a popular boy, among the others?
He was a bit of a loner, I think. I don't think he was unpopular, but the thing with Dylan was that if he decided that he was going to be interested and hold an audience of lads, he could do it, without a great effort. He spoke rather a different language to the ordinary sort of lad at that age, and they would sit round quite happily and listen ... at that time he spoke, I suppose, a normal sort of Swansea Welsh. I don't remember anything particular about it. I don't ever remember him having any sort of pseudo accent.

Was he any good at any of the chores, like making the fire?
Oh, I think he could. It was just a question that he was on holidays, and if you said "You get some water", he got water, if "Get wood", he got wood but eventually he got a bit cross about it. As others did – I'm not saying that this was a peculiar habit of his particular character ... but no, he didn't resent doing hard work. He resented the waste of time of doing it, I think. This was probably the thing, in the same way as he resented the time sort of making up and bed, and keeping the place sort of tidy. He didn't see the point in doing this, really, because he was on holiday and he wanted all the time for his own little bents, whatever they may have been.

Did he bring a lot of books?
I didn't see him do a lot of reading, but he was scribbling away part of most days ... Dylan wasn't always with us, you see. He would sort of meander off on his own – but, as I say, if there was any sort of party there, he'd would always be there.

People have described him as a delicate boy.
He looked delicate. He was rather small. But I always regarded Dylan as rather sort of a wire-haired terrier type. He had a terrific streak of determination; in some cases I would almost say obstinacy – he wouldn't give in. He'd never give in. If he thought he was being beaten, he'd still fight on, you know.

Was it the custom for the boys to go down the Strand on the weekends, or on the evenings
Yes ... we used to put mufflers on and pull our old clothes on and go down the Strand. If you went down there looking at all respectable you were probably rolled in the mud by the bods down there. The great attraction, apart from some of the lower pubs which weren't places to be found in, was when, of course, there was one of these fairs on. You know, these sort of circus, roundabout fairs.

And if you went down there, you really had to look fairly scruffy to get away with it. Dylan used to love this. I think, even at that stage, he was always searching for the other side of life. Sometimes to the extent of even the seamier side. He wanted to find out what made the lower bracket of people, as far as social status was concerned, tick. Always seemed very interested in this. But we had many escapades down there, but, as I say, these had best be left unsaid.

Evelyn Milton

The first time I remember meeting Dylan was really down in the Gower Peninsula. He was down there camping with a group of boys, and I was staying in a cottage with two other girls ...

...he had a great sense of humour, and he was lots of fun to be with, and he really brightened up their camp considerably. Having him there was an asset, even though he was a little younger than they were. He had this beautiful voice, even when he was quite a nipper ... I couldn't believe it came from this skinny little chap ... because he really was terribly thin, and he had just this mass of hair and these great gooseberry eyes ... he was a delightful little character in those days. And as far as I remember, in all the times I've met him since, he was always amusing. I always loved to be with him, except when he was very, very drunk ... of course, he was shy until he knew you. He wasn't exactly one of these people who came forward and made himself known to you, or even joined in the conversation if he didn't know people. He didn't strike me as being in any way pushing.

...I was older than he was and I think I was just about to embark on Advanced Level English, so he naturally thought I knew a bit about poetry, and he told me that he was writing poetry ... I can remember him giving me this poem to read ... we both lay on our stomachs on the grass. I can remember the kind of feeling of it really, more than the sight of it ... I told him the poetry was very good, and he was very grateful for my opinion, and when I look back on it now and think of how famous he is and that I should have dared to give my opinion of his poetry ...

...when he showed me his poetry, I think he gave me the impression even then, that this was what he wanted to do in life, and he also gave the impression that this was the only thing he cared about, and he wasn't going to do anything else. I think even from his very early days he was dedicated to this; that he knew he had this talent, he knew he was something special. And he intended not to let it go by the board. He intended to cultivate it ...

...Dylan was quite apart from politics, he was tremendously interested in people, not movements. He loved people and their stupid characteristics, and I think the sillier their characteristics, the more they were endeared to Dylan. He loved to find out something about people which was different, which made them something extraordinary or out of the ordinary.

16. Evelyn Milton

...the one great thing about Dylan was that, coming from a Welsh, very respectable background, and very much frowned upon very often by the Welsh people, he was still prepared to live the kind of life that he wanted to live ... he wasn't going to be influenced by outside people, and this is a trait to be admired ... because so many of us are bamboozled and dragooned into doing things which are not really our nature to do at all. I mean, how many of us Welsh people are square pegs in round holes, because we've got this bug of respectability?

Hedley Auckland

We started in the Grammar School at the same time, and it was necessary for me to walk to school via the top of the road in which Dylan lived. And it so happened that, on many an occasion in walking along the top of the road, I would meet Dylan and walk to school with him.

Did the fact that his father was senior English master make much difference to the way he was treated in school?

No. Do remember that Dylan was one of the boys. He was agin the government side. He was accepted – there was no question of Dylan being namby-pambied and being spoilt, oh no.

Was he active in sports and things like that?

The only sport he was really active in was running. And this was long-distance running, the mile, which for some reason he was a natural athlete. He practised very little, trained very little and he would still win the mile – he was a natural athlete. If he had taken the trouble to train and gone in for it wholeheartedly, there is no doubt about it, he would have been quite a good amateur athlete. But he'd enter for the mile, and possibly the day before he'd run around the park and do a bit of training, but that was all the training he ever did.

His mother told me that he'd had lung haemorrhages when he was a boy, a very young boy, and had always trouble with his lungs – but you don't connect this with a person who is able to run long distances.

Dylan always said that he was going die young.

How young was he the first time you heard him expressing this?

This might be at the age of fifteen or sixteen – or even later than that possibly. One day we had been out as naughty boys and possibly had had, for young boys, rather too much to drink and we went off again the next night, and the next night, and I couldn't cope with this and I said "Well, look Dylan, you're an intelligent sort of chap, you've got a future ahead of you – why must we do this all the time?" And it came out while he was in one of his low moods, that it he was sure he was going to die, most certainly before he was forty, with lung trouble. As to how true this was, I wouldn't know, but certainly this was an obsession with him.

Did he suspect he had TB?

Oh yes – yes. He was *sure* he'd got TB ... he'd had some lung trouble. I don't know how serious it was, but he was firmly obsessed with the idea that he'd got tuberculosis. Do remember that young people do get these obsessions – you and I have probably, at some time or other, at that age. But this was his firm conviction, and that is why he said "I'm going to enjoy my life while I can."

...on Tuesday afternoons we used to have study periods ... and we used to walk down to a pub at Bishopston. I can't remember the name of it at the moment, but it's at the top of the hill at Bishopston, where at the end of our walk we used to go in there for a beer. Now, as a young boy of fifteen or sixteen, this beer tasted dreadful to me, but Dylan obviously loved his beer even then – he smoked, yes, but at the age of fifteen or sixteen he wasn't heavy. It was when he became a newspaper reporter that he was heavy.

...I think that his father's ambition was that Dylan would follow in his footsteps and take up exactly as he had done. As for Dylan's ambitions, I don't know that he really had any. I think he went into the

Evening Post as being the lesser of the evils of the jobs that he had to take. He would have been terrified in most forms of industry. He just wouldn't have fitted in – he didn't want to. And I think he went into the *Evening Post* as the least of all the danger that he had to meet.

While you were at the Grammar School you and Dylan occasionally got into trouble that resulted in Dylan being expelled from home.
At odd times he was in diabolic trouble, I know, but being booted out completely was after we'd left school – we were down in a bungalow up at the top of the hill at Limeslade. A wooden bungalow for which we paid the fantastic sum of thirty shillings a week. We shared this with Max Morgan and George Bowen of the gas company. We were there for one summer.

And was this the time Dylan was working for the Post?
That's true – sometimes, if we got back into favour, we would only go back down for the weekend. So we'd only have the weekend down there. But it lasted from about April until September.

How did you manage for food?
If the funds ran to some sausages, we might manage sausages occasionally, but the usual procedure was for us to go home and see what we could get from home, and it seemed to turn out usually that I managed to swipe some tins of pears and peaches and things like that, and for some reason or other Dylan used to manage to swipe some bottles of burgundy, or claret, or something like that. A typical Sunday morning breakfast would be pineapple chunks and burgundy ... Dylan loved the water, and sometimes when we'd been out on a Saturday night and I was feeling quite jaded in the morning, Dylan would dig me up at six o'clock in the morning and go down for a swim.

In those days, did Dylan have a regular girlfriend?
There was no sort of recognised, regular courtship as such. Dylan was a good-looking young man, and the girls fell for Dylan, some of them in a big way, and I'm afraid Dylan treated a lot of them rather shabbily; promised to meet them on Friday but wouldn't turn up and things like that – he didn't lack female company.

Eric Hughes has said that Dylan really had no experience with girls before he went to London. Do you think this is true?
I know it's not true.

Did Dylan ever talk to you about his father?
Oh, he had a tremendous amount of admiration for his father. More so

than the average man, the average young boy. The average young boy might tend to brag of his father if he played cricket or whatever he did, but Dylan had a tremendous respect for his father's knowledge of English generally ... I think his father was a bit of a taskmaster; I think he was quite a disciplinarian. I think that Dylan had some fear of his father, when his father was very roused – but he still always spoke very highly of his father.

But admiration isn't love. DJ was rather a cold figure to be loved, wasn't he?
Yes. That is quite true. I don't think there was a tremendous amount of affection there. I don't ever remember DJ taking Dylan out at all, ever.

What about DJ's attitude to Dylan?
Only on one occasion really did I ever hear DJ speak at length on Dylan. It was one day when I was in Cwmdonkin Park, and I was talking to DJ and he came out of his shell a bit that day, and he spoke of his tremendous hopes of Dylan. He knew that, at that stage, Dylan was far above the average in English literature and that there was a tremendous future for him, but he was worried about whether Dylan would take it up seriously. He could see the defects, even at that stage in Dylan. He knew that Dylan was inclined to be a bit of a tearaway – and this obviously did worry DJ. But this was the only time that I ever heard him speak at length on Dylan. He was tremendously proud of him, but he was worried.

DJ was a disciplinarian in school, but also at home ...
Oh yes, there were odd days when I saw Dylan, and he said that that old man had been in a paddy, and he didn't enlarge on that, but I knew very well that all wasn't well at home.

Do you think that DJ actually sort of exerted corporal punishment?
Oh no, no, but he had a tongue like a rapier, and I think that, particularly after his illness, he was rather more short-tempered than he had been before, and he wasn't the best-natured before.

In fact, it was one of these sort of tirades, perhaps, that led Dylan to go down the bungalow with you, was it?
Oh yes, that's true. That's very true. I don't think it would have been his mother; his mother idolised Dylan, and at any opportunity, Dylan would go home to mum and she would welcome him with open arms.

Did you see much of Nancy?
Not an awful lot. Nancy was older, and of course she would look upon us as young schoolboys. She was very friendly, quite an attractive

woman and rather more on an even keel than Dylan ... she tended to
mother him a bit.

So he had two mothers – two mothering mothers!
That's true, yes. She would spoil Dylan if she could.

*Getting back to Limeslade for a moment – in the evenings, when the dark
fell and you had time together, I presume there was conversation and repar-
tee and storytelling and so forth. In this sort of thing Dylan really excelled,
didn't he? At that time, was he a storyteller among his friends?*
Amongst the friends who could appreciate his somewhat odd humour.
Do remember that basically Dylan had a very acute sense of humour,
but if he was in company who didn't appreciate his humour, he'd shut
up like a clam, and you would find that Dylan would only open up
when he was in the company of people who could understand his
sense of humour ... he was really naturally very shy, and it took a long
time for Dylan to warm up to anybody. He really only had a very small
close group of friends ... many acquaintances, but there were really
only four or five people that he was really close to.

Was he reading poetry?
Yes, of course. But this I think was done mainly in his own shell, and it
was only an odd occasion when you found odd pieces of paper left
around the bungalow that you realised that what Dylan had done in his
own time. You'd find reams and reams of poetry that he'd written.

What happened to all these pieces of paper?
He used to send them up to the various magazines and newspapers,
and on odd occasions he'd get a small cheque of two guineas or
something like that, and this meant a night out on the gin.

*Did he withdraw from the rest of the company in your bungalow when he
wanted to write poems? Did he seem to want to get away and sit down in a
room on his own?*
This was all done on his own. I don't ever remember Dylan sitting
down and writing anything – in school, for example, he'd decide to take
the afternoon off, and he'd do this, sitting on a chair somewhere.

...you wouldn't realise that he wrote any poetry at all, and you could-
n't get him to come out of his shell. But he did have a fund of stories,
and a rather warped sense of humour. Shaggy dog stories he loved ... his
great hero at that time was J.B. Morton 'Beachcomber'. Dylan would buy
the *Daily Express*, or if he didn't have a penny to buy an *Express*, he'd
borrow yours, and the first thing he went to always was J.B. Morton. And
for the rest of that day, if there'd been one or two good parts in

'Beachcomber', everybody that Dylan met would hear these.

...he was very fond of the cinema. We used to mitch from school once a week to go to the cinema, regularly – the Uplands, or there was one in High Street called the Picture House that we could get into for threepence, I believe, in the afternoon – Charlie Chaplin and Charles Laughton. He also used to go a long way out of his way to see films by the great Emil Jannings, and the Marx Brothers – he would see a Marx Brothers film five times – Greta Garbo, yes. She was his absolute pinnacle.

Did he like going for walks on his own?
Very much. Very much, yes – when Dylan went out for a walk, it could be a good ten-mile walk. Oh, yes indeed. 'Cause do remember, that to walk from Swansea to Bishopston and back is the best part of ten miles, and this he did frequently.

Was he talking about politics in that period – because you had the rise of Nazism and Fascism, and the Left was very active in Swansea?
This was rather before that. This would be about 1930, '31. I don't think that he had any tremendous political leanings at the time, but I know that we used to go down and have morning coffee in a small café at the bottom of Wind Street called Biddles and in there were always one or two chaps who loved their politics and Dylan would most certainly participate, but I don't know that he participated for the right or for the left, but whatever the man was speaking for, he would be against – he could talk quite sensibly on politics and the problems of the day, but mainly through the eyes of a young rebel.

You knew Dylan at Grammar School and then when he was with the YMCA Players. Did you have much contact with him after that?
Well, during the days he was a newspaper reporter ... for a good year, we would be out two or three nights a week together ... and we didn't have any money. Part of his job was to go along to the theatre shows and the cinema shows and report on them, on a Monday night. Of course, we went in free, and we had the odd drink there. But our main port of call in Swansea was the Talbot Hotel, which is somewhere near St Mary's Church, and we used to meet there on a Friday night and Saturday night, but he had something of a wandering bug. Dylan's idea of a good night out would be to meet in the Talbot and then start at the bottom of Wind Street and have a drink in every pub, going up, until we had got as far as we could go. We might get as far as High Street Station, having one drink in every pub. But you couldn't get Dylan to

park himself down and stay in one pub.

He was fascinated by the atmosphere on the Strand, which in those days was a rather dubious quarter, wasn't it?

That's true. His particular pub was called the Cornish Mount, which was right on the edge of the North Dock – there had been previously two rather gruesome murders down there, and for some reason or other this little area attracted Dylan. The pub we used to go to down there was a most terrible pub really, but we couldn't go out on a drinking session but that we went down to one or two of those pubs in the Strand.

...one odd night I can remember going into the Cornish Mount, and these people who owned it at the time were Catholics. And it was the accepted thing when we went into this pub that we walked into the back room – which was really the living part of the house, where the people themselves lived – and we got in there one night and all the lights were out except for four candles, which were burning on the table, and on the table was a dead body. The old man had died – we didn't know this, of course – we were walking quite happily into our private little room at the back, and there was this dead body stretched out – we left very quickly. And we didn't go to the Cornish Mount for some time after that.

Dylan wasn't a drinking man in the sense that he could take liquor, and consume great quantities of it. Actually, it had rather a bad effect on him didn't it, on his health. He got quite sick very often, didn't he?

Oh – terribly sick. Oh, that's true – he could drink up to a certain limit. There are many people like this who could take, say, six whiskies or in his case six gins, and be perfectly all right. And all of a sudden he'd topple right over. And I can remember one night when we had to get him back, and it was a question of carrying him on my shoulder, until eventually it became too much, and I found a little garage, opened the door, put him in this garage – in the car that was in the garage – he slept there. I went back in the morning and picked him up – he was only sixteen or seventeen ...

Another part of the Dylan legend is the great womaniser, lecher and so forth but it's hard to reconcile this with Dylan the drunkard – as some people think of him – or Dylan even as a steady beer drinker. It doesn't seem to go together, and I have a feeling that a lot of the legend is built up of women who carted him home to where he could sleep it off, and then established a reputation for having spent a night with the great poet.

Oh, I think on a few occasions he went home with some young lady of unsavoury character – and he probably had had something to drink to go with it as well, but as for being a great womaniser – no. I think he preferred the company of men.

Dylan acted in some plays while he was a reporter ...
Whilst he was still in school he joined the YMCA Junior Players ... Haydn James who was secretary of the YMCA asked me if I could get Thomas to come along to join – he played in a series of plays in the YMCA, and he also loved playing in sketches ... he did a whole series of those. And he was equally brilliant as a comedian.

Is this in the scripted routines, or ad-libbing?
He ad-libbed alright. As a matter of fact, Dylan never knew his words too well. He knew what the plot was about, of course, and sometimes he wandered quite a lot from the dialogue.

Dylan actually produced a play or two, didn't he, for the YMCA?
That's true. He certainly produced *The Fourth Wall* by A.A. Milne – and he also produced some of the shorter plays for our club nights.

Was he a good producer? Could he really command the attentions of the players?
He was quite a disciplinarian. He wouldn't stand any nonsense.

Dylan wrote some playlets, didn't he?
We were putting on plays for our own Society and we weren't paying the royalties – but somebody, somewhere along the line, discovered that we were doing this, and this was out – we weren't to perform any more plays but that we paid the royalties. This meant, of course, doing Shakespeare, or plays that were over fifty years old, and Dylan hit upon the idea of "I'll write a play for you". We sort of played this down, we didn't think he could do it, but he produced the manuscript. Now this play that I remember so clearly was called *Capgar*. It was never published to the best of my knowledge. But the basis of this play was that there was a very pretty girl courting three men, and she couldn't make up her mind which of these three men that she liked most of all, the one she wanted to marry. And in the play she told these three men to go out in the world and to come back some years later, and the man that had done the best, she would marry. Now I'll break away from the story for a moment here. The people who were chosen to play the three parts of the men were Dylan Thomas, George Body, and myself. Now in this play, these three young men went out into the world, came back a number of years later. George Body, in the play, had come back as a successful actor. In fact, years later, George Body went on the stage

17. The cast of *The Fourth Wall*. Dylan is seated second from the left next to George Body

professionally. Dylan Thomas, the part he played, he became a successful author and poet – and we all know what happened to Dylan. The third member of the play who became a successful businessman, and whereas I don't pretend to be a successful businessman, but in those days when we were only sixteen and didn't know what we were going to do in life, Dylan had chosen the three men to play the parts in the play who in fact became what they were in the play.[28]

How long did you go on seeing Dylan? You were starting out in business, a young business executive.

No, I was no executive. Let's not get any wrong ideas. This was the height of the Depression, when there were some three million people unemployed in the country, and we were only too pleased to get any little job, and I was working in a ship broker's office in Swansea ... my money was twenty-five shillings a week ... of course, twenty-five shillings went a long way in those days. Beer was three pence, I think, a half-pint.

Did Dylan ever talk to you about the Depression, the conditions ...

Oh yes. He was somewhat left wing in his thoughts on that ... Dylan had a tremendous sympathy ... for the miners, and he had obviously been down a coal mine and seen how these men worked ... he knew all about the conditions underground, anyway.

What are your most vivid feelings when you think of Dylan now? What stands out most about him, as a person?

A man of quite strong determination on something he so wished to do. A man who had a tremendous sense of fair play. A man who in the main would very, very rarely say an evil word about anybody, in those early days. As I say, he was terribly, terribly shy and because of that not many people really got to know the real Dylan.

1931-1934
"A weak jaw and a loose mouth, and very wide eyes and a hat at a daft angle."

Dylan joins the *South Wales Daily Post* (later *Evening Post*) as a cub reporter. He appears frequently with the Swansea Little Theatre, both in its productions in the Mumbles and in the south Wales valleys, as a touring company. He lives at home, filling his notebooks with poetry and his evenings with slouching around the streets and seashore. He travels to Carmarthenshire to holiday with his aunts and uncles in rural Blaencwm, but he also begins to venture out on the urban road to bohemia, "a bombastic adolescent ... with a thick-knotted artist's tie made out of his sister's scarf, she never knew where it had gone, and a cricket-shirt dyed bottle-green; a gabbing, ambitious, mock-tough, pretentious young man; and moley, too." In 1933 *The New English Weekly* prints 'And death shall have no dominion' – his first poem to be published in London. The same year, his sister marries, his father survives cancer, and the *Sunday Referee* prints 'The force that through the green fuse drives the flower'. He wins the paper's Book Prize in 1934, and publishes in *The Listener*, though readers complain the poem is obscene. By Christmas, he is living in London, and *18 Poems* is published.

Frances Matthews (née Morgan) and George Body

Now with me are Mrs Frances Matthews and Mr George Body, both of whom were with Dylan in the YMCA Junior Players.
FM: I was fifteen when I met Dylan ... and Dylan was fifteen ... after a little while, I began to realise that there was a little more genius about him than the rest of the cast ... Dylan had some sort of air about him. His voice was completely different from the rest of them. He seemed to act with his whole body ... so involved did he become in playing a certain part that it was simply wonderful to see and to watch him ...

And what was the first play that you were in with him?
FM: *The Man at Six*. 1931.
GB: He played in about three or four productions, all mature parts, and for a chap of his age, I think he was terrific ... he liked character parts – he wouldn't take anything else ... wouldn't take juvenile parts ... always did take old parts ...

...do you remember when we did one or two shows outside Swansea, sort of concerts? We did one at Hafod Brotherhood ... we were a bit late starting, it was a very rough and ready show. I remember Dylan blacking his teeth, reddening his nose, and putting his head out through the curtains and just entertaining the audience while we got things going backstage ...

...I remember one sketch we did, little thing about only two men in the world, and all the rest of the world were women – do you remember that? Dylan played the part of the man, and every woman in the world was after him. I played his butler. He thought it was an ideal situation, until, of course, things got too much for him and then he was glad to turn to his butler and get all the women out of it.

...we did a show once, for a garden party but it rained, and we had to do it indoors ... I don't know whether he's in that – *A Little Fowl Play* it was called.

FM: I put my eye on Dylan because he was so clever ... so terribly, terribly clever, and I admired him so terribly much. I thought "I've got to get hold of this fellow now and see what's what." I do remember that we went out for a walk together one evening, along the top of Terrace Road, where he lived, and that was about the darkest spot that you could find in those days. There were no lights there. But I can remember at that time – and this is the thing that I feel that I've never been able to tell anybody – we walked along, and he talked and he talked. And I was terribly sorry, because at that time I knew that he was drinking – seventeen years of age, and he was drinking. Now, I was brought up by my mother to go to chapel – Mount Pleasant, three times a day, Sunday School, baptised at fifteen – and I suppose at that age you feel that you're going to do wonderful things with your life, and I tried to tell Dylan that he wasn't going the right way. He took no notice of me, of course, and he just carried on. But as far as going out with a boy is concerned, I went out with dozens of fellows in my young days, but I can't remember Dylan Thomas being the sort of fellow that would do anything to a girl when you were out that you would object to. I mean, other than hold hands, there was nothing to it.

He wasn't aggressive?
FM: He wasn't aggressive, he wasn't the sort of fellow who wanted to maul you around or anything like that. *I don't* think he was terribly interested in girls.

What was he talking about?
FM: About life, I think, in general. Of course, *I* was trying to lead him into the paths of righteousness ... be a good boy, don't do this, you're much too good, try and turn over a new leaf, this sort of effort which just didn't go down as far as Dylan was concerned. He didn't object, or anything like that, but I know I felt so sad that this boy who was so clever, was drinking so deeply.

Make approaches?
FM: Oh, no approaches – let's be quite straight about that. And I wasn't the sort of person who wanted approaches ... I made a real pass at Dylan Thomas, to get him to take me out. I'm convinced he didn't ask me, I'm sure of that – I think I inveigled it ... actually, I think it was the motherly bit of me coming out when I took him out – you know, I wanted to nurse him in a shawl.

...I can remember coming home to my mother and telling her that I'd been out with one of the boys from the Players. I said "He's an awfully clever boy but," I said, "I don't know – such a pity, you know, that he has this little kink."

18. The cast of *Captain X*. Dylan is seated, far left

Drinking, you mean?
FM: At that time. Yes, even at that time, at seventeen.
GB: I can remember when we were rehearsing a show with Dylan, and he came in, one night, to rehearsals, a bit late. I think he came with Hedley Auckland, and he was quite merry. Well, normally when Dylan was rehearsing, he was dead keen, the show was the thing – as we all were in those days – I mean the show was the thing.
FM: But he more than so.
GB: He more than so. But this night he was inclined to be a bit merry – I can remember I said to Hedley "What's the matter with Dylan tonight? He's full of the joys of life." "Oh," he said, "he had a couple of drinks before he came in." I said "What – at his age?" Of course, we didn't have the permissive society then that we had now. I said "He doesn't drink, does he?" "Oh yes," he said, "as a matter of fact," he said, "he's got some sort of disease of the brain, and it may prove fatal any time." I said "Is that right?" He said "Yes – and he believes in a short life and gay one." I don't think I've told that to anyone else.

I think Dylan exaggerated illnesses, including mental illness ... he thought of himself as Blake, who was slightly mad – and he thought this fitted the great poet.
FM: Yes. This is true, as I can remember Dylan Thomas, because when he played a part on the stage, he not only played the part, he *was* the part.
GB: The sincerity that he used to put into his parts as a boy, an immature boy, was really terrific. It was wonderful.
FM: He seemed to have been in this world before.
GB: He was never temperamental. He was an ideal actor, actually, wasn't he?
FM: Oh, he was great to be on. He gave you a lift, when you were on with him, he brought out the best in you. It was a joy to be with a man who could act like he could. You really felt that you were wonderful, too.

Jack Latham

I first knew Dylan through his association with the YMCA ... apart from his acting at the Llewellyn Hall, he used to help with the lighting and the various arrangements that had to be made for these amateur productions ... from the YMCA, we used to go down to the Singleton Hotel, which is just down the road from there; it was more or less an annexe, in those days, from the YMCA.

Who was keeping it then? Was it Mrs Giles? Gwen the barmaid?
Yes, Gwen. Mrs Giles, of course, was literary sort of inclined, you know. Now, Eric Hughes was a great Singleton man, and my brother Bill, of course ... [29]

...Dylan then came more or less back into my life when he joined the *Evening Post*, at the same time as my brother, they were cub reporters together, they were very close friends, and I can now remember my brother coming home from work, and saying to me that this chap's got something ... he's got a spark of genius ...

...I had actually opened a business in Swansea, a gentleman's outfitting business, and Dylan then used to come along to my place and purchase various items of clothing – he had the artist's attitude towards dress – corduroy trousers ... he liked these Viyella-type shirts ... solid colour ... an expensive shirt ... but, on the other hand, he would, when the occasion demanded, conform to the usual sartorial requirements. I remember him coming in to me one day and saying "I've been asked by the Oxford Union to give them some readings ... I understand that it's a dinner jacket effort." So he said "You'd better fix me up with the necessary." Needless to say, it was required immediately because he was catching a train within the hour. He asked for the use of the fitting room and changed and left his gear behind, and caught the train to London and returned a few days later and collected his sports jacket and what have you.

...and the point is – this is something I feel quite strongly about – he was always a perfect gentleman in the shop, to the staff, and he always conducted himself to me as a perfect gentleman. I loved his company; I wasn't a very close friend of his ... but whenever I had any dealings with him he always was a joy to deal with, I can assure you of that. And on top of that, his voice – now this may not be very important to you, but I've got a very common name, Jack. It's a very common or garden name you know, but when Dylan said it, it was musical.

...the last time I ever saw Dylan was when he was home on holiday ... I met him in the Number Ten public house, together with my brother, and Dylan had received a cheque from, I believe he said it was, some Italian literary prize or something he'd won. And he said – we hadn't got together for some time – "Before the tax man gets this, we shall have a party!" Which we certainly did. I do want to stress the point, too, that he moved on to London and then the Americans, which I've only read about, but sometimes he seemed to me a different person – quite frankly, what happened in America, I don't know ...

...Dylan was a Swansea man. He never forgot Swansea; he never, when he did make the grade, forgot his friends; he never forgot himself, and he always addressed us in just the same way when he had nothing in his pocket, as probably when he was well-off, if you like to put it that way. But he never suffered from a swelled head ...

Thomas Taig

My first meeting with him is quite vivid. I was working in the Little Theatre out at Mumbles, and a rather wide-eyed, rather full-lipped, chubby kind of boy from the Grammar School presented himself at the stage door with a manuscript of something that he had written, a dramatic script of some kind and suggested that I should put it on.

...I took the paper and the next time I saw him I tried to explain to him why I didn't think this would be suitable in its present form – it was very lyrical and very eloquent and so forth – but from my stage point of view, much too lyrical, depending almost entirely on the words, and without any opportunity for action or visual presentation at all ...

...that was our first encounter, and then shortly after that he came along and associated himself with the company. It was an amateur company with a slight difference, because amongst this company were a number of people with professional experience ...

...we put on a major production about once a month. They varied; sometimes in the early years we might do only four in the whole season, and then that increased until we were doing six, and then we were doing more. And then that increased still further until we were doing summer productions as well, so that it was pretty well all the time. They were unpaid professionals, really, because all their weekends and everything were spent in the theatre. They used to work there from early Sunday morning until eleven and twelve midnight and so on – every spare minute.

...and Dylan then came to us in the Theatre and for three or possibly four winter seasons he was a playing member. I produced him in a number of plays ... his sister Nancy was also a member of the company; another very talented actress. They played together – oh, we had a whole collection of brilliant youngsters. There was a phenomenal group. Dylan was one of them ... I was very fortunate to arrive in Swansea just before that time. I've tried over and over again to suggest convincing reasons for those flowering periods of genius – how does one account for it? But it is a fact that at that time in Swansea it was

19. Thomas Taig

most stimulating and there was so much talent. I could call on two or three people to provide a musical score or anything. Just say the word and there they were.

...I've worked with quite a number of poets in the theatre, and there's a tendency with the poets to depend so much on the word that physical movement is almost eliminated, and in some cases they are what one would call 'hand-less'. You know, if they touch anything they make a mess of it – Dylan wasn't quite like that but he seemed to be bit uncoordinated. The movements he made were not quite co-ordinated with the speech; he tended all the time to depend on the word, naturally being a poet. But a marvellous voice as you know from his recordings – beautiful voice and very sensitive interpretation of everything.

...I must say from my dealings with him over a number of years, my impression was that, during his whole career and development as a poet, he was working steadily towards a dramatic expression and got nearer to it in *Milk Wood* than ever before, but even then he was far from satisfied with that. I know; I discussed *Milk Wood* with him later, indeed, while it was being written in the first drafts, we discussed it, and he knew very well that that was a play for voices, and not intended for stage production. I myself feel quite sure that had Dylan been alive when they began putting it on the stage he would have insisted on having it vitally altered

Dylan brought this first piece of work to you when you first met him. Did you see in that some great promise of a future poet?
I do remember feeling a very lively interest in this boy, and sensing that

this was a very fine, delicate sort of person. Delicate in the sense of having extremely fine sensibilities. Which is my impression of Dylan all through, you see. I cannot think of Dylan as anything else but the kind of person one meets about once in a lifetime, who is so sensitive, and sensitive – don't misunderstand the word – in a *spiritual* way. That's the important thing about Dylan to me. I don't mean by that some religious conviction or anything of the kind; it's living in a world which is neither physical nor mental in the strict sense; it's something more fine than that.

...no, I shouldn't call him a religious poet. I should call him a poet who was deeply religious – he's not concerned with religious themes, he is concerned with other themes, but he's always religious.

...always so sensitive spiritually. I wonder whether this makes sense, but I see Dylan as the kind of artist who is so physically in his senses, is so much alive, that he can make a direct transition from the physical to the spiritual, and express the spiritual in terms of the physical without rationalising, and without making it mental in the process – he presents it directly and this, of course, I think is a sign of his great dramatic ability, which would develop later.

...he was very easy to work with ... oh, most amenable – only the very big people are so humble as that. It's the little people who throw their weight about. Dylan was never like that; Dylan was always very easy to work with ... and *most* reliable. But I know again, from other accounts, that on occasions he could be just the reverse. My interpretation of that, for what it's worth, is that Dylan did not tolerate certain people at all. Anything in the nature of hypocrisy or show or putting on an act was something which he could not stand and if he came across somebody of this kind, he would almost deliberately go out of his way to miss the appointment or put them in an awkward situation.

...the thing that sticks in my mind is that Dylan, to me at any rate, had such a gracious manner – there was something almost aristocratic about his manner, as if it were of an earlier age altogether. This seemed so strange in the environment, say, of the Fitzroy. Perhaps I imagine it, I don't know, but still that impression remains that there was this natural grace and ease and consideration.

...the most vivid memory I have of Dylan is undoubtedly of a meeting on the day that War broke out. Sounds a trite phrase, but it's actually true. On the Sunday morning in September I had picked up Vernon Watkins and we were going over to Laugharne to meet Dylan – I think to discuss the arrangements for the plays at the Mercury, almost certainly. On the way, the war was announced and we heard it on the radio, and by the time we got to Laugharne, about one o'clock, Dylan had also heard it and then my recollection is of someone so deeply affected by the horror, the enormity of the thing, that he always recurs to me as a kind of animal caught in a trap.

...couldn't do anything and feeling all this suffering and the agonies and so on that this would mean – overwhelmed by it. It lasted, oh, the rest of that day. Dylan was as if not quite there – and that was unusual for Dylan. There are some other artists who are not there at any time, who are always sort of floating off, but Dylan was immediate and his contact was always live, but not on that occasion – he seemed to be overwhelmed ... to anyone who felt every physical sensation, everything else, as keenly as Dylan did, life from day to day and from minute to minute was almost unbearable in conditions like these.

...it has surprised me that in all those studies of Dylan which have been done in recent years, in biographical and critical studies, that very few seem to realise what an important part Fred Janes played in Dylan's whole life – especially in that London period. I look upon Fred as a sort of mentor, rather like one of the guardian spirits in *The Cocktail Party*. Sort of solid, steadying influence, with a great philosophic interest. A different approach to art altogether to Dylan's and yet so much in common. I think he, Fred, played a very important sort of formative part in Dylan's life then.

Vernon's a different person altogether – he's incredible. Vernon simply cannot think ill of anybody. He lives in an impossible world – a kind of fairyland; which isn't a fairyland really, because it's real to him ... of course, Dylan – very different environment altogether. Very different shaping influences. Dylan is represented very well by some of our meetings after a play ... Saturday evening after we finished we went along to the Mermaid Hotel in Mumbles and had some supper or something of the kind, and then with such a talented group they were all doing extempore turns and it was very witty and very varied, and one thing I remember about Dylan – his obsession with the dog. I don't know where that came from, but when I noticed he had called his book *Portrait of an Artist as a Young Dog*, I remember all the incidents when Dylan had done this doggy act.

...I was thinking now of connecting up that Mermaid incident with the gala night at the Plough & Harrow, Bishopston. Those are memorable occasions; I think comparable with the most brilliant one hears of in the Paris boulevards or anything of the kind. And to find

20. Dylan as a young man

those in an isolated little place like the Plough & Harrow is almost incredible ... I can remember a night with Wynford and Dan Jones and several people coming in and sort of serial story going on. Making up a sort of serial. There was one marvellous thing about a condemned prisoner ... Wynford Vaughan Thomas was usually very good on creating a serial. His Jones Goppa was one of our standbys. And then Dylan came into prominence with a most wonderful imaginative account of a prisoner condemned to the electric chair in Sing-Sing, and what he felt the night before and what was going through his mind. And this was all being extemporised with other people joining in and gradually building the whole thing up. Wonderful.

Ruby and Malcolm Graham

RG: I suppose it would have been at the Swansea Little Theatre, and he was then a slim, curly-headed boy, as you've heard him described so often, but to me always an attractive sort of kid – of course, younger than I – and always full of beans and lots of fun with him and that very lovely voice, of course, which he always had. And a great gift for drawing people into conversation and talk, however completely daft it might have been, which it very often was! I never felt Dylan wanted to take the stage, which he could so often have done ... he'd prod other people very often, if he started some silly game – it wasn't always so silly, but he used to love playing about with words and things – he'd always get other people to come into it, if possible.

MG: I first met Dylan when I was substituting for someone else ... who'd fallen out, in a play called *Caesar's Wife* ... Dylan was a cub reporter on the *Post*, came up after the show to see me in the dressing room – I'd never seen him before – but I was quite charmed by him. He really seemed most interested to meet me, as he was always interested, as I found out later, in meeting new people and talking to them. But I was a little sore with Dylan, the following evening, because in the paper he said "Malcolm Graham played the part of the young lover with that vacuous emotionalism common to most stage lovers." I've never really forgiven him. Anyway, we saw a lot of Dylan after that, down at the Little Theatre.

RG: It was our usual custom after a show at the Mumbles, to have a supper party which invariably had the same menu, as I remember it: cold ham and tongue, probably tea and bread and butter, but certainly jelly and blancmange!

This was at the Mermaid?

RG: The Mermaid. We were given an upstairs room there, not the normal dining room, and we used to enjoy it very much. It was a very sober affair, and usually people were talking about the play, and what they'd done, and hadn't done, during the week, and Mr Taig was there that night, as I remember, so was Wynford Thomas and we were all seated at this long table. It was at the time when there was an outbreak of rabies and the papers were full of mad dogs and what happened to you if they bit you ... Dylan was a bit bored with the proceedings ... he said "Look, I'm getting a bit fed up with this. Let's have a game." So I said "What sort of a game?" wondering what on earth he was going to say. He said "We'll take any noun, anything that's on the table, let's find

21. Ruby & Malcolm Graham

an adjective, or something to describe it that just doesn't." He rambled on a bit, so I said "Give me an example, then maybe we can carry on." He looked all round the table and said "Now, you see that jelly ... static jelly!" Oh – then we had a go round the table, saying things, taking anything there, and giving the complete opposite to describe it.

Of course, once he started that, Wynford started off, and everybody else then went round the table, it was quite a game ... anyway, they decided they were two mad dogs; they both had rabies, they went round on all fours, yapping and barking and pretending to bite you ... we were seated on low couches, lots of us then, and he nipped me, came up to me like that, just nipped the front of my leg, and I said "Dylan Thomas!" I leapt up and ran downstairs after him, and when we got downstairs, he went out into the street, and there's a lamp post ... they both made for this and I may tell you, we thought the worst, of course! But no – mad, he was going to bite it! He did do and broke his front tooth, which I think he went to his grave with, he bit off his tooth and ... afterwards he used to say, "Nice smile, and you can see this tooth is through you!"

We had a lot of fun about it ... I don't read much of what is written about Dylan and quite honestly I don't wish to. I think he was one of the kindest men that I knew, at that time certainly, that I've ever known, perhaps. When I say kind, I mean it this way: I don't think – in fact, I'm perfectly certain – I never heard Dylan Thomas say a bad word about anyone. Ever.

MG: Well, you know one hears so much these days about artists, writers and others, who drink heavily; we hear that they 'love life', that the great thing about them is they 'love life'. But it seems to me that so many of these people hate their fellow-creatures. There was none of that in Dylan ... that's the difference between Dylan and so many of these so-called artists who, we're told, 'love life'. Dylan loved life, but that's a complicated thing really, but he was never malicious. He wouldn't hurt a fly.

What about Dylan as an actor?

MG: That's very interesting to me, because I was away from Swansea for a very long time, I was out of touch with Dylan while he was making his way in the BBC as a poetry reader. Well, down at the Mumbles, Dylan had no speaking voice whatsoever. He spoke in a strangulated voice, quite extraordinary. He seemed to have talent as a comic actor, extraordinary talent – I can tell you more about that – but to me the extraordinary thing is that he seems to have made a big impression on the public in his poetry readings on the BBC. I couldn't understand where he, how he, had improved in that way. I felt he must either have had tuition, or he may have become more relaxed. He probably studied it on his own ... Dylan certainly was an individualist in his acting, and he flung himself into it wholeheartedly. Had he, at that time, been able to produce a better voice, I think that he might have gone somewhere in the acting.

I was in a pub in Chelsea, some years ago and a well known poet, George Barker, when he heard that I knew Dylan, he asked me what we used to talk about, and I said "We didn't talk about anything – we did things together." That is to say, we acted in plays, we didn't talk about things, and Dylan wasn't really a talker down there. We liked our pint of beer; we liked our oysters, in those days. We had beautiful oysters down at the Mumbles and we even toasted them in front of the gas fire in the Little Theatre.

After the last night. There was another place ...

RG: Cheese's.

Cheese's? Is that also in Mumbles?

RG: It's right at the bottom. It's immediately the first pub as you come out of what was then the Little Theatre. It is really called Fulton's, but the man who ran it at that time was Mr Cheddar, so it was obviously known as Cheese's!

MG: Some of us actors down there didn't really share in Dylan's actual life. We felt very inferior to Dylan, you know, we felt that we were on a much lower plane altogether. As we were, definitely ... we knew that he was working away at his poetry but he never intruded in any way.

Dylan was extremely witty but I wouldn't say it was on a terribly high level, you know. He had a wonderful appreciation of the vulgar joke ... he was a great player on words, of course ... there was a lot of punning, yes. Quite a lot of punning. Of which he appeared to be ashamed, he would giggle ashamedly, you know.

It seems to me that although we saw a good deal of his melancholy – and he was melancholy a large part of his time – but he had this extraordinary capacity for enjoyment. A good joke, a funny situation. You, know, he really laughed.

RG: You did ask a moment ago, whether he ever discussed his poetry. I can remember in this very room one day, he turned round, he said "I don't think you ever buy any of my poetry, you know, Ruby." "No," I said, "I leave that to Malcolm, because he would understand what the devil you're talking about." He said "What! You mean to tell me you don't understand what I'm writing?" I said "A lot of it I don't, Dylan." "Well," he said, "Who's your favourite poet?" "I don't know about favourite poet. I've got a favourite poem, and if you can call the man who wrote it my favourite poet, it's OK." He said "Who's that? And what's the poem?" I said "The poem is 'My Last Duchess' by Browning." He said "Browning! That obtuse bugger! You've got the nerve", he said, "to say you can't understand my poems!"

...piano was going one end – big long rooms, you can see, and I think there was a gramophone going the other – and a lot of people here, all talking ... and when I mentioned this poem, he said "Have you got it?" I always keep it with a mark in it, so it wasn't difficult to find. I said "Now don't try and read this, Dylan." He said "Give it to me." And I can remember it so well, and the feeling coming over me whenever I think of it. He just opened the book and he started the poem ... and you know, as he was reading, so gradually the piano stopped and in few minutes, the gramophone was turned off. Gradually, the room got quieter and quieter – people were stopping in the middle of a conversation, this lovely voice flowing across the room. He went right through it, and he shut the book, and he said "There!"

MG: What I was very much impressed with was that Nancy his sister was out living in a Channel island somewhere ... I heard he was in the habit of sending Nancy books from London, out to Lundy and I thought "Good for you, Dylan." Didn't forget his family.

RG: It was me who told you. Wherever he went he used to leave an order with his publishers that she had a supply of books – not only his own – but I think *The Times*, the choice of the month or something. He always saw that she was well supplied.

...I knew her quite well ... she was a rather practical sort of girl, and very vivacious and full of beans, and I think she belonged to the Clyne Golf Club ... but very sensible, too ... you could always have a good conversation with Nancy.

MG: She had literary inclinations, you know.

RG: Dylan always spoke very affectionately of her. Always.

Eileen Llewellyn Jones (née Davies)

I first met Dylan when he joined the Swansea Little Theatre. I suppose he was about seventeen years of age at the time, but I had known his sister Nancy many years before that, because she was a contemporary of mine at the Swansea High School. We were in the same form, and we were friends because we had quite a lot of similar interests. She was extraordinarily like Dylan in many ways. She was a very pretty girl with a shock of fair, curly hair, big brown eyes; very lively, very attractive with a tremendous sense of humour. She was a very good mimic I remember, and sometimes used to get into trouble for mimicking the mistresses. She was also a good actress; she used to act in school plays. She was very prominent in the reading circle, which we had in the upper forms.

We used to meet about every fortnight to read plays, and Nancy Thomas was a very active figure in that. In fact, there were a few of us so keen on reading plays that we started a sort of private reading circle of our own; we used to meet in each other's houses and read modern plays every Saturday night ... a circle which we called The Chinaclow ... this used to meet at her house sometimes. I knew, of course, Nancy's mother who was very charming, very hospitable, jolly sort of woman who was always most kind and welcoming to Nancy's friends and, I imagine, to Dylan's friends as well.

...Mrs Thomas was a sort of smartly dressed matron. You'd see her shopping around the Uplands wearing smart suits and hats ... always seemed interested in all of us ... extremely loveable character, and very, very kind. Had this terrific warmth of personality, which I think both Dylan and Nancy had from her.

Well, I didn't actually know Dylan as a child, except as Nancy's brother. She used to talk about him as 'My little brother' and she was

22. Eileen Llewellyn Jones

rather proud of him because he used to write for the school magazine, and there was the famous occasion when he won the race at the Grammar School sports, and had a good deal of publicity in the *Evening Post* ...

...certainly, when they were at home, when they were young children, I should say that they were very close together. I know she was very fond of Dylan ... they were both keenly interested in literature ... in the theatre, both loved reading plays, both loved poetry. Nancy was always very proud of Dylan as a young boy. I think she got a bit exasperated with him later on, when he'd gone to London ...

...when I came back from London University, I found that a group of people who were very keen on the theatre, had started the Swansea Little Theatre movement ... there was a very large crowd of quite talented people, who had belonged to other dramatic societies in Swansea, but who wanted to begin something which was rather more serious. They were people who were definitely interested in drama and the theatre. They wanted to run their own theatre, construct their own scenery, and their own wardrobe, their own costumes, and really study what theatre was all about. Well now, Nancy was one of the founder members of this, and took many important parts in the early productions.

I remember Dylan first as the young boy in *Hay Fever*, in which he created a great sensation. I can remember an absolute volcanic entrance he made in that, and played the part extremely well. Nancy was also in the play, as Jackie Coryton, and was extremely amusing, too ... of

23. Dylan's sister, Nancy, as a young woman

course, neither he and Nancy were ever very good at school work, except at English. Their mother took great care of them, and she was awfully afraid that they were delicate; rather afraid that they were going to contract TB, which was a very fearful disease in those days, and if they had a cold, either of them, or bronchitis, or something like that, they would perhaps miss a whole term's schooling ... Nancy was very original at writing, and was extremely good at English, but not any good at anything else, simply because she missed so much schooling.

...I should think for about three or four years, Dylan was a very enthusiastic and really quite hardworking member of Swansea Little Theatre. He really did love acting, and he was in play after play. He took quite important parts; he had, of course, the magnificent voice,

24. Nancy, right, with her cousin Dosie Harris at Dishley Court, Ivington, Leominster, about 1920. See Note 44

rather a mannered style of acting which wasn't suitable for every type of play, but he could be extremely good. I remember him very vividly in Masefield's *The Witch*, in which I was playing a part, and Dylan played the part of the drunken priest in that, and really brought the house down doing it. He also rather enjoyed acting in Restoration comedy, which we occasionally used to do, and he played with us in *The Way of the World*; he played the part of Witwoud in that and really did extremely well. Although he rather overdid the seventeenth century fine gentleman, I think.

112

...in those days we had an old church hall down in the Mumbles which we'd converted into the theatre; very uncomfortable, very cold and a long way from Swansea. Not everybody in those days had a car, so we used to travel down from Swansea on the Mumbles train, and walk quite a big distance from Oystermouth, and I often used to meet Dylan on the Mumbles train, used to travel down with him, or home with him ... the whole lot of us, of course, used to have long, long discussions in between rehearsing. We used to sit round a very inadequate little gas fire, and talk about every subject on earth. I can remember him talking, of course, very brilliantly and very amusingly in those days ... about literature, writing, Surrealism and all kinds of things that were fashionable at that time, and a great deal, of course, about films, in which he was terribly interested.

I think all of us knew that he was writing, during the time when he used to spend so much time, night after night, at this Little Theatre in the Mumbles, rehearsing for plays, taking part in plays. Everybody wondered what he did with himself all day, and we knew vaguely that he was writing. He had also taken to posing, rather. I think after he took part in *Hay Fever* as a very Bohemian young man, he took to wearing strangely coloured shirts, and even more strange ties, which were unusual, in those days of course, and very different then. He took to dressing in a most unconventional way, and to behaving in a very unconventional way ...

...he did take his acting seriously, and he was an extremely talented actor; I think at one time he wanted to go on the stage professionally. He liked rather rumbustious acting. I can remember talking to him about acting, on the Mumbles train one night, and he was deploring the fact that in the Little Theatre some of the people liked naturalistic acting and tended even to play so naturally that they weren't even audible, and this was rather a fashion on the London stage at the time. Dylan liked a bit of good old ham at times ...

...he sometimes perhaps drank more than was good for him, but I think that then at any rate, when he was very young, he got pulled over rather quickly. I mean a few drinks would make Dylan very merry indeed. But he preferred beer drinking to spirits. I don't think that he was ever, you couldn't call him an alcoholic. He loved drinking beer but he liked going to pubs; he liked talking to people and enjoyed the atmosphere, but then at any rate, he'd certainly not become the very heavy drinker that he was reputed to be later on. Another thing about him at this time, I should say that Dylan, between the age of about

25. The cast of *Hay Fever*. Dylan is lounging on the couch

seventeen and twenty, wasn't in the least interested in girls. I was interested to hear that Eric Hughes had said this, too. I don't think there was anybody who was less interested in girls as girls. I mean, he was friendly with everybody. He would talk to girls in the same way as he would talk to men ... it never occurred to people to flirt with Dylan because he wasn't that type at all. He just wasn't interested in girls at all. That's why some of the stories about his carryings-on when he was older always surprise me, because I never imagined Dylan as that kind of person at all!

...he was unreliable in the sense he would disappear for long periods and go to Cheese's for drinks, but as an actor he was certainly not unreliable. He would always be there, and always give a good performance on the night ... and always knew his part backwards. He really took it very seriously ... just as I'm sure he would never publish a bad poem, he would never give a bad performance in front of an audience.

Did you hear about Dylan and Nancy taking elocution lessons from Gwen James?

Yes, I took elocution lessons from Gwen James myself, and I knew that Nancy went to Gwen James, too. Gwen James was a quite extraordinary character. She was not the usual type of elocutionist; she was a highly cultured woman, extremely well trained and a brilliant teacher, and she helped a great many of us in those days ... she taught both here and in Llanelli. I think that she at one time taught Clifford Evans in his schoolboy days.[30] Lots of people who went on the stage and became quite well known had been to Gwen James for lessons when they were quite young ... Nancy probably went either when she was a schoolgirl, or during the time when she was a member of the Little Theatre, because we all took our acting very seriously in those days, and Gwen James used to help us with our voice work, our diction, and sometimes even give us help with a particular part we were studying.

Ethel Ross[31]

I'd known of him of course for many years, but I first really got to know him in the Little Theatre ... I used to make the costumes ... I was the Press Secretary for many years ... we were putting on a play a month ... and sometimes a play in three weeks ...

...I should say that generally one's attention was concentrated on his face and not on his clothes ... his eyes were the most noticeable thing and I think his curly hair ... his eyes tended to galvanise one's attention ... they were very full. No, it's not a case of being intense ... they were rather protruding and you had this circle of white right round. Most people, you don't see the white at the underneath part of the eye ... the lower lid cuts it off, but in Dylan's case the white was all the way round, which made it different.

...I, of course, was a rather retiring person and more or less an observer of this particular bunch of people. I was not a partaker in many of their festivities; I just saw them when they came back, and was on the fringe of things rather than in them. Just watching and listening. And I remember him, of course, as a member of the Little Theatre and his excursions with the gayer of the girls down to Cheeses, the pub, and I've seen him come back to the house with Hugh Griffith and Stuart Thomas and Leon Atkin ...

...I never heard him discuss literature as such. I don't think he liked doing that ... that was reserved for smaller groups, I think, and people that he knew very well. He didn't parade his work in front of other people. Not when I was about, anyway. Not in these general gatherings. The talk would be mainly social as far as I can recall.

...yes, he was a great storyteller. But then, you see, so was Wynford Vaughan-Thomas, and so was Daniel Jones, and so was Mervyn Levy, so that you had a kind of competition as to who was the best performer, and that was one of the things, of course, that made the conversation entertaining to watch. Not that one had to put forward a story; I suppose one wouldn't dare. But one did form a part of an audience which was necessary.

...they used Fred's studio in College Street as a gathering place and they'd write one another messages and leave them on the wall there ... I've got some here – some of these sheets of paper on which they wrote messages to each other ... what they were going to do, whether they were in the Kardomah or not.

...Florence Thomas had quite a good sense of the dramatic, and it comes out in this recording I've got, where she acts the events she describes, taking the parts of Dylan and her husband, and all the rest of it. I think he must have got quite a bit of his acting ability from her, and certainly some of his voice power, I think.

...well, this is something that is fairly common amongst Welsh people, this ability to act every little incident is an aspect of life in Wales that makes it so much more interesting. Everybody is putting on a turn all the time and Mrs Thomas, of course, if she was telling you anything, would act the complete thing.

...I think that if you take the average student that comes here from the Welsh-speaking part of Wales, the great majority of them are used to reciting a verse in chapel on Sunday mornings, and a large number of them are used to speaking together, choral speaking, singing and so on, so that, on the whole, they tend to be rather articulate rather than inarticulate, and I think Mrs Thomas was an articulate type, anyway, and had quite a rich voice, even at the age of seventy-five.

When did you see Dylan after the Little Theatre days?
I saw more of him then than in the Little Theatre days, because he went to London you see, in 1934...and I saw much more of him when he came to see Fred [Janes], after Fred and Mary were married. I saw a lot of him then.

Did you know of a Burmese friend, a girl who was friendly with Dylan during his early days in London when he was living with Fred?

No, I don't ... in any case, I wouldn't be told any of these things, you see, if they did occur. Fred would never gossip in this kind of way.

...I saw Dylan on his return from the States, and saw him at the Boat House and saw him at his mother's, in the Pelican and in Brown's, you know. Usual hunting grounds.

Did he change very much during those years?
He was much quieter ... much quieter, I think. In Laugharne ... more thoughtful and contemplative – I don't know what he was like elsewhere – but he was perfectly normal and ordinary. I don't know what all the fuss is about half the time.

...I don't think Caitlin was particularly friendly or forthcoming when we were about. She rather tended to efface herself and not take part very much in the general conversation at these times. I don't think we were exactly her cup of tea, you know.

...I don't think I would appeal to her at all, you see. I would be, I suppose, one of the more forbidding females ... she might have thought that I was slightly disapproving of her type of conduct. I don't know – but I wouldn't say we were to any degree soulmates.

Did you see a deterioration in Dylan's health towards the end? Was it obvious?
He became very fat. And flabby-looking. I'd always known about these stories of his health from the time he was quite small, when he had these blackouts first ... as his mother said when she was talking to me, that she often found him unconscious on the floor when he was a child, before he went to school ... I don't think she fabricated that.

...I think the people who try to discount the fact that there was some physical handicap don't really know enough about it, you see. And Mrs Thomas did say that her father died of TB ... he suffered from asthma, and died of tuberculosis ... Mr Thomas' family tended to have tuberculosis and, of course, Carmarthen had the highest incidence of tuberculosis because of bad housing and poor living conditions, didn't it, in the whole of the country? Or in the whole of Wales, anyway.

...I remember, of course, what his mother says about his schooldays. How he'd come home, especially if he was reprimanded, and develop an attack of asthma – which seemed to indicate a nervous origin, rather, and then, of course, she did mention that towards the end he'd find it very difficult to walk from the Boat House towards the Pelican, which is a fairly level walk, and he would arrive at her house unable to speak. He'd have to sit down and get his breath again.[32]

*What about the Swansea of that period? The Thirties were a period of slump
and depression – and also of the clouds of violence and war on the
Continent: Hitler, Mussolini, the Spanish Civil War and the Fascists were
active and the Communists were active in Swansea.*

It was a very distressing period to have lived through, as a child ... it
did mean the total disruption of families, of people who emigrated. My
own brothers left the country and went to America, the whole family
dispersed, leaving my sister and myself in Swansea, so I don't regard it
as anything but a very miserable time.

...there was quite a strong Socialist nucleus, I think, in Swansea –
there always has been. I think in this particular period the interest in
Socialism was really spreading amongst the more intellectual set rather
than amongst the union membership ... I think Dylan was interested at
one time. I know he attended one meeting at Professor Farrington's
house in Cwmdonkin Terrace.[33] I think it may have been the initial
meeting; I went once but it struck me as being rather precious and it
wasn't really my cup of tea, so I didn't go again.

...I can remember a particular concert in the Little Theatre – I think
it was to raise funds for the Basque children who came here – Mrs
Farrington, the first Mrs Farrington, asked us to stand in memory of
this young man who had died, and we all found it a bit embarrassing
because we didn't even know him ... we were just there as audience and
weren't involved in the movement.

Eric Hughes

I first met him when he was in school. I was some years older than he
was, and almost my first memory of him was watching him run the
Junior Mile ... it came as a tremendous shock to me, because at no time
had I ever envisaged Dylan, either then or after, as anybody interested
in physical endeavour; it was just out of his nature. But it was part of
his determination to, I don't say to become big, but to become great in
any field of endeavour in which he set his hand.

...afterwards, apart from working on the same paper in Swansea, the
South Wales Evening Post, we acted together in two or three plays in the
Little Theatre, and I produced him in one play ... in those days, Dylan
really took acting quite seriously. I'm not sure that it wasn't from this
stage that the voice, which really gave Dylan his tremendous impact on
the general public in this country, began to develop. Because Dylan, as
a boy, seemed both immature in his actual presence, and he had some

26. Eric Hughes

limitations of voice production. There was an effeminate, almost, note in his voice, until he managed to eradicate it quite successfully, so that when he played his biggest part with the Little Theatre, as Peter in *Peter and Paul*, he really managed to put on tremendously effective portrayal of a not easy character.

...I think, too, he'd inherited some of this instinct for acting from his father. Because, to my mind, D.J. Thomas *should*, and would have been, a most excellent Shakespearean actor ... I don't think that DJ had any effect at all on Dylan's voice production. I think that the voice production itself came from (a) a desire to make a good thing of acting and (b) from a natural exuberance, which to my mind caused him in most cases to overact ...

...Dylan felt every role in which he took part. And it was possibly that which resulted in an over-emotional approach to a great many of the parts he played. Nevertheless, there could be no doubting the sincerity of any performance that he ever gave ... I think that Dylan as so many Welsh people are – and in this he showed, as he may not have done in other regards, his Welsh background – he showed that, emotionally, the Welsh people can bring something to the stage. Dylan might have benefited from greater discipline as far as acting is concerned, but with that greater discipline, I quite frankly think that he might have created a name for himself, on the stage, almost equal to that he has created in the other form.

...Dylan would drink basically beer, except on special occasions. His normal preparation for a stage performance was very carefully gauged. It was usually two pints of beer, and possibly one or two what we call shorts – whisky, mostly. But I never really saw Dylan going to town on whisky ... he held his drink magnificently, and anyone who speaks to me of the sedative qualities of beer, is talking nonsense as far as Dylan is concerned. He seemed to bubble; the more beer he drank, the more effervescent he became ... he seemed to become sharper in his outlook the more beer he drank.

...Dylan joined [the *Evening Post*] some years after I did. I had the misfortune to have to sub some of his copy. He had almost every quality of a bad newspaperman. Accuracy meant nothing to him; punctuality meant less. The few occasions when he really struck his form was when he was allowed to do feature work, and that was too rare, I'm afraid, for him ... I don't think he ever graduated beyond the daily call stage, the ferreting out of routine engagements which were often followed up by more senior men ... I can't remember much about his actual work at that period.

...the minimum wage for a fully-trained reporter in 1938 was five pounds, eight and sixpence, I think ... and he, as a junior, would be extremely lucky if he was getting half of that.

...as an off-duty newspaperman, he was every bit the character, without a shadow of doubt. The rallying-point for journalists in his day was the old Three Lamps in Swansea, where most of the stories were re-lived, re-told, embellished, turned upside-down, and in that galaxy he was not only welcome but had far greater authority than his years of experience would ever justify.

What were his extra-curricular interests at that time?
Apart from the theatre, the haunting of one or two second-hand bookshops in Swansea, reading wildly, and the occasional glass of beer ... during the period that I knew him, he was less interested in girls than almost any boy of his age I knew ... I don't think he ever spoke politics, or wrote politics, as normally considered. They just weren't of interest to him.

...he was keenly interested in all of Rhys Davies' early writings ... at one time he was completely rabid follower of Faulkner ... one of the only books I ever knew him to enthuse about was *Clochemerle*. And that he read with great glee when it was first published and handed on to me almost immediately afterwards.

...I think, on reconsideration, there was certain interest in girls during the Swansea period. Nothing abnormal. I still think that the first interest in the opposite sex came with the London period ... I knew he had associations while he was in London. But the idea of the overall ladykiller, or lecher, never really came within my knowledge ... the idea of him as a dipsomaniac and a sex maniac, seem completely out of keeping with the Dylan I knew ... certainly he would never accept conventions in these things, but I have no knowledge of extremes in either case.

...the Kardomah was, at that time, the social centre of Swansea. The back room upstairs was the normal resort for the mid-morning coffee break of most of the businessmen from the heart of the town. The front room was the ladies' room, normally occupied only on Saturday mornings by mixed groups, when the men ventured out of their own fastness in the back, and mixed with the daughters of their own circle. It was, I suppose, rather a snobbish sort of place, where Russian tea was considered to be the height of civilization. Dylan certainly used it on Saturday mornings; I think most people did, but for the rest of the week, I doubt whether he had his coffee there. It's far more likely that he went to the café above David Evans' store, right away on the top of the store, where nobody ever penetrated except the *habitués*, and where they had the great advantage of giving away a free cigarette with a cup of coffee. Very good cigarettes they were, too.

Socially speaking, of course, Dylan never belonged to the 'hospital ball' class of people in Swansea. He was gregarious, but not social. And that, I think, continued throughout his existence.

...he had two very disconcerting methods of dealing with things he didn't like. He would either retire into complete silence, or else explode, and the explosion was always entertaining, except for the person who had incurred his displeasure, and that might even be his closest friend. He had a really bitter touch of satirical humour, which he vented in no small measure, if he were really upset ... if any attempt were made to reduce a flight of fancy to the hard facts, anything could happen. I think that was why Dylan could never become a newspaperman. He just wasn't interested in the conventions, the accuracy so essential for any newspaperman; the thing bored him. He was not so much unconventional as to be over-riding of convention, unaware of convention ... Dylan would never even stop to regard the damage that he'd done. He was completely disregardful – he completely disregarded the impact of his explosion. He felt that it was justified, else he wouldn't have made it. And he felt that the other people must recognise the justice of the explosion. No, I don't think he ever felt any intense sympathy for the victim of his attack.

...I can quite understand Dylan being enormously shy of any occasion that could have a hint of formality about it. Dylan in his own relaxed ground would not only meet, but could dominate, far greater people. Dylan entering into any kind of society would be almost impossible to conceive. He would meet almost anybody on his own ground, but to step off ... into a kind of formal meeting ... would definitely put him off ... Dylan did have a kind of inferiority complex. The big voice was part of it. He felt that he was himself to some degree puny, physically. He knew that he was not puny mentally, but somehow or other this business of being a small person must have got at him, because to my mind this tremendous voice, which he invariably used, was nothing more or less than a cloak for his own natural diffidence, and an attempt, too, to bolster up an ego that couldn't exist in a small body.

CFitz: I think that Dylan's smallness was a constant source – he was always conscious of it.

And his frailty.

CFitz: Yes, and his frailty.

I think that the impact of his father's quite serious illness had a tremendous influence ... his father's illness occurred when he was in Swansea. And Dylan's reaction was frightening. There must have been tremendous love between his father and himself, and during the period when his father was quite critically ill, Dylan seemed completely lost. The grief which went finally into 'Do not go gentle' undoubtedly sprang from that period. For weeks he was more or less inconsolable, and there were two or three friends who really took it in turns to try and exercise some kind of guardianship of him at that time.

...I saw him several times in London after he'd left the paper. The last time was some years after the War. He seemed, at the tail end of the War, particularly depressed. I don't know whether he was going through a bad patch then or not, but he had been doing some film script writing or something – it was very definitely against his instincts.

Did he talk about it to you, his feelings about doing it?

Very slightly. I tried to keep off it, quite frankly, because he seemed to be in the depths of despair, as far as his literary output was concerned.

You know some people have said that, and perhaps it's because he did some of his best work when he was away from London, that he hated London.

Oh, I think that's completely wrong. I think Dylan was only completely alive when he was in London. He drew from London the whole of his knowledge of life, apart from that which came to him through some extraneous means as a young man. From London he drew almost everything that London could give him. The fact that he retired to the country to work was not peculiar to Dylan; a great many other people have done it before and will do it afterwards, because London is where you live and the country is where you have the opportunity to think. I'm quite sure that Dylan, who really imposed it on himself as a sort of self-discipline, went into the country in order to be able to collect in his mind the existence of which he had experience in London. I'm quite sure that he never hated London ... as most young men of his period, he regarded London as the centre of the world, and it was in London that he really began to appreciate the characters upon whom he drew afterwards.

...without a shadow of doubt, he was a boisterous person, but no, I think that there has been a lot of defamation in many ways, an exaggeration of weaknesses that are not peculiar to Dylan; on the other hand, there has never yet been an adequate description of the tenderness that I, at least, experienced in some of my relationships with Dylan.

Trevor Ogbourne and W.G. Willis

Recording now in the offices of the Evening Post. *What do you remember of Dylan?*

TO: I should say he was about sixteen, straight from the Grammar School, and he came here a nervous little boy. Chubby. Well, rather frightened, I think, of journalism ... at that time, all the junior reporters came in to do their initial training in the Reading Room, before they went into the Editorial.

WGW: I was a copy holder, too, at the time, and Dylan was a somewhat quiet, moody type of boy. Didn't mix a great deal with the rest of us, who were football keen and keen to indulge in most sports. He was more or less particularly friendly with Charles Fisher, who was also a copy holder ... Dylan seemed to spend most of his time peering through the window in a sort of moody haze, and doodling, writing poetry on the back of copy-paper sometimes, on the walls and wherever he could get a pencil to work. He wasn't a boy who would mix a great deal, and outside of the office. I don't know a great deal about him, but there was this moody atmosphere which was there even at that age ...

...later of course, Dylan left the Reading Department and was given an opportunity as a junior reporter, where he took on the semblance of

27. Trevor Ogbourne

28. W.G. Willis

the day of a reporter, the garb, sort of arty type of clothing, and loud shirts ... as far as I can recollect, as a reporter I don't think he could be termed a great success. I mean a reporter in the sense of a police court and the average, mundane duties that reporters take upon, but I think there were, quite early on, some examples of promise of fair literary ability in reviews and articles that he wrote for our weekly publication, which was the *Herald of Wales*.

Let's get clear the job he had, this copy holder job. Could you explain that Mr Ogbourne?

TO: The news comes through in manuscript ... the boy reads that out to me. I get it in proof form after the linotypes have had it set up, and very often there are pieces left out, portions left out. Well, he read it to me, then I put them in.

What do you recall of his readings to you? Did he try and give a different reading from the average copy holder?

TO: No, he was very good reading ... his speech was very plain. Which is one requisite of the copy holder ... not a strong accent, no. He didn't have a Welsh accent, definitely Swansea accent.

He had particular friends among the staff, that he went out with, didn't he ... some of these are mentioned in 'Return Journey' ... Freddie Farr.

TO: He was a reporter ... Fred Farr was rather short. Very well dressed reporter, dressed for the day with black coat and waistcoat and trousers, pinstripe trousers, and bowler hat and wherever he went, or

29. The *Evening Post* offices, Swansea

wherever Freddie was, he had a cigarette hanging from his lips. He was permanently with a cigarette. He was a fair billiard player; liked his pint and could always be found either in the billiard hall or in the pub ... and I think Dylan might have been somewhat impressed by Mr Farr in his early days, because it does appear that later, according to what he has said, that Mr Farr introduced him to some of the things like having a pint and frequenting some of the places where it was thought that was an ideal situation for newsgathering. The sort of the pubs and hostelries of those days were the sort of places where you could pick up stories, you see? Mr Farr was a very good reporter, and I think Dylan probably felt that it would have been to his advantage to have this sort of benefaction of Mr Farr's in his early days to help him on his journalistic career.

What is your outstanding memory of Dylan?
TO: Well, I should say, as a dreamer ... in the hustle and bustle of newspaper life, he was a dreamer.
WGW: Yes ... he had a faraway look and he seemed preoccupied most of the time. Although he followed the copy as a copy holder, there was that overawing preoccupation which you couldn't fail to miss every time you were in contact ...

Ronnie Thomas

...vivid memories of Dylan Thomas to me were of a schoolboy actor ...
there was something outstanding about Dylan on the stage. I
photographed him in several of the plays ... I remember Dylan as an
actor, and a voice, more than a writer ... I saw Dylan afterwards in
practically every production he took part in with the Little Theatre. I
was practically their official photographer ... if Dylan Thomas had gone
for the stage, he could have done all that Emlyn Williams did. He could
have written the plays, and acted them, and directed. No question.

Dylan became your colleague in 1931, on the Evening Post, *as a cub reporter.*
JDW [J.D. Williams, the editor] hired him ... Dylan had made an
impression on the editor by his Grammar School record ... there's no
question that his stage performances had impressed JDW. And his
writing in the School magazines.

...it was the usual story of the young photographer and the young
reporter going on the ordinary jobs, which a provincial newspaper has
to cover. Even then, it did appear to me that he wasn't born to cover
the ordinary job. There was something different about Dylan. Very
often I went out with Dylan, but very seldom did I come back with
him.

You lost him on the way?
And quite often lost him on the way back ...

What do you mean – he'd stop at a pub on the way?
Oh no, no, no, no – Dylan's drinking, as a young man, to my memory,
has been exaggerated ... I never saw Dylan in the office when he had
been drinking.

What happened exactly?
If it really was a job that Dylan didn't think in his own mind there was
a lot in it, he simply didn't go ... and he would say "Look, I don't think
I'll come, Ron." He'd go his way, I'd go mine ... he wasn't sent on
anything which was considered important by Mr Job, who was the
Chief Reporter of those days.

...Dylan was no man for the ordinary job. Mr Job, a very efficient
newspaper man, recognised that ... and I believe Mr Job was instru-
mental in Dylan leaving the office, but with the certain knowledge that
this man was a writer and was going to make his way in the world. And
I believe that the advice to leave the *Post* was more from that angle, that
it would develop his talent for writing more than to be stuck in a job.

Which for three or four years meant routine, and Dylan wasn't born for routine.

What time did the reporters start work in the day?
Oh, nine o'clock ... Mr Job was a stickler. And then, till five, remembering that the junior reporter always had one or two evenings, especially in the winter, in which there were small jobs that had to be covered. Dylan would be covering many of them ...
...I covered cricket, and played cricket with Dylan ... Dylan played for the *Evening Post* cricket team – his great virtue was making the number up. Making the number eleven. Because we were a good side, but we had to get eleven ... Dylan did not distinguish himself on the cricket field ... the worst part of Dylan's cricket was his fielding. I was a bowler at the time and I can remember two or three balls going through Dylan's legs which didn't amuse me in the slightest ... I can recollect quite a fair crowd at St Helens being amused at that ... I think his mind wasn't on the game, but he liked the game ... I can recollect him playing at St Helens twice ... against Beau Nash Cricket Club, which was then the Sidney Heath Cricket Club ... Dylan was not a regular performer, but he did turn out on the occasional game.

He left the Evening Post *in 1932. Did you see much of him after that?*
Oh, I met him very often, yes. We were always good friends ... I met him in Swansea quite often, and drank ... at the Duke Hotel with Fred Mann [the licensee] ... the Duke in Wind Street was one of his haunts...

He had worries about money, all the time, didn't he?
He didn't show them.

He didn't cadge, sponge on his friends?
No – no, no never. No, never. Never. No. Never. Never. I met him in The Duke quite often ... never, at any time, did he appear to be short of money to me.

What was the last time you saw him?
I'd have seen him in between his American trips.

How would you describe him in those last years?
He was starting to ... deteriorate. Yes. The face had gone fuller ... there was weight about him. He was always a fleshy little type, you know, but he had gone, towards the end, unhealthily fleshy ... yes, gone a bit pallid, yes.

Was he drinking too much already, then?
I'd have thought, yes.

He'd started taking spirits, had he?

Yes, I saw him once or twice, even before going to the BBC for programmes ... I think there was one programme [October 24, 1949], I think it was a picture ... of Daniel Jones, Fred Janes – you see, I took that picture ... And Dylan was definitely happy at the start of that interview. He had been hitting the bottle before that. Because I was there before the interview started.

Bill Latham

I was serving a six years apprenticeship with Northcliffe Newspapers, whereas Dylan came in under a different scheme, as a learner, or junior reporter. But we were of equal status, but by reason of the fact that he joined the paper a little later than me, he came with me for several weeks, day by day, just to learn the technicalities of the job ... but very soon it became apparent that he was quite capable of going around under his own steam, and he began to be given assignments completely on his own ... it was at that time when Britain went off the Gold Standard and almost every day we ran a series of articles describing how people had been hoarding golden sovereigns or golden half-sovereigns in their homes, were digging them out and taking them to jewellery shops, and realising three or four times their face value, and I well remember that Dylan wrote some brilliant news stories describing some of the remarkable incidents which were then occurring in every jeweller's shop in Swansea.

The first impression he gave was as if a cowboy had walked into a four ale bar. He looked so incredibly innocent; he had a chubby face, and those curls were still golden, in those days. But he almost immediately broke the illusion by beginning to chain smoke, to recount saucy jokes, and to come in reeking of beer at noon. So the first impression he gave was shattered after about two days.

...the attitude of the older reporters towards him was one of friendliness and, as they got to see his work more and more, one of respect for his work, but nevertheless in the old tradition, the older reporters pulled his leg just as they pulled the legs of the other junior reporters.

...one particular evening we pulled his leg unmercifully because poor Dylan had been to the dockside and seen a corpse hauled ashore which had been in the water for many, many weeks. He went with the police, the dock police, and ambulance men and actually penetrated into the mortuary where the corpse was laid out on a cold slab ... this

30. Bill Latham

experience for a young man of nineteen, left him pale and trembling and he came to join us shortly afterwards and drank at least three pints one after the other.

...Freddie Farr knew the dockside pubs of Swansea inside out and I know that several times he took Dylan on tours ... I don't know whether you know Swansea docks well or not, but in the Thirties there were some very remarkable goings on ... there were pubs where homosexuals got together; there were pubs where sailors met dockside tarts; and there were pubs where people got together, many of them sailors, many of them Welsh colliers, to sing, of all things, Welsh hymns. And when they did so, it was with a fervour which one would imagine more appropriate to a chapel than to a public house. But to those of us who know Wales, we know what this means. We appreciate what this stands for, that this is part of the way of life ... anyway, I remember Dylan telling me that he went with Fred Farr to a pub in Swansea where they saw several sailors knitting pullovers and behaving in an effeminate way.

In some of the recent writings about Dylan, there's been a suggestion that he had indulged in it [gay sex] once

...also that he indulged once with an MP or some such thing ... I would say that's completely out of character. He was completely normal ... as boys of seventeen and eighteen, we were both very normal. We both drank beer, we both smoked a lot, and we both had love affairs, which more often than not lasted a few weeks at a time. But I would say that it would be completely out of character for him to have had any kind of practical experience of homosexuality. In fact, the very idea really revolted and disgusted him. Just as it did me.

*You have a voice in 'Return Journey', saying "Look, he's blushing now ... "
Was Dylan capable of blushing in those days?*
In those days, believe it or not, he was capable of doing that. At seventeen or eighteen, he was ... but at nineteen or twenty he was not ... the hardening process came in between eighteen and nineteen in Dylan's case.

...Dylan was a fine all-round reporter – although he never bothered to learn shorthand as the rest of us had to do, but then he was rather a special character – he was capable of taking a quick summary note, writing in fast longhand, which was usually quite adequate ... Dylan covered one or two rugby or soccer matches for the *Evening Post*, and maybe he covered a boxing match or two, because when Freddie Farr 'Half Hook' was on holiday, for example, one of the junior reporters would be assigned to take his place to cover a boxing bout; and it may well be that Dylan covered a boxing match in the Mannesman, for which he was not technically qualified, shall I say. He certainly was not technically qualified to cover a rugby or soccer match, although the editors tried him out once or twice and then decided that his talents lay in other directions ...

...Dylan could be very gracious and very kindly in assessing other people's work. Mark you, there were times when he could be a very harsh critic. But I well remember one occasion where he warmed my heart when I was dictating a running commentary on a soccer match, by telephone, to Dylan, when he interrupted me to say. "Bill, that's a *damn* fine report you're giving, and I don't care *who* says so – who I say that to!" Now, frequently he was capable of making kindly gestures which mean a lot.

...there were occasions when he would read an article or a gossip note or something I had written, and he would go out of his way and say "Bill, I liked that article. You've put something really good into that. I liked it." And believe me, getting a little tribute, or a little compliment from him, meant more to me than if it had come from the editor himself ...

...it was a wonderful experience for me to live for twelve months daily with Dylan, to be doing the same kind of work ... to sit with him having coffee, when we used to do word games and tear pages out of dictionaries to learn, to extend our vocabularies ... to spend a whole evening drinking with him, because in drinking we would also be discussing very profound matters, and we often discussed ideas which frequently I've seen reappearing in his works fifteen years later.

...he confessed that he had been very largely influenced by a book by J.B. Priestley called *The Good Companions*, which he read over and over again, and he was also a great lover of Wodehouse ...

...a typical morning, when we were on the calls together, would be to go to the British Legion, then to the Hospital, then to the Kardomah for a coffee, and to meet the kindred spirits of our age, between eleven and twelve, and then, after we'd written what we had collected, to go to have a pint of Number Six and the cornish pasties in the Singleton Hotel ... run by Mrs Giles, who used to keep pewter tankards for special clients, and Dylan and I were among the favoured few who, when we appeared at the bar, Gwen, the barmaid, would immediately produce the pewters and fill them up with Number Six, which was our favourite drink ... a heavy, dark brown beer, which had almost the texture of stout.

He mentions various pubs where the reporters used to hang out, and one was the Three Lamps. What were these pubs like?

The Three Lamps, had a character of its own because the landlord sat in a corner and he controlled proceedings, and he would be very deeply offended if anyone even held his glass of beer up to the light, to allege that it was cloudy or anything of that sort. I've seen Old Mac I think his name was – but I speak entirely from memory on that – I've seen Old Mac in a blazing fury when one man had held his glass up to the light, alleging that the beer was cloudy, because when that happens in a crowded bar, it frequently means that several other people hold their glass up to the light, too, and people begin to think "Is there something wrong with this beer or isn't there?" And the very sight of one man holding his glass up to the light was enough to send Mac into a complete rage ... Dylan sometimes held his glass up deliberately to provoke him!

There was another pub called the Bovega ... directly opposite the *Evening Post*, in Castle Bailey Street ... it was extremely popular with newspaper men and bookmakers, particularly. So it was rather a sporty crowd and it was there that Glynne Lowry held sway. Now Glynne Lowry was a tall, powerfully built man, but with a nature as gentle as a dove, but he was a fine sporting journalist and later went to Fleet Street to become the Press Association's chief boxing correspondent ... he used to say at quarter to six, "I'm going on the quarter to seven bus to Gorseinon," where he was living. And then quarter to seven would come and then he would say "Gentlemen – I'm going to my home in Gorseinon at quarter to eight." At quarter to eight he would say, "Gentlemen, I'm going on the quarter to nine." And so it went on. And so we called him 'Last Bus Lowry'.

There was another fine old character who also lived in Gowerton I believe – George Harry. He was an old journalist, a very experienced journalist ... a dear old character, and one of the characters that Dylan used to love, because to Dylan the more bizarre, the more eccentric, a character was, the more Dylan loved him ... George was one of those dear, congenial, happy characters and Dylan, in such company as that would respond, because he, too, loved playing the clown. And so some of those evenings in the Bovega were the funniest things that one could ever imagine.

...Charles Fisher was rather a flamboyant character ... I do remember that Charles wore a monocle at one time ... Charlie and Dylan were very friendly, but their interests were rather wide apart in that Charlie was a great fisherman and he wrote a splendid weekly article on fishing for the *Evening Post*.[34] Charlie also loved poetry, but I think that he, like most of us, developed an inferiority complex about our own work, because of the fact that it couldn't hold a candle to the superb verses that Dylan was already producing in his teens.

...the editors' attitude towards Dylan was avuncular. They recognised, after a while, that this was not just another junior reporter, but someone who seemed to have the seeds of genius within him, and so they each, in their turn, took every opportunity to encourage him to produce creative work such as book reviews or to try his hand at poetry, or to encourage him to write special descriptive articles on subjects which appealed to him ... this was obviously his field instead of straight reporting. But, nevertheless, a straight news report by Dylan had something in it which lifted it above the ordinary run of even first-rate journalism.

...he may have been unreliable in some ways, in small ways, about making appointments to go to the cinema or go and have a drink or something of that kind, but he certainly was not unreliable or slipshod or haphazard in his work. He would go to the most extraordinary lengths to get even his news stories right.

...I've no evidence that he ever took up any kind of politics seriously. In fact, he used to treat politics as a complete joke. He was never particularly interested in one party or the other. Whenever elections took place in Swansea, and we reporters had to spend our evenings going from one parish hall to another, to cover political meetings for the *Evening Post*, he considered it a crashing bore, and he did so, just like the rest of us, just as a job and he was very glad to get it over with.

...he was smoking a lot ... he began to drink so heavily, even in his teens, that he started taking hard liquor long before one would have thought it advisable to do ... I have played the part of the – what shall I say – almost that of a sackman in returning him and depositing him on the doorstep of his home in Cwmdonkin Drive.

What about Dylan's girlfriends?
He had several.

Did you ever see him altering his behaviour according to the company he was in?
No, because he was no snob. I was with him almost every day for twelve months, in the company of many different kinds of people, and it seemed to me that, as they came along, he enjoyed their company ... he preferred the bizarre, the eccentric, and the unusual, no matter what social category they came from.

...it would be quite wrong to say that he was a sponger, but it would be quite right to say that there were times when he was short of money, when he would borrow half a crown and he may be quite a long time repaying it, but it would be wrong to categorise him or brand him as a sponger, because there were times when he could be extraordinarily generous – when he was generous, he would be outrageously so, to an extent far beyond what was really required of him. In other words, he was so unusual he was difficult to pin down.

What was the effect of London on him?
Oh, the impact of London was beginning to speed up the process of deterioration physically. I saw him in London about 1947. That is to say, about ten years after our *Evening Post* days. I was then a reporter with the Press Association, and one day I met him in Fleet Street, and we went out on a large-scale pub crawl. It was probably three o'clock in the afternoon when we began, and when the pubs were closed we were in clubs, and when we got fed up with clubs we went to pubs, we did a tremendous pub crawl, and then we lost each other somewhere.

Gwen Bevan Courtney

I was about seventeen to eighteen ... Cliff Williams and I promised to meet by the Kardomah in Castle Street ... of course, I was working in an office in those days, five shillings a week ... and I don't suppose that the cub reporters had very much more ...

...now, you've got to realise that in those days, to go on beyond Castle Street down into Wind Street, I mean it wasn't done, it wasn't the thing

31. Gwen Bevan Courtney

... and as I say, we didn't have much money and we invariably went Dutch. So we were going down to Gower. And in those days Taylor Brothers, I think, was running the buses and the Gower Inn wasn't the Gower Inn as it is today, mind. The Gower Inn was seats, wooden seats, you know. No, nothing posh about the Gower Inn. It was a typical farmers' pub. And you couldn't afford to drink anything else, only beer.

Heavens above! Who should be coming up Wind Street but our friend Dylan. And he looked dreadful! All I can see is the yellow of his lips. His hair untidy, he hadn't washed, and his collar and tie squiff and his hat on the back of his head. Remember, pork pie trilby on top of these curls and he was coming up Wind Street – of course, he spotted us. Well, I thought "Oh, this is it! This is it! He's had a reject." You got to know when he was down ... anyway, he just tagged along, and he doesn't ask you, he just tags along, you see.

So he came and caught a bus. Of course, he had no money. Oh, and he was miserable. And dejected. And morose. Ooh, he was a little swine. So we got out and we weren't very happy because our bit of money going Dutch, you understand, was going three ways, and our cigarettes as well. So anyway, he came down and followed us, not a word out of him. He sat on the bus ... and we were working out how far our money'd go ... I think the Gower Inn, if my memory serves me rightly, was open until half-past three in the afternoon. So it was only a case of having a drink and just having a walk round.

...so we had a glass of beer. Not a word out of him – oh, and he'd obviously been drinking. He'd had no food and he looked as if he'd been out on the tiles all night. So I said to Cliff "This is great, isn't it? We've got him tagged behind us now." What we used to do, even if it was cold, in those days, you walked, you used your feet, I mean there was no such things as cars, you walked. Well, we used to walk back to the Mumbles, call in the Pier, and the Pier at that time was not the Pier as it is today, of course, have a drink and catch the Mumbles train home.

So anyway, that's how it was in those days. Dylan had his drink with us. We had to make it last a long time, because we had no money, so he was there and this drink and he was really miserable. So I said to Cliff, look – let's walk him over the dunes. So we walked over the Parkmill dunes – do you know the dunes of Parkmill going up to Pennard Castle? There's a ramp up to the Castle. Well, as you know, this castle overlooks the sea, and of course you've got a wonderful view right round.

So then Dylan – I can see he's got on top of the ramp up to this castle and Mr Haughty he was standing on top, like this, trilby off – he took it off – and the wind was blowing his coat, you know and he was going "Yes – they're rejecting Dylan Thomas today! But the day will come," he said, "when the name Dylan Thomas will echo from shore to shore. But Dylan Thomas won't be here to hear it." So I just looked at him, you know, and it was cold. "Ooh," I said, "for Heaven's sake, monarch of all you survey, come down from there, will you?" I said "Listen – you'll live. The devil looks after his own."

Down he came and we got him down walking, hauling, walking behind us, scrounging our cigarettes, till we got to the Pier in the Mumbles. We got there, in time for another half a glass of beer. And then of course, we got the bus home.

...I never saw Dylan other than being, you know being rough. Then he'd come up here. Then he'd start – rejects.

Up to your house?

Yes, to this house. Into the middle room ... oh, he'd start and he'd go on and he'd cry and he'd throw himself ... we had a sofa ... he'd come and he'd fling himself on that sofa and he'd cry and he'd throw his rejects at me and he'd –

Carry on, in other words?

Oh well, you know, as Dylan could carry on. Well, the only thing you could let him do was to carry on, and he would still go on and say about the time will come when he'd be famous. Anyway, you just listened to this. Then he'd come and we'd have some serious times, and then we'd talk. Now, this is where I am convinced that he was deep down, deeply religious. We'd talk about socialism – not a political socialism, we'd talk about a Christian socialism, and he really believed in a classless society ... in my view, I was convinced, and am still convinced, that he was chasing a faith – what faith, I don't know. Maybe it's the sort of faith that I am trying to find.

...we used to talk about religion. That's where I'm convinced that he had this religious belief. We used to talk about politics, but I can't call it politics, you see. We used to talk a lot about socialism. And our real true belief in socialism – as we believed socialism. Which I suppose you could call it politics, but not what they call socialism today.

Were you talking about the economic structures, like nationalisation?
Oh no, I mean, oh no, no ... we never thought of those things. That's a Fabianite thing, that has come out. When we talked about socialism we used to talk about the socialism of Christ, the good Samaritan and we used to discuss the Bible a lot. And we used to have terrific arguments on, more or less, the Christian socialism of Christ. That's the socialism *I* believed in ... we used to discuss the Tolpuddle Martyrs. Well, we'd argue about Keir Hardie ... we both had the same idea in our heads ... this classless society.

I loved company. Like Dylan, I loved a damn good argument. I used to really like Dylan, I used to enjoy going out to these pubs – Pontlliw; oh, I'll name them all for you ... you take the Penllergaer Inn ... the Castle in Pontlliw. Go on into the Hendy – well, you go in with the Welsh collier ... a few Welsh farmers, and have a darned good argument and listen to their views of life ...

Did Dylan have any girlfriends of his own in those days?
No, I never knew him have any girlfriends ... Dylan seemed to be spending his time down the Cuba and around those places, but I never knew him to bother with any girls, only to tag round with us.

...I'm not speaking about Dylan in his later life ... but somehow I am convinced that Dylan wasn't the *roué* that they're all making him out to be. Because it's very seldom you'll find a man who is interested in drink, interested in women. They're not compatible with each other ... he may have perhaps gone out with one woman and she's probably exaggerated it and added on, and added on, as they do – but I'm convinced deep down in my heart, that Dylan Thomas was *not*, and I repeat it, *not* the horrible sexual maniac that people make him out to be.

You knew him when he was eighteen. Some people have said he was an innocent then, some people have said that he was already experienced sexually. What do you think of that?

Oh no, I'm not going to say that he was innocent; I'm not saying that by any means. I don't say that for one moment ... but I cannot believe honestly that he was as rotten as they've made him out to be.

Dilys Rowe

The first I remember hearing about him when I was very young and he was perhaps sixteen, seventeen, I heard that he was taking out a girl from Woolworths, and this was very shocking, because his father was a Grammar School master and, you know, the word Woolworths was somehow ... my mother, the shock that one had on hearing this.

...I didn't really talk to a member of his family until very much later, when I met Mr Thomas, DJ, in the square in Llansteffan ... it was some time just after the War ... we knew that Dylan was in Italy, and at the time there was a story going round – which I don't think was true, but it was being said in London – that while he was staying in this villa in Italy, the tapestries were cut up in order to make clothes for the little girl ... we asked Mr Thomas how Dylan was, and he said he was in Italy and he didn't think it was a particularly good thing, and so I said "But this is what he always wanted, to have the sun and to have somewhere to live and to write in peace." And Mr Thomas said, yes, but it was a bad thing and we said "Why?" and he said "Because the red wine doesn't agree with him."

...I used to see him in London, yes. I remember being struck by how different his behaviour was from what one thought of as his behaviour in Swansea. Although unconsciously he probably outraged people in Swansea, he never *consciously* did so but I think he did consciously outrage [in London] ... he had a public face, in a more extreme sense than most people have it, and a private one, and I always think, perhaps I'm over-simplifying saying this, that in the Swansea behaviour and the London behaviour, there was such a contrast. But this may be because I knew him in two distinct periods, and there was hardly anything between.

...as far as the Depression was concerned, I think he adopted the attitude that was adopted by people in Swansea, and by many people who were more involved in the Depression, older people, and people who suffered from it more, that you laughed so that you didn't weep, and this is certainly what little that I remember of the Depression in the middle Thirties, that everybody had a kind of false gaiety ... perhaps he couldn't have been the rather peculiar mixture that he was of almost hysterical wit and sort of depression, if he hadn't been born at that time in that particular place.

The other thing, of course, that's terribly important about his makeup – and this is probably a truism – the religiosity of the place, the way that when one is very young, up to perhaps the age of seven, one is taught about hell-fire. It has its value – there's beautiful imagery, and Welsh *hwyl*, even at that age, is a wonderful thing to hear from the pulpit, but it's a terrible guilt-creator for the rest of one's life ... I think one could characterise the part of Swansea where Dylan lived as suffering from the bourgeoisie of the suburbs and the non-conformism of the nation ... it's a terrible combination.

...the first thing that occurs to me about Dylan Thomas' poetry is that it shows this tremendous tension of a person who would like to think about religion, and to make his own decision, but who being born where he is, with the parents he had, or with the mother he had perhaps, doesn't stand a chance, that it's all decided for him ... he wasn't encouraged by his father, apparently, to believe, and if he were going to take his father's side of ideas, he certainly wouldn't. I think this must have created enormous tension which he never quite resolved. You know, we've talked about guilt and I think this is one of the springs of his creative drive.

Leon Atkin

I met Dylan a dozen or fifteen times over a period from 1931 until just two or three weeks before his death. Never by appointment – always by accident, as most people did meet Dylan. You couldn't make an appointment with him, because it was seldom kept. You collided with him or you'd have to meet him in cafés and in pubs ...

...I went into a café and he sat there and was very depressed ... I suppose he'd be about eighteen. Very worried about his health. He had spits of blood, which he imagined was a very serious symptom, and I argued with him and said "Lots of people spit blood from a tonsil or something like that, that's been infected and burst." And that was our first meeting ...

...Swansea was, of course, the pre-war Swansea, pre-blitz Swansea. Grand town. Friendly, with far too much smug, non-conformist hypocrisy in it, but even then, owing to the Depression, we had twenty-eight thousand unemployed, which meant a tremendous section of the people living hungry ... I spent most of my time working on

32. The Revd. Leon Atkin

unemployed demonstrations. So much so that I used to have a private detective come to my service on Sunday nights, to take notes. They thought perhaps we were subsidised from Russia and trying to instigate an uprising.

...there was a tremendous cleavage between certain religious people who thought that the unemployed were unemployed because they didn't want work and one or two churches [that] identified themselves with them. They paid very dearly; they lost all the well-to-do people for doing it ... we ran a soup kitchen here. We collected all kinds of things, old clothes. The young men, the men of Dylan's generation, avoided the main streets because the bright lights showed up their threadbare trousers. They walked in the back streets. But there's one thing about Dylan's generation. Although they suffered deprivation, although they had no pocket money, many of them, cut off on the means test because their father was working three days a week, migrated. Went into the Army, Navy, went on the roads. And the church's job, although it was only done by a few, was to try and keep that family together, try and keep the boys at home. Yet we had no real outbreak of crime. In proportion to the added incentive to steal – you know what I mean, the privation. We had very little, if any, thuggery or violence ... the unemployed in Swansea and in Wales, were marvellously well-controlled. They demonstrated; they made a hell of a noise, but they did it with a drum. And a brass band. An amateur one, very often, but they made a hell of a noise. But, it was their protest. They didn't smash windows, they didn't attack people. They didn't even beat the police up ...

...hungry men are angry men, and even business people who are interrupted in their money-making tend to react in an ugly way, irrationally. There was disillusionment everywhere. The established political parties seemed self-discredited. Novelty, anything new, would attract attention. We remember the sudden rise of the Social Credit Party, and then the more dramatically-advertised British Union of Fascists. They came to Swansea; they took a room in Walter Road. And outside stood two black-shirted sentries, or so it seemed. So strong was their appeal, so attractive the novelty of this new idea which was apparently at that moment rebuilding a Germany on a firm foundation, that local businessmen and men of good repute were attracted, and even joined. Town councillors, business people, and others less able to see beyond the veneer and the exploitation of political extremities. And then there appeared all over Swansea large posters, thirty feet by fifteen, with the slogan 'Mosley speaks! Plaza Cinema – Sunday'.

...as a minister of religion and as one interested in local politics, I was given a complimentary ticket to sit with the élite in the first three rows. The Plaza Cinema, since demolished, was then the largest picture-house in Wales. It held three thousand five hundred people, and on this particular Sunday night it was filled to capacity. Outside on the forecourt, buses and charabancs from Rhondda and Merthyr, full of political agitators and people out for trouble, unable to get into the hall, waited. Of course, my special ticket enabled me to sit in the front. At that time, being a young minister, I wore a frock tailcoat with my clerical attire. And there I sat. The stage was bare apart from a table draped with the Union Jack, a decanter of water and a glass. The hall lined, downstairs and in the galleries, with hundreds of blackshirts – stewards they called them ...

...and then Mosley came to the platform, spotlighted. Then in the prime of his days, a handsome man, I should say six foot two. Neatly attired in his black shirt and bright belt with brass buckle, he gave the Fascist salute, which was answered by the chorus already prepared, and a mixture of other responses. And then he began to speak. For an hour and a half he spoke; from beginning to end, his speech consisted in a tirade against international Jewry. The Jews, he argued, were responsible for everything bad on the planet, including the weather and not exempting the position of Swansea Town in the league. When he had finished, he announced that, owing to the brevity of time, he would take a few questions – not oral questions ...

...I could not resist writing on the back of my special invite, my question: "I have been working for a Jew for quite a number of years. Ought I to change my employer?" And by a miraculous coincidence, it was the first question to come out of the hat. Drawing himself to his full six foot plus, the would-be dictator read the question "I have been working for a Jew for so many years. Ought I to change my employer?" "Certainly," he said. "I am sure if you looked round, you would find a far more reliable Gentile." Rising to my feet in the front row in full clerical attire, I said "Mr Mosley, could you give me his name and address?" Mosley turned the colours of the rainbow. "Is this man a *bona fide* parson?" he cried. "Course he bloody is!" shouted someone. It soon became a chorus. In the gallery, the Welsh Nationalists started singing 'Mae hen wlad fy nhadau'; the Communists sang 'The Red Flag'; the wavering patriots sang the National Anthem, and within a few seconds pandemonium reigned. Escorted by the strangest bodyguard a parson ever had – Communists, Welsh Nationalists, members of the Labour Party, Liberals, and Conservatives – I was ushered down the gangway and out of the hall, into the vestibule, now a congestion. Free fights were breaking out everywhere ...

...through the years Dylan came to call me 'his parson'. He never came to church, not to my church. The only time I saw Dylan in a church was when his coffin was taken in for the funeral service. As to him being fundamentally religious, I'd say no; you could never fit Dylan into a creed or to a denominational conception of religion. That was to the good, because he was far too big. But I think his whole response to the realities was religious, for the simple reason it wasn't commercial. It wasn't materialistic. He had to live, and he lived, I suppose, more on faith than most parsons ever have tried to do. He wrote, he created ... he travailed with it, he worked hard and it was floated. And no one could ever accuse him of daring to submit his talent to commercial interest. In fact, there were times when he looked like a tramp, and I suppose he didn't eat much more than a tramp.

The critics say it was his own fault; he preferred beer. He did drink a lot, and I am prepared to admit he drank too much. In fact, I think he drank in proportion to the ugliness of the world in which he lived. He was so hypersensitive, as the poet always is, that its contradictions and its cruelties were a little bit too much for him and he just used to hide behind a barrel, or try to drown his sorrows. He found they could swim, as they mostly do.

...he always struck me as a man whose soul was so much alive that he suffered. He suffered a lot, I think. But every action he seemed to make was, according to my unorthodox view, a religious action. It was an attempt to evaluate and appreciate and express beauty and something that was lovely ... he says in his poem, the one where he speaks of being young and in the mercy of his means ... whose means? To my mind that's a wonderful approximation to a healthy theology. Life lived within in the mercy of God's means ... I think that things like that could never be classified in terms of orthodox theology, or credal expression, which made Dylan a most religious man in that sense ... in fact, his religion was, I suppose, repulsive to the orthodox religions, because he was so free. He always used to remind me of King David.

Did Dylan ever discuss his concept of God with you, in any way directly or indirectly.

No. No. No. No, the nearest we got to my job was very kind mimicry of deacons and parsons. I suppose I met Eli Jenkins a thousand times before he got into *Milk Wood* ... we used to have a lot of fun together – fooling – I used to pretend to preach to him, you know. He would do the deacon stunt, and then he'd preach to me, that kind of thing. Well, looking back now, I can see old Eli Jenkins. He was being made then, I suppose. Perhaps there's a little bit of me in him, I don't know. Not as orthodox as he was ... Dylan was never unkind in his discussion of parsons and deacons. He gave them some thumps, but they were never below the belt.

Someone who knew Dylan when he was in Grammar School said that, unlike the other boys, who usually were out in the countryside or one of the playing fields, he would be spending his time roaming around on the Strand, which was quite a disreputable area of Swansea at that time.

The poet's got to find material; he's got to live so close to human life, he's got to keep his finger on the pulse of humanity ... he'd want material, he'd want to see life in the raw so to speak, and at that time in the early Thirties, the Strand still retained some of these crude, riotous lodging-houses, where Dylan would find the characters that he was interested in ... all I can say is that Dylan, as a poet and as a student of human nature, would always be attracted to human nature in its more violent forms – the prostitute, the thug, the thief, the outcast, the tramp. Naturally, those were the raw materials that he had to understand if he was to make a true assessment of life. But I think he looked upon the prostitute, the tramp and the down-and-out more or less as the debris, the victim of a society which he hated so much, and he wanted to assess the true damage that this horrible, money-idolatrising society was costing ...

And he wanted to communicate his sympathy to them, too, which is one reason he went, and was with them.

Yes. And that's one reason why I, as perhaps an unorthodox parson, would identify Dylan as extremely religious. He was not afraid of contamination. He was not afraid of being criticised because of his association with the down-and-outs. Lots of people have a professed affection and compassion for the unfortunate, but it's at arms' length. It's generally handed out on the end of a clothes prop – the sop, the vinegar and the gall, which after all was a kind of a sedative to keep them quiet, lest in their crying they disturb the peace of their night. But Dylan had none of that; he would identify himself with them, and never seemed to worry as to what people thought. Why should he? He was so near to the essential and vital truth, he could afford to say "I don't care a damn." And he didn't, and because Dylan didn't care a damn, he was loved by those who truly understood humanity.

...we're all to some degree the same – will behave in a way that seems so out of character, so destructive, so cruel, and yet underneath as I would say "He sinned; and yet he sinned so delicately, that even God must find it hard to punish him."

...it has been said that a friend is one that knows all that is bad about you, and loves you as though he didn't. I knew a lot that sometimes used to make me uncomfortable, embarrass me and make me want to blush; and yet underneath I knew that there was so much that was essentially good and clean and right. And I would sooner spend an hour in the company of a Dylan Thomas, than an eternity with some of the professing Christians that I have suffered under.

...he had a terrible hatred of hypocrisy. But I liked him ... the night before he went to America on the last trip, he was in the Westbourne, the pub on the corner by the hospital, and I just happened to pop in about eight-ish, as I usually do. He was there, accompanied by this American. And he was in a nice, merry state. "Let me introduce you," he says to the American. "This is my parson." At that second, an old chap sitting in a seat called me across – these things happen very often in a pub. "Sign this form." – he was reapplying for a new pension book and wanted the signature of a minister, and I had to leave the two of them. And it appears that while I was away, this youngster said "Is that chap really a parson, or is he taking part in some kind of rag or something?" And Dylan went furious; he said, "Indeed, that man is the only parson I know! You will apologise!" – he was getting a bit oiled – "Apologise," he says, "to my parson!" "Oh," he says, "I'm awfully sorry, I don't get about – we don't see these kind of things back home in the States." Well, I appreciated that, although it was all fun, but underneath that, if you can see it, there was Dylan's regard for not only a friend, but a friend who as also a parson.

Do you know anything about the American who was with him then?
He was a tallish fellow, young. He struck me as being a kind of a private bodyguard to see that Dylan turned up.

Brinnin?
He might have been. But he didn't appear to have been a literary man of any ability, or he wouldn't have been so daft.

...there was a group of them used to go to the Bush sometimes – Dylan, Dan and the painter man. Of course, all great writers like Dylan, they get a following of young aspirants who would like them to read one of their poems, you know. And there was a chappie who worked in the market, a businessman, and he had an idea he could write poetry and bless him, he couldn't, but he wanted to ... he'd written a bit of stuff and he came in the pub one day, and he said "Do you think Dylan would read this, or let me read a line to him?" And it was just like the bringing of little children to our Lord – the disciples rebuked them. One of the others – I won't say who it was – said "Don't bother with that bloody tripe ... " He was half-drunk, being very crude, and the poor chap – he was hurt, you know. It was doggerel, I know, but Dylan looked at it. "Oh," he said. "Carry on working," he said. "Not bad – carry on," he said, "keep at it." It struck me then that – and the text came bump to me because I thought, what an illustration of it, suffer little children – because he was a little child compared to Dylan.
... I've never heard him talk in terms of party politics, or political theories. But his compassion for people as people, irrespective of class distinction or anything, makes him what I would call a Christian Socialist. He believed in the essential unity and family of men, and men were men and it didn't matter ... he was always concerned for the underdog ... he hated any injustice, he hated hypocrisy. And although he may have been as big a hypocrite as the rest of us, he would never condone it, justify it.

Some people have said that one of the reasons for the end of his life, that Dylan was in a state of near despair because his poetic genius was drying up and he was afraid that he was finished as a poet. I don't believe that, do you? No. No, I don't. In fact I've got my own theory, which may be miles and miles from the point and it might sound crude, but I think Dylan ... was so super-sensitive that the internal spiritual vibration of that personality – if you can think of such a crazy phrase – eventually broke itself. Fused ... he worked up to a pitch of sensitivity, and in travail for something even better than he'd ever done before – and, you see, he was a perfectionist ... I think poor old Dylan, he did just explode. That's a crude word, too ... you could almost say that he died in childbirth. Couldn't you?

W. Emlyn Davies[35]

Well, he wasn't a politician, but he was intensely aware, and became more intensely aware, of the kind of world in which he was living. As a reporter, he was in touch with the Depression in Swansea, in south Wales, and in the world ... I do know definitely that he read Whitehead's *Science and the Modern World*, which gives you the background to the modern attitude of science to our life, and also the revolutionary manifesto, *Communist Manifesto*, of Karl Marx. He did try to read Marx's *Kapital* itself, but like everybody else he ...

...so far as being aware of the life of that time, nobody could be more aware of it than Dylan was. Only recently I've met some young people who went about with him, unknown people, people who couldn't be quoted, but mixed with him and found that he was almost like the 'angry young men' that you've had amongst teenagers in the last five years. To say that he was merely a poet in an ivory tower is quite absurd. He would have been, if he had been born in another age, but the facts of life made that impossible.

...and you met his mother?
She was a person who was constantly in touch with people about here. She was a very gregarious person, and she knew most people, and she was aware of what was going on in the world. Nobody could at that time not be aware of what was going on in the world. You had the two big things that counted in the lives of people; you had the economic depression and you had the growth of Nazism on the Continent, and it was at our doorstep. We were part of it.

...and that's why I do feel that to regard Dylan as a non-political, non-economic, pure poet, is rubbish ... he lived too much in contact. He *had* to – I mean, his daily assignment in the *Evening Post* was in the police courts, and then from there to the pub ... there are many ways in which you can show how he shared the life of the ordinary people, young people of his time, in Swansea. The hints are there over and over again, and even in his books, his early books, describing his life, where he describes Swansea, the foreshore, the Promenade and these places, he's describing a life which anybody who had lived in Swansea at that period, or a generation earlier, would appreciate, would know. That's why I like to feel that Dylan was never an ivory tower poet.

...he went to the Grammar School here. He was mixing with people and, of course, the Grammar School in those days was rather different from what the multilateral or the big kind of school is today. It wasn't a catchment area for one particular spot but rather boys from all over the town ... and he would pick up the accent, the idiom, the approach of these people, when he was in school. Then, when he went – well, he could not go to a better sounding-board for the way people thought and talked in Swansea than in the *Evening Post*.

You mentioned he got his voice from his mother.
Yes ... I knew her, you see, back in 1937, '38 ... a very lovely woman. She had a rich voice – it wasn't from his father. It was from the mother. Also appearance, by the way.

What about his father?
Of course, his father was ill – we know that now – and was ill for a long time and was removed, was withdrawn, was very difficult to get at him. The mother was the extrovert. And the mother was the home, in a very strong sense. I think it was a matriarchal system rather than the patriarchal, and I think that the sympathy and the feeling, and also the encouragement for Dylan, came from his mother.

Tom Warner

I met him at Dan's in about 1931 ... he was about eighteen at the time and I was about twenty-three ... my brother was in Dylan's class ... in fact, I think they were very good friends, because Dylan didn't prepare his Latin – my brother did.

...Dylan was a young choirboy-looking boy. He was very gay, very full of life. Wonderful mimic, and, of course, those were the days when we had quite a lot of music. We discovered that if you fit an old

33. Tom Warner

loudspeaker into the back of a gramophone, you can broadcast from the top of the house to the bottom, and we played each other concerts very often. Dylan's great turn was sitting at the piano and doing a whole opera, in soprano and bass.

And there was the famous trio that we used to have in those days. Dan and I would play violins and Dylan would saw away on the cello, and we'd put in the notes above him. And, at times, we sounded like a trio. We looked like a trio, and we sounded like one ... we called ourselves 'The Twitterers'.

You mean Dylan could handle a cello?
He handled it, yes. You realise it's the only instrument that a chain-smoker can actually hold without burning a hole in it. He would start on the cello, play a note. I could put a note in above it, that was musical, and Dan could put another one above that, and we played for hours on end ... he'd follow a tune, yes ... it was rather like the sort of Javanese music where you extemporise.

...there were two girls, Dylan used to take me along to play the piano for them. One was slightly crippled – she's made a wonderful recovery since then – she had a tubercular spine or something, and he knew them very well. I think they were old family friends, and some evenings he'd take me along there and I'd play the piano for them.[36]

...then Dan left to go to London and Dylan used to call in for me. We used to go to the pictures every Monday afternoon, it was absolutely a fixed rule for a year ... he was passionately fond of Greta Garbo. "The greatest emotional actress you or I will ever see," was one of his sentences. And then he'd come back to my house – I lived in Mirador Crescent – for tea. Boiled eggs on Mondays, always ...

...the first time Dylan came, we noticed that he was just sitting in rather a helpless way with his egg untouched, and by general gestures we realised he wanted someone to take the top off for him – he'd never done it himself. So my aunt just took his plate and cut the top off and then we went on with tea quite normally.

Did he talk much then about an ambition to write something for film, and to work in film? Because he later did write documentaries, during the War.
I don't think he ever thought of it, no ... he thought of himself just as a poet, and he couldn't see anything further than that in those days. He used to make up documentaries ... in the course of conversation, someone would mention Canada and he'd sort of put his special booming voice on, and 'do' a bit of a documentary on 'Canada – Land of Wheat'.

...he was telling me the story of *The Death of the King's Canary*, the thriller. That arose from the fact that in those days he was reviewing thrillers for *The Telegraph*, and he'd be sent so many a week, and I think, unfortunately, he found three rather bad ones in a row, and they turned out to all have been published by Collins. So Collins, funnily enough, sent him a very nice letter saying they were very interested in his reviewing, which was, obviously, first-class, and that he showed such a knowledge of it, he *must* have a manuscript somewhere, and could they see it. So he started writing this thriller ... I think it got written in the end, but not by Dylan – the poetry wasn't written by Dylan!

...I remember how excited Dylan was about *The Postman Always Rings Twice*. He was thrilled by that book, I know. And just about those times, we were reading the new Evelyn Waughs, as they were coming out ... *Scoop* and *Black Mischief*, I think, came out that year ... he was fond of Donne at about that time, too.

Are there any other little pieces of poetry that you recall him mentioning?
The drill would be he'd work all day, and I'd meet him in the evening, and he might try something out. But it's so long ago I can't really remember anything very much, except that once I remember he had some phrase like 'my leafy alphabet', and I asked him what it was, and he said "Well, can you imagine, you have leaves falling from the tree, and each one has a letter on, and they could fall in such a way as to become a poem." I saw it when he explained it.

...he showed me a poem he wrote once. It ran 'I like my bike'. He'd written on a sheet of cardboard. You know, he wrote all his poetry on the card you get out of shirts back from the laundry – it's a lovely white expanse of paper ...

...he seemed as fit as a fiddle all the time I knew him. I think he had 'flu once; I came to see him and he was lying in bed, looking *very* small and frail, reading novels which I helped to supply, but obviously he must have had a very strong constitution to go without food as he did, and one thing and another, in London.

...there was a time when his father gave him somewhat of an ultimatum about his drinking ... Dylan came to see me, and his father obviously knew everything that was going on, and much to Dylan's very great surprise. He knew every fact about him, over the past four or five years, and threatened him that he'd get him more or less into an inebriates' home – he must have been under twenty-one at the time, mustn't he? He was very worried about it, he must have promised to reform or something.

...I remember meeting him late one night because I'd had to go somewhere else, and had this famous conversation. He said "Maida Vale", and we were in Swansea at the time, so obviously he wasn't trying to get to that district of London. And I said "Maida Vale?" "Made a veil mistake – had two whiskies." – or something like that. He was explaining why he couldn't articulate properly ... if he'd had some friends with him, and his keeping to beer, he'd have been quite safe all his life.

...I know one amazing morning, walking up Wind Street and on the kerbside of the pavement was obviously a sort of tramp man, and on the other side was a man carrying a briefcase and with a Homburg. And they both said, absolutely simultaneously, "Good morning, Dylan!" One was one of his father's friends, I suppose, and the other was a drinking friend.

...they were a very happy family. Delightful ... he loved his mother very much, and he also had a lot of Victorian respect for his father ... on one of those occasions where Dylan hadn't been seen for about a year, I met his mother in the Uplands, and she said "Daddy and I know he's a bit of a genius, so we just have to put up with it."

Trevor Hughes

We went to stay at a boarding house in Llandrindod Wells once, and found that D.J. Thomas and his wife and family were staying ... but Mr Thomas would not mix with anybody else; they had their private

34. Trevor Hughes

rooms upstairs ... he had been my master in the Grammar School, and I had such a great admiration for him, but I had no chance to speak to him at all. He was aloof; he spoke to nobody ... it was not a churlishness, it was simply a reticence, a shyness.

...but we got very friendly with Mrs Thomas, and she came in the room one day to speak to us, and I saw a little face of a boy about three years old peeping out from behind his mother's skirt, and a mass of light curly hair and these great eyes staring at me. And that was the infant Dylan Thomas, the first time I'd ever seen him.

...she delighted to come in our room and have a chat with us. I had a brother who was a great comedian in his way and Mrs Thomas used to say "I'd give anything if we were here with all of you, we could enjoy ourselves so much."

...there was an advertisement, or rather a paragraph, in the *Evening Post* – it was in June 1931 – saying a local man was thinking of starting a magazine, in English, to be called *Prose & Verse*, and he'd like to hear from anybody who was interested. It gave no indication of who it was at all. So I was very curious, and I replied. I had a very nice letter, asking would I call at 5 Cwmdonkin Drive where he lived then, so I went up and met this Adonis of a boy. A most remarkable looking boy. And I said immediately then that, the look about him, his eyes, you could see the lamps of genius in his eyes then, at the age of seventeen. Tremendously alert face, you know?

...I soon became very friendly with him, and later on I found that his father was Mr D.J. Thomas, the literature master at the Swansea Grammar School, a man who had had a great impression on me. I

150

thought he was a most remarkable character, a most beautiful charac-
ter. He used to recite Shakespeare to the class, and he'd walk up and
down the room reciting. You could tell he wasn't there – he was on a
stage somewhere. And he put so much feeling, so much expression
into it, and you could really see that he had tears in his eyes, he had a
job to control his emotions.

...of course, he [Dylan] had read all the other poets, particularly
fond of some more than others. John Donne, for instance, he was very
fond of him ... and he liked D.H. Lawrence ... Yeats ... it has been said
that Dylan was influenced to some extent by Francis Thompson.
That's absolutely not true. Because I was very fond of Francis
Thompson ... I think *The Hound of Heaven* is a very remarkable thing,
and I spoke to Dylan about it on more than one occasion, and he was
never interested at all ... I think he was rather impressed by Poe ...

...at the end of September 1931, I was to move to London. We'd met
several times in the meanwhile, and become really firm friends. And I
was going to leave on the Sunday ... on the Saturday morning Dylan
asked would I spend the day with him down the Gower Peninsula. So
we got down to Rhossili – that was a glorious day. We walked out to
Worms Head ... I sat on the edge of the cliffs ... Dylan had some paper
and a pencil with him and he would say "Well now, you give me the
last word in each line, and I will write a poem." And he kept doing that
sort of thing.

And he could do it so easily, you know. We spent some few hours like
that and became absolutely absorbed in the subject, and then we
turned and walked slowly back across the Worm to see the tide sweep-
ing over the rocks, and we clambered down as hard as we could go for
quite a distance. It was too late; we could see we couldn't risk it. We
were marooned till one o'clock in the morning and then the coast-
guards came and they got us off.

...we walked home through the night. Dylan got very, very tired
because, of course, he was still very young, only seventeen – he got
desperately tired. A few times he sat down in the middle of the road
and declared he wasn't going another inch. I remember we walked over
Fairwood Common; we saw the dawn rising ... and I could remember
about the lean, non-conformist God stalking the sky at dawn ... we
walked fifteen or sixteen miles to Upper Killay, and we got some
conveyance in from there. We had walked all night. Later on, Dylan
wrote a story about that. About the incident, about being on the Worm
but he didn't mention me by name and it was more or less a caricature

which I thoroughly enjoyed. [Hughes was the original for Raymond Price in 'Who Do You Wish Was With Us?']

...I introduced him to the Fitzroy Tavern ... the first time he came to London, just about the end of 1931 or it might have been early in 1932 ... he'd heard so much about these Bohemian pubs in the West End. Did I know of any typically Bohemian pub where I could take him? I thought immediately of the Fitzroy. I was not a drinking man at all in those days but I had to come up to London to work; I was staying in Bloomsbury at the time.

...I can only speak about the young Dylan Thomas when he was really Dylan Thomas and not what people make he became in later years – more or less a reprobate. He did, from his earliest days, love the atmosphere of pubs ... it was not due to any inordinate desire to drink at all. He liked the social atmosphere, and I do know that, so far as he and I were concerned, we could sit in the Fitzroy Tavern on a Saturday night – it would be absolutely full of people. Somebody playing the piano in the old tinky-tonky way, you know. Tremendous hubbub all about us. And in that atmosphere, Dylan and I could be more alone and less self-conscious than we would be anywhere else. And in that environment, we could discuss things without embarrassment that we wouldn't have dared, we couldn't have discussed, in a Lyons Tea Shop.

...and on such occasions we sometimes got very close together – I've never had this experience with anybody else in my life – we'd be talking in a very animated way on a subject which was very close to both our hearts and both, there's no doubt at all, absolutely sincere with each other. And perhaps, I would say something, practically knowing that that would lead Dylan to say something else, and I waited for his words and they came exactly as I expected. And we were both playing the same game. On those few occasions when we came very, very close, there seemed to be an absolute community of thought between us. And that is one of the most enjoyable experiences in life – it's a great experience and one which you very rarely get. I think when people scoff at people who sit in pubs drinking and all that, they're not aware of such experiences. Well, that night probably we'd had half a pint; at the outside we'd had a pint of beer – eight penn'orth.

...and Dylan did not want to drink – no, he wanted to talk, he wanted for us just to communicate as we always did. We were so very close to each other in our letters, and then we he came to London and we'd go and meet in the Fitzroy as the most convenient place in town and to fulfil all the promise of our letters ...

...I remember once in the Fitzroy, we'd just sat there for a little while and he said "Oh, I'm expecting so-and-so." I'd heard of this person, I'd never met him, and I said "What on earth did you invite him for?" Because, of course, I was jealous. I couldn't share Dylan with anybody, you see, I just wanted the whole evening to myself. Naturally, I didn't want to share him with other people. "Frankly," he said, "I thought I might be able to touch him for five shillings."

So this man came, and he was ... the pompous type of person. I couldn't stand him and neither could Dylan, and I think we turned the conversation as we wanted it. We tried deliberately to shock the other man's susceptibilities, and we were not at all surprised about nine o'clock when he said "Oh well, I shall have to be going now." So I left the bar for a moment. I went downstairs and when I came up he'd gone, and Dylan was standing at the bar ordering beer. He looked at me and held out his hand – there were two half-crowns in his hand. That was his reward for the night's work. Whether the man got his five shillings back, I don't know, but I will say, any time Dylan borrowed a few shillings from me – the most he ever borrowed was five bob, I couldn't spare more in those days – he was scrupulous giving it back. It might come shilling at a time, but he'd never forget and always pay it back.

...Dylan did tell me one amusing story ... of the time when his father came up here for an investigation of an illness ... Dylan took his father to the Fitzroy Tavern and his father said "What are you drinking?" And Dylan said "Beer, please." So his father said "One pint and one half, please." And Dylan was very amused about that – of course, the half was for Dylan ... well, Dylan could have drunk ten pints, even then.

...to say that Dylan was then drinking to excess was absolute piffle – that wasn't Dylan Thomas at all. He drank in company; but I have often said this, and this is the truth, we had many nights together in the Fitzroy – oh, they were glorious nights, and I still have wonderful memories of them – often we were both absolutely broke. I met him once, and I do like this story. I had about two shillings on me which was to last me to the end of the week, and I had enough responsibilities – I had a job to get by. Dylan had nothing at all. So I ordered two half-pints of bitter, and we spent, I suppose, about an hour and half drinking these two half-pints of beer. And then I couldn't spend any more money – it was only fourpence a half-pint in those days ... and Dylan saw that I had my gold cuff-links on. He said "Give me your cuff-links. I'll go and pawn them so that we can buy some more beer." Now, you can call me a weak-minded fool, or say I was very shrewd, or what you will. I took them out without a word and gave them to him. And he went out, and he came back in about ten minutes looking very crestfallen. The pawnbrokers were shut, you see. I'm not quite clear at the time whether I was quite certain the pawnbroker *would* be shut before I gave them, you see.

...when Dylan was young, when I knew him first, he had not the remotest interest in girls. I was amazed to read in later years where he talked about following girls along the street and then – I'm quite convinced that he was just writing of something that he had read elsewhere, that he had never done such a thing, and I can speak from actual experience of this, because on a few occasions I saw instances of girls trying to get off with Dylan. He'd just brush them aside ... in the Fitzroy one night, it was getting late, near to closing time, and there was a girl sitting on a bench seat a couple of yards from us and she sort of gradually edged nearer and started talking. Well, I was between her and Dylan and she was quite passable – not the usual type, you know, quite a decent sort ... she ended by suggesting we should go on to their place and have a few drinks. I spoke to her and, very briefly, and this is the truth, that Dylan took no notice of her whatsoever. He pulled out a piece of paper and a pencil, and he doodled until I got rid of that girl. Refused to take the slightest notice of her. And that was not the only incident. He was at that time absolutely scrupulous in that way. It was true – he had no interest whatever in girls.

...I wrote to Dylan ... and I told him about a very strange experience I had had, a truly psychic experience, and something happening to me for the first time in my life ... I was full of it at the time I was writing to him ... he was writing a short story and then, apropos of nothing, he took a sentence or two from the context of my letter, and just dropped them in the middle of his short story ... a little while ago, somebody in Cambridge wrote a book criticizing Dylan ... he seized on this very extract from my letter as a proof that Dylan simply did not know what he was writing about. If he'd only had any idea of how he came to write it, it would have been a different story.

There are a number of times when Dylan picked on something from a letter of yours that prompted him to write a poem, for instance.

There's one particular occasion I had received a letter from him when he told me that his father had to come up to London for a medical examination ... it was his usual very charming letter ... I was also very upset to hear the news about his father's illness, because I was so fond of his father also. And throughout that day I'd thought of nothing else but this letter and when I got home at night I wouldn't eat my dinner or anything, I just went upstairs and got my typewriter and just slammed as I always did, you see, never stopped for thought at all. They were terrible letters, but then again I would just strike the right note and the right paragraph. And discussing something I'd get a bit of what you'd call the Welsh *hwyl* ... in talking about a certain type of people I had written "And they shall die in darkness, die in the night and move to eternal fields of darkness. Foster the light and God be with you." Well, Dylan was so impressed by that phrase, that he immediately wrote the poem 'Foster the light', which he handed to me when he came to stay with me six weeks later.

...I was rather pleased by that incident. And, of course, he was like that. When he read anything that I had written, he'd seize on a phrase like that. Not often – I'm not claiming that I could often do that sort of thing. I remember one story in which I'd written about "a churchyard's mounded field", and Dylan seized on it – he was delighted. Another story I'd written about an old man, and I said "His limbs were beginning to remember the rainy seasons," and Dylan seized on that in the same way.

...he had so very, very many qualities, you know. And as a boy, he had an innate wisdom, and it always seemed to me that if he read of some harem experience, it immediately became his own experience, if you understand me, and if he came across such circumstances in life after that, he could understand because he'd read it and made it part of himself ... he did seem to have an infinite fund of understanding and I think that was one of the things that most impressed itself upon me when he was so very young. Where other boys would be talking school-boy stuff, no, when Dylan and I were together it was always funda-mental. He wanted to be talking all the time about things that mattered in a most serious way – not a solemn way, but serious.

...they were his formative years. They were the years when he could write poetry so very, very easily. You know, when I met him first I got to his house and he said "I'll read you some poetry", and this was just a schoolboy ... didn't want to talk about football or any of the usual schoolboy subjects. He would lie down on his stomach on that mat, you know, schoolboy-wise, and all his papers spread in front of him, and he would read a poem ... sometimes I wouldn't say a word – he'd just look up at me, just to get the look in my eyes, and, satisfied, he would then start reading the next one. And I remember him coming across one poem, which was incomplete – and he just got down on the floor and completed it. It was a poem of no importance, no doubt, but that's how he was. He was never lost for words at all.

You were perhaps the first person to see the 'Poem in three parts'? ['I, in my intricate image']
I think that's quite possible. I'd arranged to meet Dylan at the Fitzroy as usual one night – I think he'd phoned me at the office, he'd come to London very unexpectedly, and of course I was thrilled and couldn't wait for the day to pass, to go and meet him. And that in itself is rather remarkable, because he was simply a boy and I was twenty-seven years old, a man with heavy family responsibilities and so on. The thought of meeting this boy, it was surely like anyone meeting the young Keats or the young Shelley. It was of great importance to me. And I went along to the Fitzroy and, most remarkably, he was not there. As a rule, he was sitting there watching the door, waiting for me to come in, and the moment I went in he'd reach for a pencil and say "Have you brought anything?" It didn't matter what it was, I'd have had to write something and take it with me, just something for him to read, something for him to discuss, words we could argue about.

...I went outside and I walked a little way ... and, of course, I met him about fifty yards from the pub and, in his usual shy way, with his usual great humility, he said "I've got a poem to show you." And he handed me 'Poem in three parts'. And I stood in the street and I read it through – I just could not stop. And, as I looked up, he was waiting and watching my eyes, you know, and just caught the look in my eyes, and he seized my arm so excitedly "Come on, Trevor – let's go and get drunk." He had no intention at all of getting drunk; it was just Dylan's way of expressing his extreme pleasure that I liked the poem – he knew I would like it. And he said "Of course, you know, Trevor, that's a big advance on anything I've ever written before." I said "Yes, I know that, Dylan." It was a most remarkable achievement.

Are there any other poems which you recall about which he talked to you?
"Especially when the October wind with playful fingers punishes my hair." – do you remember that one? In the very first version of that, it is "Especially when the November wind with playful fingers punishes my hair". Well, he got that from Bert Trick ... a theory about the explosive quality of words, and I'm quite sure that led him to alter the "November" into "October" – a more explosive type of word.

What about the later years – you kept the correspondence up with him?
No. Not after the four or five years ... it just lapsed. And then, of

course, the War came and everything was so different. The world had changed entirely. When Dylan and I met first it was still the old world.

Bert Trick

> Then I went on my way from the sea, up Brynmill Terrace and into Glanbrydan Avenue where Bert Trick had kept a grocer's shop and, in the kitchen, threatened the annihilation of the ruling classes over sandwiches and jelly and blancmange. ('Return Journey')

I'm not exactly sure of the date. It would be either late 1932 or early 1933...a young man arrived at my house ... he had a trilby hat hooked to his little finger and a Woodbine stuck in his mouth. He said "I've been told to come and see you by Mr Taig ... I've been writing some poems." – he always called them 'pomes' ... So after a little more ordinary conversation, we decided that he'd come along in a couple of evenings' time at seven o'clock ...

...he turned up, and in his pocket he had a roll of school exercise books ... he came into my sitting room ... I said "Shall I have your poems to read?" "Oh no," he said, "poems have to be read aloud."

...he was very self-assured and very mature for such a young-looking person. So I sat back and waited for the reading to commence, and, of course, in a matter of minutes I was absolutely enthralled. I just sat there listening with astonishment, first of all to the wonderful way he read poetry, and certainly the poems themselves ... then he rolled up his books and he said "What do you think of them?" And I said "I think they're very good indeed. I'd like my wife to hear them ... " So I went in the other room and I said to Nell "I want you to come and hear him read his poems. This is a genius we got. This is the real goods."

...and that was the beginning of a friendship that lasted for roughly ten years ... and, without any planning at all, it led to what became, for the next few years, regular meeting nights. Wednesday night up at 5 Cwmdonkin Drive, and Sunday afternoon and evenings, until the early hours of Monday morning, at the Tricks'. And there we had a nucleus of people who were the sort of permanent group ... Fred Janes ... Tom Warner ... John Jennings ... and then, around that, we had a changing circle of people like Charles Fisher, Gwyn Thomas, Gilbert Evans ... on a few rare occasions, Dan Jones.[37]

...I may have been a steadying influence or not, I wouldn't care to flatter myself on that, but Mrs Thomas on more than one occasion told

Nell that she was always happy in her mind when she knew that Dylan was in the Tricks', because she knew he would never come to any – involve any escapade or get drunk and so forth. So I did know that there was this sort of reputation ... he certainly never drank to excess when he was in my company.

...during the years I knew him, until he met Caitlin, I have no knowledge of him being involved with girls. He certainly wasn't a girl-chaser. The only incident I know of – which is quite an innocent one, I think – a little barmaid in the Mermaid Hotel in Mumbles, where he used to go in for a drink, and I think he used to make passes at her, but on the right side of the counter. I doubt very much whether Dylan was involved with girls at all, prior to leaving Swansea. And he was in my company, and I was with him so much during that period, that I would have known if he was involved with anybody. I'm certainly sure he wasn't. None at all.

...Mrs Thomas, of course, was a typical Welsh mother. I can only put it in those words – what we say a 'Welsh Mam'. She was a loveable person, and she certainly mothered Dylan. And there was a strong bond of affection there. I remember one night we were having our usual session, and about nine o'clock Mrs Thomas would bring in a tray with coffee and sandwiches, you see. But on this particular evening, we'd only been chatting for about ten minutes, when Mrs Thomas come in and said "Mrs Morris" – or whatever the person's name was – "She's telling the cups – come on, Bert, Dylan!" They used to have a woman to come in once a week to wash and clean, and she could tell their fortune in the teacups. And Dylan sat there absolutely absorbed and thrilled, having his fortune told in the tea leaves ... anything of that sort really appealed to him.

...Dylan's father and Dylan – this is rather harder to assess. I should think there was a very deep love there, a tremendous respect for each other's personalities, which were so different. And there was also, I think, on the part of the senior Mr Thomas, a complete lack of understanding of what Dylan was trying to do as a poet ... I remember going there one Sunday evening – Dylan hadn't turned up at our place and I went up to find out if there was anything wrong. Dylan's father was in a dressing gown; he invited me into his study, and we sat there and chatted and smoked, and he was very concerned then to know what I thought of Dylan's poems. This was when he was just beginning to get published in various magazines and that ...

...he's said to me "Mr Trick, I'm told by the people who should know that Dylan's poetry is very good. Now, I can't make anything of it; I belong to the old school. What is your opinion of it?" I merely mention that to show that there was this sort of difference in the senior English master and his son – but a tremendous family tie, family bond; they were a very close family, in short.

...Mr Thomas was considered a very able Greek scholar, incidentally. I remember some of the boys who took Greek with him at the Grammar School for state scholarships at Oxford or Cambridge ... Dylan used to tell a story ... that his father and his great crony [W.S. 'Soapy' Davies] used to go down to the Fultons in Mumbles and they'd fall out, they wouldn't speak, and they wouldn't meet for a pint, and they wouldn't speak for week ... they would quarrel about the translation of a Greek word or a Greek verse or whatever it might be. Now again, how far that's true, I don't know. That's what Dylan told me.

...there was a profound respect for each other, and Dylan's father did tell me that when Dylan was stuck for a word or for some information about some Classical reference, that he would go to his father and ask him, rather than go searching through the necessary books and documents to find it. I think there was that affinity between them ...

...DJ was a very austere, very aloof sort of person. When you got to know him he was a very charming, very cultured man. But he was no mixer, and there was never any great show of affection, not demonstrably at any rate, between Dylan and his father. They always sort of treated each other with a great sort of respect, as it were. There wasn't that 'father and son' relationship, which you expect, particularly in a Welsh family. Mrs Thomas was the complete opposite ... very buoyant, a real chatterbox, delightful person, as bright as a button. And, of course, she idolised Dylan. If Dylan had never written a word of poetry, she would still have idolised him. He was the apple of Mrs Thomas' eye, there's no doubt.

...I can say this from my own knowledge, that it was a source of great grief to Mr Thomas, at the time I am speaking of, that Dylan would go on these outrageous benders from time to time.

And his mother too, I suppose. Did she know about these, or was she blithely unaware of it?

Oh, I think Mrs Thomas would be one who would cover up. She'd shield Dylan, I'm quite certain of that. Because, there's no doubt about it, that she really worshipped the very ground that he trod on; there's no question about that. The show of affection there was unmistakeable.

...every room you went into in the Thomases' house was strewn with books. Even in the kitchen, they'd be under the kitchen table, up on the sideboard, piled with books. Well, that was Dylan's background. I don't think there was any sort of direction; it was merely his own leaning towards certain things which led him in his reading. But, in certain areas, he was tremendously well read ... it was in these days that he discovered Caradoc Evans, and was very enthusiastic, for a time at any rate ... we both read Joyce's *Ulysses*. Which was very hard to come by in those days ... I think that influenced Dylan very considerably. I think he was also influenced tremendously by T.S. Eliot ... I don't say that he ever imitated, but the influence in thinking ... there were things which stimulated his thinking. I think I mentioned a very pleasurable evening reading out of Logan Pearsall's *Trivia*, which he enjoyed enormously. And then he also had a tremendous love for children's books, even at that stage. He used to come down to our house and Pamela then, she couldn't read, she was only three or four, but nevertheless he'd bring books down ... he also had a period where ... we had a whole spate of Anatole France – we went through the lot.

...his interests were so catholic in reading, and it was only in conversation with Dylan, or very often what would boil up into possibly an argument, that he'd suddenly surprise you with a wealth of knowledge of an aspect of reading which you'd never thought he'd even seen or heard of. He was a very astonishing person like that.

...one of the things that we did repeatedly ... Dylan would fish out one of these exercise books which he always carried around with him – in those days – and he'd write what could be a line of poetry. And he said "Now, Bert, you write the next line." "What's it supposed to mean?" "It doesn't matter about the meaning; let's get the words."

...he's given me credit in, I think, the *Daily Herald* report, that I influenced him in words. Of course, that's a piece of sheer loyal buttering up, because Dylan had the gift, it was innate, this gift for words. But one thing we were agreed upon, and that was if you wanted to make even a sentence of prose hit, stand out, mean something, you had to play around with those words, make them explosive in a new context – which he did extremely well. He used to practise, I mean quite frankly, as a technical practice.

...he had what he called his dialectical method. He would get a phrase and the meaning of this phrase, and then he would immediately have a next phrase which was the antithesis of the first one. The two would be more or less paradoxical, or contradictory. Then, out of that, you would get the synthesis, the old Marxist dialectic ... he used to claim that he always worked towards meaning through words, rather than used words to express the meaning.

...a phrase would be the inspiration for a poem with Dylan. He very rarely had a theme and wrote a poem about it. He'd have a phrase, and then from that phrase he'd probably counterpose another phrase – might be, in fact, the antithesis of that. And gradually, out of these, as it were, the agitation of these conflicting images, so the poem would evolve. The divine essence would eventually emanate from that. He worked from words to meaning and Dylan always said "I'm not so much concerned about meaning as the sound I like."

...words that have been repeated in sentences ... [become] pedestrian and flat-footed by being used too often. But the same words used in different juxtaposition, suddenly start to explode. In other words, words themselves were not just flat, ordinary objects, they were round, explosive things which, if mixed in the right way, could produce an entirely new effect. And this was the sound that both Dylan and I were so concerned about.

...we worked out a theory that words, through constant use, had become flat-footed, like an old spavined nag, and down-at-heel. In fact, these words wanted a 'retread'. We held the theory that there was nothing new to tell, there were not new things to communicate. The only thing one could do was to communicate in a modern idiom, and these words wanted new life poured into them. Another theory was that they were phials, that the meaning had been half-emptied, that we must pour new meanings into them. And the way to do that was to juxtapose words, so that instead of being trite, platitudinous if you like, that by changing the position of a word in a sentence, you suddenly got jerked, you were alerted. The words began to bounce and bubble again ...

...we held the belief that the academicians had emasculated a lot of the meanings of our words, that the grammarians had gutted them, they had made them frigid with their fondling, and we had to unfreeze them. And this is the way we set about it; we used to experiment, fill up sheets of paper, write a sentence and then re-write it, transposing words so that you got this new meaning. Another thing we used to do was to take any well-known aphorism or proverb, and by changing one or two words, get an entirely new meaning into it ...

...where Oscar Wilde would take a platitude and twist its tail and make an epigram, Dylan ... would change a word, or invert a word – for example, instead of "once upon a day", he'd say "once under a day".[38] To read Dylan, either his prose or his poetry, and especially as he read it, which flowed out in a lovely stream of words, you would think that these words, and these sentence build-ups, came easy to him – but they didn't. They were the result of meticulous craftsmanship; he was almost like William Blake doing engraving over and over until he got exactly what he wanted. He'd repeat, change, amend, until he got exactly the sense, not so much the sense as the sound of what he wanted. And then, of course, when he read it, it just flowed off in this wonderful, lyrical poetry that he wrote.

...I've known Dylan to bring a poem, read its first draft to me – and he read all his first drafts to me – and then he would say "Do you like this line, Bert?" He'd read it through ... and he'd read the alternative. And another alternative. And another alternative. And we'd talk about this, and what we liked was, if I can use the expression, the sonority of the word. For example, we both loved words that had a flow of vowels in it. There was something sonorous about a run of vowels that flowed, rather than words which would appear to be 'chopped up'. We had a theory, which we discussed – indeed he mentioned it in some of his letters to me – we reverted back to his belief in the miracle of Christ, the compassion of Christ, and what Dylan called the "four stations of the breath", his almost innocent belief that he and God were on direct speaking terms.

...the doyen of English letters at that time was ... *The New English Weekly* – if Orage [A.R. Orage, the editor] recognised a poet, that was the cachet of acceptance ... I told Dylan all this and rather grudgingly he decided to send a couple of poems ... I had to nudge Dylan's elbow many, many times because he was the most un-commercial person I ever met in my life. But eventually, standing over him, I helped him to select two of the poems which we'd submit to *The New English Weekly*. He came into my shop some time later. Usual Dylan, he felt in his pockets and out came bits of crumpled paper, and a very crushed and rumpled piece of paper ... it was a letter from Orage, speaking most eulogistically about the poems – these were "excellent poems. Could he send him some more?" So I said "There you are, Dylan, you're home and dry, you've been accepted." "Ah, but they don't pay anything," he said. "That's no damn good to me." And as far as I thought at the time, that was the end of it, but I understand later that he did actually submit some more poems to *New English Weekly* ...

...he was writing a story, and the title was 'Daniel Dom', as I remember. And the father's study was being decorated, so instead of going to the study, which was our usual meeting place, we went into the front room and it was the room on the right. It wasn't used very much, I think, because there was damp coming, a big patch of damp on the wall ... when I went in, Dylan said "What do you think of my first couple of pages of 'Daniel Dom'?" And he pointed to the wall, and as you came in through the door, pinned with a drawing pin was this piece of cardboard. I said "What on earth have you written these on, Dylan?" He said "Well, my mother got them from the draper's shop. These are the covers of blouse boxes." And as the story progressed, so you walked around the wall and read these murals.

...I can say without fear of contradiction that when I knew Dylan, round about seventeen, come eighteen, that his political knowledge was very rudimentary. In fact, I think that's one of the influences I may have had on him, introduced him to socialist thought ... I would say that in that period in the Thirties, he was politically illiterate ... anything which was left of Cwmdonkin Drive was all the same to Dylan.

...for the ten years I was intimately acquainted with Dylan ... he was never what I would call a politically conscious person. What Dylan did have was a tremendous compassion for mankind. It was something that one admired. Anyone who was mentally or physically lamed, or oppressed, or treated contemptuously, he was one who would sort of fly to his defence. I don't think there was a down-and-out or a strange character in Swansea which Dylan didn't encompass within that tremendous compassion of his. It was all part of the Swansea which, undoubtedly, he loved.

...it was a salient part of his whole character. Anyone who was handicapped in any way, Dylan had a sort of fellow feeling. And one thing that he was outraged about was any show of violence. I remember on one occasion, we were sitting on the verandah at 69 Glanbrydan Avenue, lovely Sunday afternoon, looking over the park ... and there was a young fellow with a black spaniel dog, and the dog either dallied, or strayed off the pavement or something, and this fellow got the lead and he simply leathered this dog, and Dylan got up, clutched the verandah, and he shrieked at this fellow – he called him all the names he could think of. He was absolutely trembling in rage and outrage.

Wales was in a pretty sorry economic plight during this period, and yet Dylan didn't seem to address himself to this in his writings very much.
I think that's perfectly true. Dylan was never interested in the economic or the political side of this. That's why I keep emphasising that this flirting with the idea of his being a Communist I think is quite out of character. I'm sure it's quite wrong. What he did see is the

effects, and I think in his short stories ... you get these composite characters of the beachcombers on the sands, and the dogs, the naughty boys and so on. He was very conscious of the atmosphere of drabness, of poverty, of almost starvation ...

...one of our favourite pursuits on a Sunday evening round about seven or eight o'clock in the summertime ... the Swansea sands, known as the Sandfields, was an open forum, and you got these soapbox orators, every conceivable thing from spiritualism to Trotskyists, and every conceivable cult on the lunatic fringe were there. Some of them, of course, were quite proper and orthodox ... we used to stand around and listen to these boys ... these were glorious evenings. We've laughed and enjoyed, and we've repeated it. He'd come home to supper at our house, and then he would mimic some of these speakers, for Nell's benefit, you see.

...it wasn't so much what was being said by the speakers that interested Dylan, as the audiences that gathered round. Here were these shabby, underfed, ill-looking Swansea citizens, dressed in the proceeds of a thousand jumble sales; young men without any teeth in their head, looking quite cadaverous, coming there for the cheap entertainment.

...I think quite a great deal can be made of the fact that, in the very short period when Dylan was a reporter on the *Evening Post* he certainly absorbed, in that period, a tremendous feeling for Swansea, particularly the seamier side of Swansea, down in dockland, which in those days was a pretty rough quarter.

...you could never pin a label on Dylan and say that he was a Socialist or a Communist or an anarchist or anything else – he was far out on the left in politics. He believed in the freedom of man to be man, that he shouldn't be oppressed by his fellows, and that every man had the stamp of divinity on him, and anything that prevented that divinity having full play was an evil thing.

...in the orthodox sense of being a church-going Christian, one could answer very definitely 'no' ... but beyond that, in a mystical sense, he was very religious. I remember on one occasion in the Mermaid Hotel in Mumbles, there were three or four curates present ... I remember him in full spate, he held everybody spellbound, both with the gift of illustration and the point he was making – which was purely intuitive, of course. He felt that there was a supreme being with which you could get in touch direct. That you hadn't to wait for benefit of clergy and that sort thing, that in each one of us – well, what's the word I want? "The green fuse" you know, his poem. That through nature this identical stream running through all nature and you're part of that. Which would be very much sort of paganism, wouldn't it ...

...if I'm dealing with Dylan at all, I emphasise one aspect of both his poetry and his prose: it was religious in the sense that I understand religion. That is, that at the core of religious consciousness are the concepts of infinity and eternity. Dylan would agree with me, I know, because we discussed this so many times, it was a recurrent theme in all our talks – that man is the creature and creator of his own world, and that means that there's frustration and commitment ... he must attempt to penetrate the eternal mystery and, being finite, he must accept defeat. And that I think is the real way to understand what made Dylan tick.

...not only in his poetry, in his short stories, even in *Milk Wood*. Because, if you take *Under Milk Wood*, the linking theme there is the character of Eli Jenkins. And Dylan himself has projected his own personality into that character. He's got the same un-judging innocence ... that simple innocence that William Blake has in his *Poems of Innocence*; that even the Negro spirituals have ... that, I think, is the very touchstone of Dylan.

...the embryonic *Under Milk Wood* he had written in 1933, and he read it to Nell and me in our bungalow at Caswell around the old Dover stove, with the paraffin lamps lit at night ... the story was then called Llareggub, which was a mythical village in South Wales, typical village, with terraced houses with one *ty bach* [lavatory] to about five cottages, and the various characters coming out and emptying the slops and exchanging greetings and so on; that was the germ of the idea which ... developed into *Under Milk Wood* ...

And he wasn't living at Laugharne then?
Oh, no – Dylan was living at Cwmdonkin Drive.

But none of the characters were formed at that early time?
I wouldn't remember that. I know among the characters there was a parson, because Dylan always had the Caradoc Evans complex about the Welsh parson. That had to come into it, of course.

...and the interesting thing was, of course, that Dylan, as a small boy, together with Nancy, was taken every Sunday to Mumbles and attended all the services at Paraclete. One of Dylan's proudest posses-sions was a framed certificate for passing a scripture examination, which hung in his bedroom, as far as I know, all his life.

...[DJ] was a professing agnostic ... this is all very interesting, because

35. Bert Trick's bungalow, where a first version of *Under Milk Wood* was read in 1933

here you get the tensions which actually developed Dylan's personality. On the one hand, he was in revolt against his father's agnosticism. On the other hand, he was in revolt against the narrow Puritan conventions of his mother's Congregational background, and it was from these tensions that the personality of Dylan Thomas developed.

In one of the American editions of his collections of his short stories, there's a whole section given to some of his early short stories ... there's a dark element in them. Reminds you of Edgar Allan Poe, but set in the countryside ... superstition, witchcraft and everything. He went through a period, then, didn't he?

I used to tell Dylan in those days – and I'd be quite frank with him in my criticism, because that's what he wanted – that to me, at that time at any rate, in that period of development, there was streak of morbidity. His obsession with these things of witchcraft, black magic ... seemed slightly morbid.

...you know the poem, 'When, like a running grave'? That poem was written in 1933, thereabouts, and at the time Dylan – whose reading was very wide – he'd got hold of a book of Italian mediaeval legends, which really absorbed him. I was at his house one evening and he read one of these stories to me, and as far as I remember it was about an Italian count who had a dread of when he was dead, of being boxed and lain in the ground and to stay there for eternity. So he decreed in his Will that he should be buried in a steel coffin with the base of the coffin projecting forward like a spade, and that the coffin should be lain in the grave at an angle of about forty-five degrees, so that the temperature action of the soil, and the chemical reaction and so on, that from time to time that this steel coffin would jink – "the running grave".

...Dylan held the belief that from the moment you were born you started to die. I think that's the whole theme behind his poems. This cycle of life ... for example, take one of the lines of his very early poems: 'I see the boys of summer in their ruin', a line which, when he read it to me at the time that he wrote it, appealed to me very much, and I said "What image have you in mind?" "Well," he said, "you go down to the beach in Swansea in a summer evening ... and the city man, the office worker and so on, they'd strip off there ... and get into a pair of the old-fashioned bathing trunks and waddle down to the sea – and there were the boys of summer in their ruin." Bunion on the toe, a potential pendulous belly starting, a slightly balding of the head – they were in the summer of their years, but he saw them also in their ruin ... many of these telling lines in Dylan's poems are images which he saw so clearly in his Swansea.

...I had a postcard from a young man named Leslie Lewis ... he was a member of John O'London's Literary Circle. Some time later, he asked me if I thought Dylan would be prepared to give a talk or read a paper to the Literary Circle ... he broached this subject, and Dylan said "Oh, yes." – much to my surprise – "I'll come along."

...so the next time I went up to Dylan's, which was on the Wednesday night, I said "What about this John O'London's – are you going to do something with them?" "Oh, yes," he said, "I've already started. Would you like to hear it?" And in that little crabbed writing, he had a big sheet of paper which he'd covered with this small writing, he read this out to me, and it was so outrageous that I thought it was a leg-pull and I just laughed ... I've forgotten the title of the paper that he intended to give, but it could very well have been 'Pornography in Nineteenth Century Literature'.

...eventually the famous night arrived when Dylan was to give his paper. They met above an ironmonger's shop owned by a Mr Bates in St Helen's Road, right opposite the General Hospital ... Dylan arrived at my house, accompanied by Fred Janes and Gilbert Evans ... altogether we were about six or seven who turned up. We were all in the kitchen there, ready to go, and I'd lined them up and I said "Right turn, quick march!" and we all marched out into Oakwood Road, and Dylan was in great style. He'd got a silver-knobbed stick, and that was to defend himself from the irate company when he'd finished with them, you see. Well, in this sort of spirit we marched down and we got to the Westbourne Hotel, which is just opposite the General Hospital at the bottom of this hill that leads from Walter Road. So as we got near the Westbourne Hotel, Dylan said "Let's go in and have one drink before we go in," he said, "just to loosen up." So we all marched into this pub and we had a few rounds of beers.

By this time, we had warmed up and were getting a bit hilarious, and I said "Come on boys, we'll be late for this. It's eight o'clock; we're due at this Circle." So I led the way out of the pub and across the road, and coming out of the bright-lighted pub into the semi-darkness of St Helen's Road ... it so happened at that particular time that there was a very major public works thing going on, a new main drainage system for Swansea with an outflow at Mumbles. And across the hospital was a deep trench that had been dug, and there were red lamps placed there.

...next thing, I landed flat in this ditch. And of course, before I could give any warning, the rest of them had landed in on top of me! We were in a real pickle, covered with clay – we did look a disreputable lot. We scrambled out, and we had to go round the side door of this business premises. So I rang the bell and, I think it was Mrs Bates, she was the secretary, came to answer it ... we were led up the stairs, beautiful carpeted stairs, and landed in a big lounge with big settees and easy chairs set all around, and what they thought had came in I'm sure I don't know. Some navvies off a public works job.

After the introductions were over, the chairman, who was a Mr Mitchell, I think, the manager of the Llandarcy oil works, he introduced Dylan, who sat at a little card table, and pulled out his sheets of paper, held this silver-topped stick in his hand as a weapon, and then proceeded to read, in that glorious cathedral voice of his, this terrible paper that he'd prepared, and which I never thought that he was going to read!

The first reaction, of course, was one of unbelief of the audience. I looked around, and I confess my own embarrassment, I never thought he'd do this on us. And the look of unbelief was followed by one of deep shock. And that in turn was one of stupefaction I would say, because they were speechless. And so it went on and on and on, each following page getting more and more outrageous as we went along. And then he finished up, and with that angelic look that he had – Dylan in those days had a very angelic face, his mop of curls and his big, blue wondering eyes – and in all innocence he said "If there any questions, Mr Chairman, I'll do my best to answer them." There were lots of questions asked ... but one question I do remember, and it was a lady who asked the question. She said something along these lines: "Well, judging by the morals which Mr Thomas has outlined," she said, "what would be the position if I were locked in a room with a rough, uncouth man who had designs on my virtue?" Without any hesitation, he said "Try wearing tin drawers."[39]

...there was a friend of mine, a Labour alderman and his wife, who had expressed a wish that she would very much like to meet Dylan Thomas ... Well, I made the biggest *faux pas* of my life in telling Dylan about this some days later ... of course, it was fatal. On that particular Sunday night, fourteen people turned up ... and the Alderman and his wife ... by eight o'clock, it was obvious that Dylan wasn't going to be there. No explanation. And by about half-past nine, we all went down and had supper which Nell had prepared, and, of course, as far as Dylan's appearance was concerned, it was a complete wash-out. I was rather disappointed about this, but I realised it was my own fault because he would not be the lion of the evening, he would not be on show, he would not be the exhibition piece.

...when Dylan went up to London, he was very much the little boy ... behind his defensive mechanism of his Bohemianism, and his outrageous conduct at times, all deliberate and of a set piece, he was a little Welsh boy, and very frightened. He was very frightened. He was very frightened of meeting – this American tour, I'm quite sure, put the breeze right up him, and all his booze, and all that sort of thing, was a defensive mechanism – of that I'm convinced. Because from my own experience of him, he was the most charming, the most loveable character you could meet. But if he were here now and doing what I am doing, he'd shut up like a clam. You could never put him on show; he wouldn't have it. All Dylan's natural talent had to grow up in the moment. And it had to be amongst people *he* liked ... Dylan hated being put on show.

...this question of the annihilation of the ruling classes ... you remember it was the Thirties, when I believe the total unemployment in Swansea at that particular period was running about twenty-eight percent of the working population, and we were literally jumping mad that the ruling classes could be so stupid, so inept, that they allowed whole communities in Wales that we knew to rot and rust, become apathetic and to decay before our very eyes.

...it's hard to realise now, looking back, but I remember in Swansea market then it was the usual thing to see pyramids of condensed milk, condensed skimmed milk, and printed on it was 'unfit for babies', and these were being sold at tuppence ha'penny a tin, and I knew of families where they bought these tins of milk and spread them over the bread for children because they couldn't afford butter or even margarine.

...there seemed to be no purpose, no drive. In fact, at that time they were more concerned, the ruling classes, with preventing a morganatic marriage than they were with being present at the *accouchement* and the birth of a single new idea. Dylan and I at that time, we wrote in the local journals, we preached, we cajoled, harangued, we did everything that was in our power, as any intelligent and sensible young people would attempt, but I am afraid to very little purpose. Unfortunately, our boot wasn't big enough to crush the stupidity and ineptitude that seemed prevalent in the ruling classes – you know, no-one can feel so strongly or morally indignant as the very young, and I am afraid that we were both very young in those days.

You were an active member of the Labour Party weren't you?

If you want a catalogue of my activity – first of all, I was an executive member and minutes secretary of the Swansea Labour Party. I was editor of their monthly journal, *New Outlook* – and in saying 'editor', in fact, in a very short time, I appeared to be writing all the contributions from the poetry column to the funny stories. This, of course, was purely a voluntary effort on my part. During that period, too, I was Chairman of the Swansea Peace Council, I was Secretary of the Swansea Left Book Club – oh, dear, what else was I? I was up to my eyes in it. I carried on a regular campaign in the *South Wales Evening Post* against the local *gauleiters* of the Mosley Party, and it was with some trepidation that I went with Dylan to Mosley's meeting on the Sunday night, when he arrived with his fairies in the lorries covered with chicken wire ...

With his what?

Fairies. They were known as Mosley's fairies. They were the ex-prize-fighters and thugs from the east end of London ... they stewarded the hall ... it was the Plaza Cinema. I decided that discretion was the better part of valour, I was too well-known as an anti-Fascist in the town, I'd better keep away, but a neighbour of mine, Jim Davies, a schoolmaster who lived opposite, came over about tea-time. He said "Are you going to the meeting, Bert?" I said I didn't think it would be wise for me to go, I shall probably get beaten up. "Oh, nonsense," he said, "let's go along and hear Mosley." I said "I'm expecting Dylan here, it's Sunday evening, it's our regular session – I'll tell you what I'll do. We'll call for Dylan and see if he will come. If he would like to go, then yes, we'll go." So sure enough about six o'clock we went up to Dylan's house.

...he'd evidently been busy writing; he looked as though he'd come from a session either with the typewriter or correcting proofs. So I explained that there was a Mosley meeting at the Plaza, and he thought it might be worth going along. "Oh, I'd love to sit in – wait a minute." And in less time than it takes to tell, he'd gone into the house and changed into another suit, and off we set for the Plaza.

That was the largest cinema in Swansea, wasn't it?

...at that time it was the super cinema of all Wales. Now, I was on a committee of the National Council of Civil Liberties – another of my activities – and on that Council – drawn from people of all political parties, but liberal and progressive in outlook – I remember there was a minister of the Unitarian Chapel – I've forgotten his name; the Reverend Leon Atkin ... Professor Benjamin Farrington of the Swansea University; and Mrs S.E. Harris of the Liberal Party. In fact we held several meetings of the Council at her home in Eaton Crescent, I think it was. And we had petitioned the local council to stop this Mosley meeting being held, but as was the general answer one got in those days, that in a democratic country you mustn't suppress any minority view, the council felt they were not in a position to ban the meeting.

...well, when we got there the Labour and trade union elements from all the Swansea valley had come down for this, and there must have been as many people outside the Plaza Cinema as were inside. While we were waiting, these lorries pulled up. Oh, half-a-dozen probably. They were converted lorries with wire netting almost like a chickens' coop, and out of these poured these Blackshirts. Great, lusty, tough-looking mob.

...there was a lot of booing as they came, the crowd shouting and I think someone started to sing *The Red Flag*, which was taken up with great gusto by the crowd. The Chief Constable and some of his senior officers were there in mufti – bowler-hatted – mingling around to see that there was nothing started. Anyway, by this time we started to go in. The hall was absolutely packed and down every aisle, both upstairs and downstairs, within touching distance of each other, were all these young Blackshirts, which belonged, I take it, to Swansea and district. These weren't imported, these were the local Mosleyites. Then the hall was blacked out; a spotlight on the stage, a black back-cloth, and Mosley came on the platform.

...all you could see was his hands, his face and the silver buckle on his belt. A very tall man, very commanding-looking fellow and the stage effect, of course, was quite effective. He immediately stood there in front of the microphone, when these lads gave the Nazi salute, the raised arm, and spelled out M-O-S-L-E-Y, and then shouted at the top of their voice "MOSLEY!" I felt I was already in Nazi Germany. This in my own home town of Swansea. Mosley spoke for well over an hour, and he was a very good speaker in the sense that he could rouse the crowd – a rabble-raiser. Then it was said that he would take questions. Somebody got up and asked a question, which he answered at some length, and then there were some questions which were asked which were questions really to start trouble, and somebody was forcibly ejected from the gallery. So then the gallery, solid as one man, stood up and started to sing 'The Red Flag'. Then the fighting broke out. So I nudged Jim and I said to Dylan, come on, this is where we scram. So we scuttled out – dignity was left to the four winds – we scuttled out of the Plaza, got outside – there was a very large foyer at the Plaza, with glass cases in which local trades-people like Ben Evans had on display expensive fur coats, that sort of thing – well, they were smashed to smithereens because coming down like a human avalanche, down the stairs from the galleries, were all these anti-Mosleyites, arms linked, singing 'The Red Flag' and coming down in one solid mass. So at a signal, the Mosley fairies ... started to converge in the foyer at the bottom of the stairs. Then I saw, I think it was, Chief Constable May and some of his senior officers, still bowler-hatted like rather overgrown civil servants, elbowed their way in and they just bashed these Mosley fairies, and that's the last I saw of it because we by this time had reached the exit.

When you say they bashed these Mosley bully-boys ...
They got in between the fairies ... and the boys from the valleys, you see. In other words, they formed a barrier between the two elements which could start a civil war at any time. Well, the crowd outside were chanting by this time. This crowd had increased to several thousand – including those who had come out of the cinema – and they were shouting for Mosley and there would have been real trouble, I think, real rough trouble. But they sneaked him out through the back entrance ... Dylan and I started to walk home up Walter Road and just as we got opposite what is now a funeral parlour, I believe, in Walter Road, half-way up, that was the local Mosley headquarters, and some elements in the crowd had formed a gang and they started shying

bricks through the window and generally causing a commotion, but that was more or less the end of it. I'm telling you this story because I've heard from other visitors I've had, who are familiar with the correspondence that Pamela Hansford Johnson had with Dylan, that he wrote about this incident but he built it up into quite a fairy story where he had been thrown out and almost fractured his ribs or something – well, that's absolutely fiction.[40]

...Fred [Janes] was telling us about one of these little episodes when they were in London. The three of them [Dylan, Janes and Mervyn Levy] had been somewhere, and they were returning by Tube. It was very late at night, probably about the last Tube back that they'd caught ... there were a couple of what we call now Teddy-boys. They weren't known as Teddy-boys in those days; they were just layabouts, the razor-boys. And because Levy was a Jew – and it was obvious from his beard and that sort of thing – they were making these comments about it. Well, Fred is a big chap, and in a rough and tumble ... he could probably give a good account of himself. Anyway, they thought it was wise not to start ... because these boys were the razor-boys. Things got so unpleasant that they decided to get out at an intermediate station rather than go the whole journey, before things really developed. So they got out of the Tube station, and there was a long passageway out from the Tube station and these three razor-boys got out as well, and chased them, and when Fred was telling me, the perspiration was running down his face still, for the memory of it, you know. And they belted as hard as they could go until they got out of the main street, and I think there was a bobby about or something, but it clearly frightened Janes.

Was there any recollection of Dylan's reaction to this?
I know what Dylan's reaction would have been. He'd have taken to his heels, and he could run, too, believe me. A lot of people have got a mistaken idea about him, that he was a sort of hypochondriacal, but he wasn't, you know ... he could run like a hare ... not only could he run like a hare, but he walked very fast. A very quick step ... he was a great walker ...

...although Dylan was so many years younger than I was, there was a maturity of mind, even at seventeen there was a certain maturity. I always described it that Dylan had an intuitive intelligence, without being scholastic in any way. He seemed to sense a problem, not by going though his logical processes, but an instinctive, intuitive touch for getting to the root of things. And I think all that was conditioned by the fact that I've never met, in all my acquaintances, anyone who had such a really, deep compassion. I have described it, I hope not sacrilegiously, as Christ-like. Anyone who was lamed mentally or physically, anyone who was misused, exploited – and so many of our fellow Swansea citizens at that time were depressed and exploited through unemployment – and Dylan had this deep compassion, he had an identity with all people who were deprived. Deprivation of liberty, deprivation of opportunity, deprivation of health and that sort of thing, immediately found a response in Dylan. He had a tremendous feeling for his fellows.

Waldo Clarke[41]

It seems to me that Dylan Thomas is perhaps the most perfect example in modern times of what one might call the pure poet – unaffected by intellectual considerations, moral considerations. He seems to me to be solely concerned with conveying the poetic experience to the reader, to his listener.

But can a poet detach himself, as Dylan did, from what was happening around him? Dylan was growing up in a period of intense suffering – yet he did not use this as a subject ...

No, he didn't ... the great lyric poet – although he may be aware of suffering and tragedy (something of that suffering and tragedy will affect his imagery and his rhythm) – he's not primarily concerned with drawing people's attention to the suffering and tragedy of his time. I think he's probably concerned with the great art of singing in the words ... of conveying experience.

...I think they feel they are too near to it, that's the trouble. They want to get away from what is immediate to some kind of universal experience, what you might like to call the human condition throughout the ages. It comes out in what is perhaps one of the most moving lyric poems written in English literature, 'In my craft or sullen art', where he says "Not for the proud man apart/ From the raging moon I write/ On these spindrift pages/ Nor for the towering dead/ With their nightingales and psalms/ But for the lovers, their arms/ Round the griefs of the ages," That's the "grief of the ages", not the grief of the one particular period in time. Or one particular personal grief. It's a universal suffering that he was aware of, as I think the true poet always must be.

Isn't it a bit of a cop-out, not to deal with the things that are happening in their own time?

Yes, but if you contrast the poets who didn't cop out, like W.H. Auden and Stephen Spender, or Day-Lewis, compare them with Dylan, and although W.H. Auden is technically a great maestro I don't think he ever once hits the high tragic note that Dylan has achieved in that little poem, and in many others besides.

But this is because of a difference of talent. What if Dylan had addressed himself to these things, had decided to take it on – now Lorca tackled the things of his time, and look what a fantastic effect he had.

True – it has been done. I am quite prepared to admit that. But it seems to me that Dylan is somewhere near the very great poets like Keats and Shakespeare, as far as English literature is concerned, and in both those cases you have a rejections of the immediate, of the contemporary, in favour of some kind of universal approach to grief and tragedy and pain.

...the poet is still like the composer of music. He is not really concerned with immediate tragedy; he's concerned with something much more remote, something more universal if you like, something which has existed ever since man has existed, and I feel in a way that Dylan wasn't running away. What he ran away from was the danger of becoming involved in politics, didacticism and such matters, and that he wanted to remain a poet, a pure poet in the truest sense of the word. I can read his poetry, as I can read the poetry of Keats or Shakespeare, and many more, for the pure pleasure of the sound, the imagery and the deep feeling that comes out from them. No-one, I think perhaps in modern literature, has achieved more in the expression of emotion than Dylan.

I only wish that he had been able to show us how a great poetic talent can address itself to the suffering of the time, completely independently and originally, but free of propaganda. I'm waiting for a poet who'll do that. I think Lorca did it – magnificently.

Yes, Lorca did it. Yes, he did. But Shakespeare didn't.

I wish Dylan had been the Lorca of Wales, you see.

Part Two: The Records

Introduction

During the late 1960s, Brinley and Olwen Edwards helped their son Colin by travelling around Carmarthenshire interviewing people about Dylan's family tree. Brinley's research was aided by his own roots in and around Llanybri – his uncle had farmed Pentrewyn and Preswylfa farms. It also helped that Brinley spoke Welsh, and had some experience as an amateur historian.

Brinley's notes are now in the Edwards archive in the National Library of Wales, Aberystwyth. I have used them to prepare Part 2, which also includes material taken from Colin Edwards' interviews.

Chapters 1 and 2 are not for the faint-hearted: they form a database, a consanguineous concentration of facts and figures, names and addresses, interspersed with some comment and a little biography. They are probably best regarded as a resource to be used for specific enquiries, rather than for reading 'at one go'.

I have used the Notes to include material on family members only distantly related to Dylan in the hope that this will help Carmarthenshire historians, as well as people researching their own family trees.

1. Dylan's Family Tree

I bow before shit, seeing the family likeness in the old familiar faeces, but I will not manure the genealogical tree.
— Dylan to Vernon Watkins

The young Dylan Thomas spent many holidays with his mother's relations around Llangain, Carmarthenshire. He was, too, a frequent visitor to the area during the 1940s, and also came to the pubs in Llansteffan and Llanybri when he and Caitlin were living at the Boat House in Laugharne. Yet, fifty years after his death, we still know little about the people and places that were important in his own development as a child, and an influence on his early writing.

Brinley Edwards' notes provide an opportunity to find out more about the family members that Dylan knew as a child and teenager. They don't tell us much about the personalities and characters of Dylan's relatives, but they do provide some basic information on identities, family relationships, places of residence and occupation. Dylan's roots were firmly in the Carmarthenshire soil: whilst his grandfathers were railway workers, one of them had started out as an agricultural labourer. Of Dylan's great-grandfathers, two were farmers, one a gardener and one a farm labourer.

Brinley's data must be treated with a little caution. Some may require further verification from birth, marriage and census records, though I have tried, where I can, to verify as much as possible. For example, a date I have found in a census return is shown as '1845*c*', and as '1876*b*' where I have taken it from a birth certificate or, before 1837, parish records. A date followed by a '*g*' (1913*g*) indicates that either Brinley or I took the date from a gravestone.

Ages given on census returns can be inaccurate and can vary through a person's lifetime by a couple of years, so if a date is particularly important it should be checked against a birth certificate. Gravestone birth dates, and even those in family bibles, can also be inaccurate.

I have made many additions to Brinley's data with information given

179

to me by Dylan's second cousin, Mrs Haulwen Morris of Llwyngwyn farm, and Susan Deacon, a descendent of John and Anna Williams of Pen-y-coed farm, and to whose mother Theodosia Rees was godmother. On the Thomas side of the tree, Tom Elwyn Thomas and Eleri Bearne, whose grandparents were first cousins to Dylan's father, provided data. I have also taken extensively from census returns, electoral registers, rate books, parish registers, Wills, obituaries, funeral reports and birth, marriage and death certificates. Carmarthenshire graveyards also yielded information, particularly those at Llanybri, Llanllwch, Llangain, Llangynog, Llanybydder, Llanfihangel Rhos-y-corn and Union Street, Carmarthen.[42]

The Williams Branch

Dylan's mother, Florence, was the daughter of *George* and *Anna Williams*. We learn from George's birth certificate that his parents – Dylan's great-grandparents – were George and Mary Williams (née Davies) of of Alltycnap. Llanllwch. George senior, a farm labourer, was born in 1813*c*, and Mary in 1798*c*.[43]

Anna's parents – Dylan's maternal great-grandparents – were Thomas and Anne Williams. Anne (née Thomas) was born in 1815*c* and died in June 1902*g*. Thomas, who was born on March 10 1816*b*, d. July 14 1890*g*, was the son of John and Anna Williams of Lambstone farm (SN335.159), Llangynog and, from the 1820s, Pen-y-coed farm.[44]

Anne and Thomas Williams were married on November 5 1835. They farmed at Pencelly Isaf from at least 1836, and then at Waunfwlchan. Florence's mother, Anna, was the third-born of their eleven children:

1. *John*, b.1836*c* at Pencelly Isaf, d. September 21 1918*g*. Unmarried. He farmed Pen-y-coed from the 1890s and, at the time of the 1910 land values survey, he owned Mount Pleasant, as well as 2, Blaencwm and a cottage in the parish of Llangynog called Myrtle Hill with an acre of land. He also owned Berllan-newydd, a cottage near the entrance to Waunfwlchan. Buried at Capel Newydd, Llanybri.

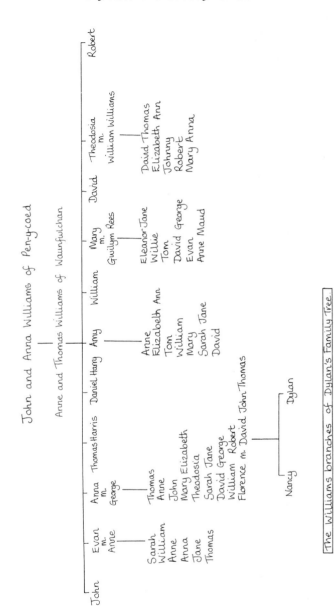

The Williams branches of Dylan's Family Tree

2. *Evan*, b.1838c at Pencelly Isaf and d. December 2 1897g, who married his paternal first cousin Anne Thomas, b. February 4 1852, d. April 14 1924g, at Union Street chapel, Carmarthen, on February 28 1871. Anne was the daughter of William and Sarah Thomas of Pen-y-coed. Evan and Anne farmed Tirbach for about fifteen years, and then went to Llwyngwyn farm. Both are buried in Capel Newydd. The Llwyngwyn family bible tells us that their children, Florence's first cousins, were:

   i. Sarah, b. August 11 1871 at Pen-y-coed, d. February 25 1954g. In 1895, she married Thomas Evans, b.1862, d. August 6 1937g, and they lived in Maesgwyn farm. Their daughter, Sarah Anne, died in 1897g, aged eight months. They are buried at Capel Newydd.

   ii. William, b. November 11 1873 at Tirbach farm, d.1942g, unmarried. Buried at Capel Newydd.

   iii. Anne, known as Annie, b. October 21 1879 at Tirbach, d.1951g. She married William Evans, b.1875c, d.1951g, son of Josiah and Mary Evans of Pencelly Uchaf farm. Anne and William had no children. Buried at Capel Newydd.

   iv. Anna, known as Hannah, b. March 27 1882 at Tirbach, d. May 24 1925g, unmarried. Buried at Capel Newydd.

   v. Jane, b. December 1 1884 at Tirbach, d. April 19 1913g, unmarried. Buried at Capel Newydd.

   vi. Thomas John, b. March 21 1889 at Llwyngwyn, d. March 18 1960g, buried at Capel Newydd. In September 1929, he married Mary Ann Davies, b. November 24 1898, d. July 6 1991g, daughter of Sarah and Evan Davies of Penparcau, Llangynog, and then Pen-y-coed. Thomas John and Mary Ann had three children: Thomas and Olwen, who were still-born, and Sarah Anne Haulwen (b. March 5 1934) who married Phillip Emrys Morris in 1955, and had eight children – Janet Rosemary, Philip John, Sara Rowena, William Thomas, Audrey Anne, Eirios Lynwen, Olwen Eireen and Ifan Dylan.

3. *Anna*, known as Hannah, b. March 19 1840b at Pencelly Isaf, d. July 5 1913g. She married George Williams, an agricultural worker then a railwayman, b. August 16 1838b at 'Danyrallt', St Peters, Carmarthen, d. November 7 1905g. They were married on September 15 1860 at Lammas Street chapel, Carmarthen, two months after their first child was born. At the time of their marriage George was living, and presumably working, on

Pilroath farm. George and Anna moved to 29, Delhi Street, St. Thomas, Swansea, in the mid-1860s. They are buried in Capel Newydd. Their nine children were:

i. Thomas, b. July 18 1860*b* at Waunfwlchan, d. May 27 1938*g*. Minister of religion. He married Emma Davies of Swansea, b.1861, d. April 15 1944*g*. Both are buried at Bethel, Sketty. No children.[45]

ii. Anne, known as Annie, b. February 26 1862*b* at Llwynhelig, Llansteffan, d. February 7 1933*g*. Dressmaker. On September 16 1893, she married James Jones, b. July 17 1864*b*, d. September 3 1942*g*, the son of Richard and Rachel Jones (née Morris) of Pentrewyman farm. Jim and Annie lived at Tirbach, Pentowyn and Fernhill farms. Their only child was Daniel Merthyn Idris, born at Tirbach on April 24 1897*b*. He died on 11 November 1959*g*. Buried at Capel Newydd.[46]

iii. John, b. September 6 1864*b* in Penalltycnap, Llanllwch, d. October 4 1911. He married Elizabeth Ann Evans on December 21 1903. They had one child, Theodosia, b. October 5 1904*b*. John worked on the railways and the docks. After his death, Elizabeth Ann and Theodosia moved to New Quay in the late 1920s. Theodosia married George Legg, and had three children: Margaret (1930-1998), George (1932-) and Anne (1935-).

iv. Mary Elizabeth (Polly), b. February 9 1867*b* in Swansea, d. March 13 1946. Music teacher, unmarried. She lived at 29, Delhi Street, before moving to join her brother Bob at 1, Blaencwm in 1928. Buried at Capel Newydd.[47]

v. Theodosia, b. June 30 1869*b* in Swansea, d. April 15 1941*g*. She married the Rev. David Rees, who died February 19 1939*g*. After Paraclete Manse, they lived at 2, Blaencwm from 1933. Both are buried at Smyrna chapel, Llangain. No children.

vi. Sarah Jane, b. March 18 1872*b* in Swansea, d. September 19 1879 at Waunfwlchan (death certificate). According to Brinley's notes, she was brought up by her relations at Tirbach and Waunfwlchan.

vii. David George, b.1874*b* in Swansea, d. April 5 1892, a student of medicine, according to the 1891 census. Buried at Capel Newydd.[48]

viii. William Robert (Bob), b. January 22 1877*b* in Swansea, d. September 17 1962*g*. Coal trimmer and shipper, unmarried. Moved from 29, Delhi Street to 1, Blaencwm in 1927. Buried at Capel Newydd.

ix. Florence, b. April 28 1882 in Swansea, d. August 16, 1958. Seamstress, married David John Thomas on December 30 1903. They had two children, Nancy Marles, b. September 2 1906, d. April 16 1953; and Dylan Marlais, b. October 27 1914, d. November 9 1953. Nancy married, first, Haydn Taylor and then Gordon Summersby – there were no children. Dylan married Caitlin Macnamara, and had three children: Llewelyn b.1939, Aeron b.1943 and Colm b.1949.

4. *Thomas Harris*, b.1842*c*, d. June 10 1872. Brinley missed Thomas but he is shown on the Waunfwlchan census returns for 1851 and 1871.

5. *Daniel Harry*, b.1845*c* at Waunfwlchan, d. February 23 1913*g*, who worked as a 'shop walker' in the Ben Evans store, Swansea, unmarried. He was known as Dr Dan. Ferris gives some information about his ill-health and drinking (1999, pp.10-11). The 1901 census return for Pen-y-coed describes him as a 'Retired Draper'. He owned 1, Blaencwm. Buried at Capel Newydd.

6. *Amy*, b.1847*c*, who had a daughter, Anne, b. January 12 1866*b*, d. May 24 1922. Amy then married, first, a publican and, second, David Jones, the Ferryside coxswain and pilot. Amy's other children were, Tom, William b.1876*c*, Elizabeth Ann b.1882*c*, Mary b.1884*c*, Sarah Jane b.1887*c* and David b.1889*c*.[49]

7. *William*, b.1849*c*, d. 1888*g*. Buried at Capel Newydd.

8. *Mary*, b.1851*c*, d. January 1890, who married Gwilym Rees b.1848*c* and farmed forty-two acres at Cryganfach (1881 and 1891 census SN423.129) and then Cwmafael (SN418.127, 95 acres), both at Llandyfaelog, across the estuary above Ferryside; their children were Eleanor Jane b.1878*c*, William b.1879*c*, Thomas b.1881*c*, David George b.1883*c*, Evan b.1887*c* and Anne Maud b.1890*c*. According to the Edwards archive, one of the women in this family kept the Rose and Crown in Llandyfaelog.[50]

9. *David*, b.1854*c*, d. May 8 1871*g*. Buried at Capel Newydd.

10. *Theodosia*, b.1856*c*, who married William Williams of

Moelfre, b.1854*c*. They lived at Tyrnest (SN404.167, 38 acres) in Croesyceilog, then at Coedlline (SN421.123, 112 acres) and Cilmarch (SN405.130 143 acres), near Llandyfaelog; their children were David Thomas b.1875*c*, Elizabeth Ann b.1877*c*, Johnny b.1880*c*, William Robert b.1888*c* and Mary Anna b.1890*c*.

11. *Robert*, b. May 16 1859*b*, d. October 28 1859*g*.[51]

Missing Sisters, Family Scandals

Amy Williams' first daughter, Anne, was brought up at Waunfwlchan by her grandparents. Anne's father was George Williams, whose wife, Anna, was Amy's elder sister. Amy was eighteen when Anne was born in 1866, about the time that George and Anna moved to 29, Delhi Street. It seems their move to Swansea was as much the consequence of family scandal as economic necessity.[52]

Anne first married John Gwyn of Cwrthyr Mansion, and had a son, the Rev. Mansel Edward Gwynn. They lived at Plas Ucha, Llanybri. After Gwynn's death in June 1893, Anne married a second time on February 3 1895 to a distant cousin, Robert Williams of Waunffort farm, and they lived at Rose Cottage, Llansteffan; their children were William David, who was drowned at Llansteffan in 1917, aged twenty, and Doris, b. January 29 1902*b*, d. August 14 1967, who married a dentist, Randolph Fulleylove. Brinley's notes describe Anne as "Talkative – energetic – nicely spoken – liked reading"; and Robert Williams as "Did not like work – bit of a traveller, or packman. Quite educated man."

The second child brought up by Thomas and Anne was Gladys Mary, born at Waunfwlchan on March 4 1885*b*. The 1891 census return for the farm describes her as a granddaughter but gives no information about her parents, and nor, surprisingly, does her gravestone at Capel Newydd. This made me curious enough to search for her birth certificate, which tells us that her mother was the above Anne Williams – Doris Fulleylove had a half-sister. Gladys, whose father is not named on the birth certificate, died in March 1893*g*.

The Williams Settlements

There were three primary settlements of the children of Thomas and Anne Williams of Waunfwlchan. The first was in St. Thomas, through the migration of their daughter, Anna, and her husband, George. Their daughter Florence, Dylan's mother, was an urban child, brought up in industrial St. Thomas, born there some fifteen years after her parents had left Carmarthenshire.

The second settlement was in the triangle formed by Llangynog, Llangain and Llanybri, where Thomas and Anne's sons John and Evan lived, as did all of Evan's children. This settlement was later re-enforced by 'returners' from Swansea, including Dr Dan in retirement, Annie Williams through marriage, and then her siblings Bob, Polly, Theodosia and Florence in retirement.

Llandyfaelog was at the heart of the third settlement, associated with Thomas and Anne's daughters, Mary and Theodosia, their husbands and children. There is no information in the Edwards archive about the Llandyfaelog cousins, or about what contacts, if any, Florence and her children had with them, but Robert Williams, Theodosia's son, was at Annie Jones' funeral in 1933.

The Thomas Branch

Dylan's father, D.J. Thomas, was the son of *Anne* and *Evan Thomas* of Johnstown, Carmarthen. Their marriage certificate shows that Anne was the daughter of William Lewis, a gardener, of Lime Grove, Carmarthen.

Evan's mother was Anne Jones, born in 1808*c*, of Esger Onnen who, in books about Gwilym Marles, is said to be related to the 'well known' Llwyncelyn family of Abergorlech. Evan's father was William Thomas, the son of David and Hannah Thomas of Gelli Grîn, Brechfa, a holding of about a hundred acres.[53] William, who was born on May 7 1804*c*, had a number of siblings who are detailed in Note 53, and they are also shown in the family tree opposite:

Dylan's paternal great-grandfather, William Thomas, was a farmer and according to the 1851 census he and Anne worked forty acres at Glan-rhyd-y-gwiail, Brechfa, Carmarthenshire. Dylan's grandfather, Evan, was the first-born of their five children:

1. *Evan*, b.1832, d. February 12 1911*g*, a miner then a railway-man. Known as Thomas the Guard. He married Anne Lewis, b.1835, d. January 23 1917*g*.[54] They had eight children, five of whom survived infancy:
   i. Jane Ann, b.1864*c*, d. August 1903. She married William

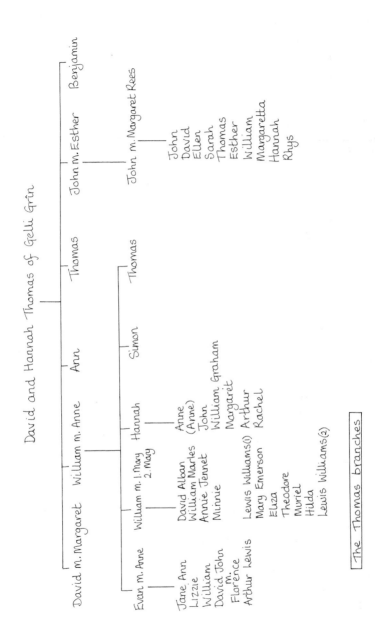

David and Hannah Thomas of Gelli Grîn

The Thomas branches

Greville of Pontyates (d. about 1938/39), who was a grocer, according to the 1901 census. They lived in Cross Hands at Carreg Hollt, which was both their home and the shop. At some time, William was an alderman and a JP. There were four daughters:

– Lizzie May, who married Dr David Henry Griffiths, and lived in Cross Hands, first at Isfryn (*Register of Electors*, 1919-1928) and then Derwydd, until the late 1940s; they had at least one child, a son W. Greville-Griffiths. Lizzie died in 1962.

– Minnie Olive, b.1890*c*, who lived at Carreg Hollt with her father until his death. She married David James Bowen and lived at Maes Del, Forest, Pontarddulais during the late 1940s and early 1950s (*Registers of Electors*), before moving to Weston Super Mare.

– Dilys Irene, b.1892*c*, unmarried, who also lived at home with her father until his death, and then lived in Isfryn, Cross Hands, until the late 1940s. Later, she moved to Weston Super Mare.

– Florence Evelyn, b.1895*c*, who lived at Carreg Hollt until about 1927, and then married a Wyatt.[55]

ii. Lizzie, b.1866*c*, d. May 10 1900*g*, unmarried, buried in Llanllwch.

iii. William, b.1869*c*, lived in London, and was, says Thompson (1965), in the drapery business.[56]

iv. David John, b. April 8 1876*b*, d. December 16, 1952, school-teacher, who married Florence Williams.

v. Arthur Lewis, b.1880*c*, d. October 15 1947, unmarried. A guard at GWR's Dyffryn Yard, Port Talbot and then Traffic Supervisor at the nearby North Bank Docks. He lodged in Aberavon and, from the 1930s, in 37, Beverley Street, Port Talbot with relatives, Ken and Hettie Owen.[57]

2. *William*, b. April 7 1834, d. December 11 1879, better known as Gwilym Marles, cobbler, classical scholar, Unitarian preacher, headmaster and teacher, a writer of stories, essays and hymns, a poet, editor, and radical leader. After studying in Glasgow, he lived in Llandysul and in 1858 married Mary Hopkins, b.1829, d. January 4 1867, and had four children born between 1860 and 1866: Diana Alban, William Marles, Annie Jennet and Minnie. In 1868, he married Mary Williams, b.

36. Evan and Anne Thomas, seated, with Nancy. Florence and D.J. Thomas, standing right. Arthur Thomas on the far left.

November 22 1834, d. June 12 1903, and had seven children born between 1869 and 1877: Lewis Williams (1), Mary Emerson, Eliza (Lisa), Theodore, Muriel, Hilda and Lewis Williams (2).[58]

3. *Simon*, b.1838*c*.

4. *Hannah*, b. June 10 1848*b* at Glan-rhyd-y-gwiail, d. about 1897. She was "six feet tall, fair hair and very intelligent." She often helped with the organisation of the parties and hunt balls held in the big houses, and at the lunches put on at the Forest Arms, Brechfa, for estate fishing parties. It is also said that she taught the children of the families she worked for. Hannah's descendents told me that four of her children were love-children, thought to have been the offspring of the local gentry: "they were not ordinary, they had a different manner to the Welsh way of life."[59] Hannah's seven children, first cousins of D.J. Thomas, were:

   i. Anne, b.1868*c*, d.1956, known as Annie. By the 1901 census, she had moved to Swansea and had married William

Righton, a ship runner and then a ship store agent. They lived at 8, Burman Street, just off Walter Road in Swansea. They had five children, including Clara known as Clarrie and Carrie, b. March 12 1894*b*; Dolly b.1897*c*; and Jessie b.1899*c*. Clara married Alford Auckland, and had at least two children, including Nancy Barbara, b.1914, who later married a Treacher, and was interviewed by Colin Edwards.[60]

ii. Anne, b.1871, d.1937. She was brought up by Hannah as her own daughter, and may have been a love child from somewhere else in the family. She married Tom Thomas and from 1920 they lived at Aberduar farm, Llanybydder. There were eleven children: Dafydd who farmed at Cwm Cothi, Brechfa; Ifan Tom and Daniel (both of whom went to America in 1921); two sons who died young; and Lettitia, Sarah Jane, William, James, Ben and Agnes, all of whom lived in the area around Llanybydder.

iii. John, b.1884 who went to America and farmed in Idaho.

iv. William Graham, b.1887*c*, d.1951*g*, who married Esther Davies of Rhiw-saithbren, Llanfihangel Rhos-y-corn. They farmed Rhiw-saithbren, and then, from 1933, Gwargraig, Llanybydder. There were three sons:

– Ifan Tom b.1903, d.1910.

– William John b.1904, who married Hannah Jones in 1926. They farmed Llainoleu Uchaf, Llanfihangel Rhos-y-corn (1926), Pentre Evan (1933), Brynllofawr, Llanybydder (1939), and Gwargraig (1951). They had four children: Elizabeth Megan, Gwilym Marles (Brynllofawr), Tom Elwyn (Blaen-nant-y-mab, Llanegwad) and Eddie Arfryn (Gwargraig).

– David Arthur b.1906 who married Eira Mary Lewis; they farmed Pentre Evan and Rhiw-saithbren, and had two children, Elizabeth ('Betty') Esther, b.1928, who married Ernest Jones; and Sarah Mary, b.1934, whose husband, Ralph Tucker, was instrumental in establishing the tri-ennial production of *Under Milk Wood* in Laugharne, commencing in 1958, and took part in performances. He was a bearer at Florence Thomas' funeral.

v. Margaret, b.1889*c*, d.1962*g* who married John Evans of Abergorlech. They farmed around Llanfihangel Rhos-y-corn, including Ty'r-cwm, and had four children:

37. DJ's first cousin Margaret Evans, her husband John and their children, Glanville and Bessie.

- Idris and Eunice, who died young.
- William John Glanville, b. March 18 1914*b* at Glan-capel-mair, Brechfa, d.1971*g*, who married Elizabeth Margaret Daniels. They farmed in the Gwernogle area, including Gwernogle Bach and Abercwm Bach. They had two children, Gareth b.1943 and Eleri b.1956.
- Bessie b.1919 who married Noel Howells, a tailor, and lived in Brechfa and Llanybydder, and had a daughter, Val.
   vi. Arthur b.1891, d.1957*g*, unmarried and lived at Gwargraig farm.
  vii. Rachel, b.1897, d.1977*g*. She married Tom Evans of Whitemill, and had four children: a son, 'Jackie', a baby who was was still-born and two others who died young. They lived at Llwynmarles, Wellfield Road, Carmarthen. She was interviewed by Colin Edwards.

Arthur and Rachel were the children of Evan Jones of Tirlan, Brechfa, with whom Hannah set up house, and may have married.

5. *Thomas*, b.1852c, who lived at 185, Aldersgate Street, London. He was alive in 1905, and is acknowledged for the help he gave O.M. Edwards in his book published that year about Gwilym Marles, which gives the address.

The Thomas Settlements

There was no significant settlement of DJ's relations around Johnstown, or that part of Carmarthenshire. There would have been few of them, if any, for DJ to visit with the young Dylan – DJ's brothers were in Port Talbot and London, his sisters were dead, as were his parents. His four nieces – Dylan's first cousins – were brought up in coal mining Cross Hands in the east of the county, and continued to live there for many years. There is no mention in the Edwards archive of Dylan and his parents visiting the Cross Hands relations, although Lizzie May Greville had been one of the witnesses at DJ and Florence's wedding in 1903.

There is no note by either Brinley or Colin Edwards of DJ's relationships with the Llandysul settlement. DJ's aunt, Mary, the second wife of Gwilym Marles, died in 1903, and it is unlikely that DJ had much contact with his first cousins, the eleven children of Marles. Three of the children died young, and Lewis (2) died during the First World War. By the end of 1934, only three of Marles' children were still alive, and one of these, Eliza, later recorded that she had not seen DJ after 1897, and had never met Dylan, largely because she had lived in India.[61]

The Brechfa connection remained live, however, and there was some contact with three of the children of DJ's aunt, Hannah Thomas. In her interview with Colin Edwards, Barbara Treacher describes the continuing friendship between DJ, Florence and Dylan with DJ's first cousin, Annie Righton, the eldest of Hannah's children. Annie's house in Burman Street was not far from Cwmdonkin Drive, and Treacher describes the weekly visits of Annie's children and grandchildren to the Thomases. The friendship went on even after DJ and Florence moved to Blaencwm in 1941, because Annie and her family moved to Carmarthen, living at 8, Wellfield Road, next to her half-sister, Rachel Evans, before returning to Sketty in the late 1940s.

DJ, Florence and Dylan sometimes visited Ty'r-cwm farm, Brechfa, the home of DJ's first cousin Margaret, who had married John Evans. Their son, Glanville, was the same age as Dylan, and there is a photograph of the Evanses with Dylan as a boy, probably taken at Ty'r-cwm.

38. Rachel Evans

Glanville and his sister Bessie also used to go for tea with Florence when she lived in Laugharne.[62]

DJ's first cousin, Rachel Evans, was brought up on farms around Gwernogle, Brechfa. Rachel told Edwards that she didn't meet Dylan until after 1945. It was Rachel who in the 1950s helped to look after Florence Thomas, and was a beneficiary of her Will.

There was also an Abergwili/Llanllawddog settlement of the Brechfa Thomases with whom Dylan kept some contact. William Thomas' brother, John, had a granddaughter, Margaretta, who married David John Evans, a school attendance officer, Labour and trade union activist, chapel deacon and competitor at local *eisteddfodau*, where he enjoyed success with his hymns and poems. Their daughter, Megan, was Dylan's third cousin, and she married Eynon Lloyd Hughes, a keen local historian and writer of short stories, some of which were broadcast on the Light Programme in the late 1950s. Eynon would meet with Dylan in the Drover's Arms in Carmarthen in the years after 1945, and particularly when Dylan was in Laugharne from 1949 to his death in 1953.[63]

According to Brinley Edwards' notes, DJ had another cousin, Mrs Marjorie Owen, living in Swansea. She lived for some time with David and Theodosia Rees in Newton. In her interview with Colin Edwards, Addie Elliott mentions 'Maggie' living with the Reeses, and describes

39. John and Margaret Thomas and their children. Margaretta is behind her mother.

her as the niece of DJ's mother. Brinley says that Marjorie was the mother or grandmother of Ken Owen, with whom Arthur Thomas lodged in Port Talbot. She is listed as a sister-in-law at Annie Jones' funeral in 1933, and living in the Mumbles.

Evan Thomas and the Young DJ

Little is known about Evan Thomas the Guard, nor about the young DJ. The following extracts about them are from Brinley Edwards' notes and Colin Edwards' interviews:

> Evan Thomas ... lived at the Poplars, Johnstown, was of medium size. He had a beard and moustache. Very quiet and very distant type. Did not go about much – always at home. He was a very good gardener and had great pride in his flowers and veg. – most of his neighbours were also good gardeners. He and his wife were well

known and respected. She, too, was always at home. They were a very happy couple and lived a good life ... [he] was a man that kept a lot to himself. There was a good bit of ground around the house ... he was a man that you'd always find about there, doing something, pass his time. You'd never see him like with the men of the village here now, playing quoits and all that sort of game. You'd never see him out and about, nor even going to the pub anywhere. Always at home. Proper home manner ... he was well-spoken. I should think, by the way when you talked to him, that he was a well-read man. (D.J. Thomas, a family friend)

I used to think the world of him [DJ: Dylan's father], because he used to teach me so well ... I learnt a good deal from Johnnie Thomas because of the way of his expressions ... he explained things in a simple manner, you know. And mathematics – he would teach me far better than anybody else ... he used to teach in all the classes, he used to go round the classes that were best ... he was a very good speaker ... he didn't do much poetry, not to my knowledge. But he was a very good speaker, and very able. He used to talk a lot about history and that sort of thing to me, but chiefly on music. I was very interested in music from him ... he used to play for our morning service ... a little harmonium ... when he left school, Mr Brown, who was the Principal of the Training College at that time, wanted him to go to his College and be trained there, but he wouldn't have it, he wouldn't go to the College. "I'm going to Aberystwyth," he said ... he wanted to go to university very much indeed. I know he was very ambitious." (Albert Savage on DJ's time as a pupil-teacher at the Model School, Carmarthen.)

Arthur who was not of the same type as his brother DJ. Arthur was tall, happy go lucky and quiet. DJ ... was smart and active – played football at Johnstown. DJ's friend was the son of Mr Townsend who had a woollen factory near Johnstown. He and DJ went to Aberystwyth University together.[64] Another friend of DJ was Dan Jones, a well known tailor who made his clothes for him. Dan used to visit DJ in Swansea often. They were both fond of football. DJ understood the Welsh language and could speak the language. (D.J. Thomas)

Dan Jones the tailor appears in Dylan's story, 'A Visit to Grandpa's'. In his interview with Edwards, D.J. Thomas, describes how Dylan's father, DJ, kept in touch with his Johnstown friends, including Dan Tailor and Emyr 'Evie' Lloyd, the carpenter and undertaker. In the interview, D.J. Thomas describes DJ as a "very nice, very sociable feller ... "

A Child Alone

It's clear from the data on Dylan's family that he was the baby in a 'greying' nuclear and extended family. When he was born in 1914, his father was already thirty-seven, and his mother thirty-two. More to the point, his father was in his fifties when Dylan was a teenager. Of his many uncles and aunts, the youngest, Arthur, was already thirty-four when Dylan was born – the oldest was fifty-four.

Despite the number of uncles and aunts that he had, Dylan had comparatively few first cousins, and none of his own age. His three maternal cousins, Idris, Doris and Theodosia, were very much older than him. Dylan's five paternal cousins must have been much older, too, since their mother died in 1903.

Three of Dylan's grandparents died before he was born; the exception was Anne Thomas of Johnstown, but she died within three years of his birth.

A Molly-Coddled Child

By all accounts, Florence Thomas was a loving but over-protective mother, who appears to have been extremely anxious that Nancy and Dylan would fall victim to some fatal childhood illness, and she seems to have been particularly worried about pulmonary illnesses. Florence's anxiety may well have been grounded in family tragedy: two of her siblings, Sarah Jane and David George, died as youngsters. Their death certificates show that David died of 'Phthisis', almost certainly pulmonary tuberculosis, and Sarah Jane of 'Chronic abscess 6 months. Typhoid fever 9 days'. Then in 1897, the child of Florence's first cousin, Sarah of Maesgwyn, died at the age of eight months from 'Epilepsy'.

On DJ's side, three of his siblings died in infancy, as did six of the children of his first cousins, Anne, Margaret and Rachel, thought to be from pulmonary illnesses. Such illnesses, especially asthma, were extensive throughout Hannah Thomas' children and grandchildren, and still affect the families of some of her great-grandchildren today. Pulmonary illness also affected the Williamses to the present day – Evan Williams of Llwyngwyn was so 'chesty' that his doctor recommended he take up smoking as a cure.

Young But Not So Easy Any More

Dylan started at Swansea Grammar in the autumn of 1925. He went there from the dame school in Mirador Crescent, where his fellow pupils had included girls, and his teachers were women. The Grammar school was boys only, and the teachers all men. The move to the Grammar school also brought him even more within the ambit of his father's influence.

Ferris (1999, pp.38-39) has noted that the next few years of Dylan's life were marked by various forms of petty delinquency, including theft. The details provided by Brinley Edwards enable us to see how this early teenage delinquency coincided (and one can put it no more strongly than that) with a number of significant changes in Dylan's extended family. First, the St. Thomas side of his mother's family broke up: his uncle Bob and aunt Polly moved in 1927 and 1928 to Blaencwm, and, at the same time, his aunt-in-law, Elizabeth, and his first cousin, Theodosia, left for New Quay. There was then no close family left in St. Thomas. Second, Fernhill was also lost to the young Dylan, as Jim and Annie Jones left the farm in about 1929. If this was a blow, then it may have been worsened by his aunt Rachel leaving nearby Pentrewyman at the very same time – see Chapter 2 for details. Moreover, Dylan's cousin, Doris Williams, left 5, Cwmdonkin Drive in 1928 to marry Randolph Fulleylove – she had been a regular feature of Dylan's childhood both at Llansteffan and in number 5, where she had stayed after the death of her mother in 1922.[65]

Thus at the very time that Dylan was dealing emotionally with the all-male environment of the Grammar school, his ties to several female members of his family were significantly loosened, and the heedless days and ways at Fernhill had come to an end.

Death's Dominion

The death dates given in Brinley Edwards' notes present other opportunities for investigation, such as the incidence of disease and illness in the family. Take cancer as an example. According to Brinley's notes, both Gwilym Marles and his brother Thomas died of cancer; we know that their nephew, Dylan's father DJ, had cancer of the tongue, from which he recovered. Brinley also tells us that DJ's brother Arthur died of cancer. Dylan's maternal aunt Annie of Fernhill had cancer of the womb. Dylan's sister Nancy and his son Llewelyn both died of cancer.

The availability of the dates of death now allow us to establish, through a search of death certificates, which other members of the family died of cancer, or, for that matter, of other illnesses. For example, the death certificate of Dylan's uncle, John Williams, shows that the cause of death was 'General Paralysis of the Insane. Exhaustion'. Dylan's grandfather, George Williams, died from pneumonia. It's possible that searches of death certificates may yield information pertinent to Dylan's own death.

2. The Insanitary Farms

Despite some inevitable repetition of material from the previous chapter, it might still be helpful to set out who lived where in the cluster of farms and cottages that Dylan knew from childhood onwards. I have taken most of the data from sources in the Carmarthenshire Archives, including *Registers of Electors*, the 1945 *Rural Housing Inspection Report* (RHIR), providing data on the rooms in properties, and the 1910 *Duties on Land Values* survey, which gives acreage.

The large majority – some seventy per cent – of land holdings in Carmarthenshire from the 1870s to the 1920s were under fifty acres (Collins, 2000). But most of Florence Thomas' Llangain relations had much bigger farms than this. Evan Williams, the second eldest son of Waunfwlchan, married into Pen-y-coed with its 128 acres and then accomplished the difficult transition from farming 59 acres at Tirbach to taking on Llwyngwyn's 190 acres. His two daughters, Sarah and Annie, married into large farms at Maesgwyn (132 acres) and Pencelly Uchaf (93 acres) and his youngest son Thomas married, as Evan himself had done, into Pen-y-coed.

Whilst Jim Jones was himself a poor farmer, his marriage to Annie Williams in 1893 meant that the Williamses also successfully aligned themselves to the Jones family holdings that spread north from Waunfwlchan – Pentrewyman, Fernhill and Dolaumeinion in particular. This was a powerful family network – by 1929, the various Joneses and Williamses farmed over 800 acres of Llangain countryside, and much of this is still intact today within the family.

Fernhill's squalid poverty has been much dwelt upon by Dylan's biographers (and by Dylan himself), obscuring the real achievements of the Llangain relations. The important story about the Williamses is their self-improvement through hard work and strategic marriage, upon which was based the kind of inter-family co-operation once eesential to successful farming, and which led the Williamses to comparative prosperity.

Many of the Williamses were still living on their farms during the

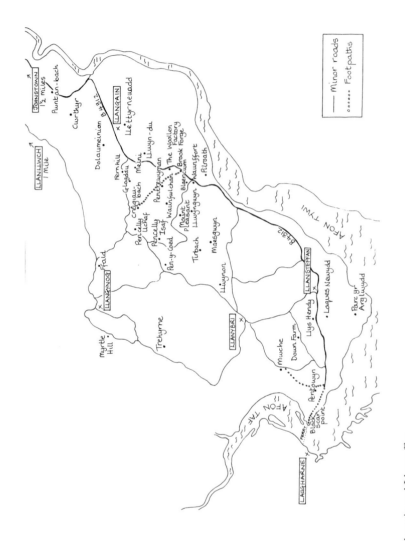

The Family Farms, Llangain and Llansteffan

40. Thomas and Anne Williams of Waunfwlchan, Dylan's maternal great-grandparents

young Dylan's holidays, though it is impossible to know what contact he had with them. Evan's wife, Anne, was alive at Llwyngwyn until 1924; of their children, William lived until 1942 and Annie until 1951, whilst Sarah and Thomas John survived Dylan. The Llangain family circle may have given Dylan a tangible sense of place and family, but at times it may have seemed claustrophobic. Imagine, for example, the teenage Dylan coming on holiday in 1928 – his mother's siblings were at Fernhill and Blaencwm; her sister-in-law at Pentrewyman; and her first cousins at Pencelly Uchaf, Llwyngwyn and Maesgwyn. Even when Dylan came to Blaencwm in 1945, nine of his mother's close relations still lived clustered within the family circle, with many more relatives living in the triangle formed by Llansteffan, Llangynog and Llangain.

If any one of the Williams farms is to be considered as their 'ancestral seat' then it must be Pen-y-coed, inhabited by the Williams family or their relatives from the 1820s to the present day, with Llwyngwyn and Maesgwyn not far behind, in continuous Williams occupation since the late nineteenth century.

In the following descriptions of the farms, I have tried to show the principal way in which the inhabitants of each property were related to Florence, and to identify who was living there during Dylan's childhood and teenage years.

Pencelly Isaf (36 acres): Farmed by Thomas and Anne Williams, Florence's grandparents, from at least 1836. Florence's mother, Anna, was born on this farm in 1840. Anna's two brothers, John and Evan, were also born here.

Waunfwlchan (kitchen, two living rooms and six bedrooms, 120 acres): After Pencelly Isaf, Thomas and Anne Williams farmed here from 1841.[66] Florence's mother, Anna, was brought up at Waunfwlchan until the mid-1860s, and Florence's brother, Thomas, was born here. Thompson (1965) was told that Florence and her siblings came here from Swansea for holidays when they were children. In Dylan's childhood, it was farmed by David and Ann Evans, who were at Waunfwlchan from at least 1918 to 1925, as the *Register of Electors* shows. Their daughter, Lettice, married David Jones, the half-brother of Jim Jones Fernhill, bringing Waunfwlchan briefly back into the wider family fold.

Pen-y-coed (128 acres): From the 1820s, Pen-y-coed was farmed by Dylan's great-great grandparents, John and Anna Williams. It was then farmed by their daughter, Sarah, and her husband, William Thomas, until his death in 1886. The farm was taken over by Sarah and William's daughter, Hannah, and her husband Joseph Thomas, who were here at the 1891 census. In the early 1890s, Florence's uncle, John Williams the eldest son of Waunfwlchan, took over the tenancy, and lived here, as the 1901 census shows, with his brother Daniel (Dr Dan), and their widowed mother, Anne, who died at Pen-y-coed in 1902. By about 1912, there was a new family at Pen-y-coed – Sarah and Evan Davies, parents of Mary Ann, who married Florence's first cousin, Thomas John Williams of Llwyngwyn. After Evan's death in 1930, Sarah stayed here until her own death in about 1939. The farm was then run by her son, Russell and his wife Annie, until his death in 1991, when it was taken over by their son, Roger, who farms it today.[67]

Tirbach (59 acres): Florence's uncle, Evan, and his wife Anne, lived here from about 1872 to about 1886, and their children William, Annie, Hannah and Jane were born here. They were followed at Tirbach by Evan's brother Dr Dan. Sometime after 1891, Florence's sister, Annie, left Swansea to live in Tirbach as a housekeeper to Dr Dan before marrying Jim Jones in 1893. Dr Dan moved to Pen-y-coed, and Jim and Annie came to Tirbach after their marriage; their son Idris was born here in 1897. By 1920, the farm had moved outside the Williams family.[68]

Pentowyn (216 acres): Jim, Annie and Idris rented this farm overlooking the Taf estuary after their stay at Tirbach. We don't know the date they moved in, but they were here in 1901, as the census return confirms, together with a cook, a domestic servant and three farm workers. They are also shown as resident here in the 1906 *Register of Electors*. The Rees Davies interview notes that DJ and Florence visited Pentowyn on holiday. Sister Polly was staying here at the time of the 1901 census. After Jim and Annie left, Pentowyn was taken over by David and Anna Evans. In the report of Annie's funeral in 1933, Anna Evans is described as a cousin; she was related to Annie and Florence through Sarah Rees of Llettyrneuadd, to whom Anna was a first cousin – see Note 71. We can see from the *Registers of Electors* that David and Anna were at Pentowyn throughout Dylan's life. There may have been some contact between Dylan and the Evanses because, after crossing from Laugharne in the ferry, he would walk past Pentowyn on his way to Llanybri or Llansteffan – see Chapter 6.

Fernhill (kitchen, two living rooms, four bedrooms, 15 acres): Jim, Annie and Idris moved here from Pentowyn sometime between 1905 and the 1910 land tax survey, which shows Jim as a tenant farmer at Fernhill, paying rent to a Mrs F.M. Blumberg of Southport – see Chapter 5 for more on Mrs Blumberg. The Joneses probably came to Fernhill in 1909 and stayed until about 1929.[69] "Many summer weeks," Dylan told Trevor Hughes in February 1933, "I spent happily with the cancered aunt on her insanitary farm. She loved me quite inordinately, gave me sweets & money, though she could little afford it, petted, patted, & spoiled me."

One of the living rooms was 'the best room', kept for special occasions. In 'The Peaches', Dylan describes the room in some detail, and further information can be gleaned from his poem 'Fern Hill'. As for facilities, Fernhill was no more or less 'insanitary' than the other family houses that Dylan knew around Llangain: the RHIR tells us that there was an outside earth closet, water was carried from a dipping well two hundred yards away, people washed in the kitchen and cooking was on an open fire with an oven. The house suffered from "extreme rising dampness", a defect noted by Dylan in 'The Peaches', in which he also describes the dilapidated farmyard and buildings. Watt Davies told Colin Edwards that Jim and Annie kept ten cows and two horses.

Mount Pleasant (kitchen, bedroom): Owned earlier by John Williams, son of Waunfwlchan. Jim and Annie lived in this cottage from about 1929 until their deaths. Idris inherited Mount Pleasant from his father, and continued to live here until he moved into 2, Blaencwm in 1948.[70]

Pentrewyman (kitchen, living room, three bedrooms, 110 acres): Jim's half-brother, David Jones, farmed here from at least 1910. Jim's sister, Rachel Jones, and her son Albert, then took over Pentrewyman from about 1919 and were here during Dylan's visits as a boy to Fernhill. She appears as 'Aunt Rach Morgan' in 'The Peaches'. Brinley Edwards' notes describe her as "very dark, medium size, slow moving, nicely spoken and nicely dressed. Only fair in English." The 1891 census return says that Rachel, like her parents and siblings, spoke only Welsh. Rachel was helped on the farm by Watt Davies and May Bowen, who described Rachel as being "on the brownish, how you say, tarry side, then". Rachel and Albert left Pentrewyman about 1929 to live in Johnstown, as the *Registers of Electors* confirm. Another set of Florence's relations then took over the farm – William Jones and his wife Margaret Jane, who was the sister of Annie Lewis, Llettyrneuadd (see below and Note 71). William and Margaret lived at Pentrewyman with Annie's daughter, Glenys, until 1953, when all three moved to Peniel, just outside Carmarthen. Glenys remembers Dylan in Llansteffan, and told me about Florence's visits to Pentrewyman to see William and Margaret.

Llettyrneuadd: Mrs Annie Lewis of this farm was related to the Williams family, and used to visit Polly and Bob in 29, Delhi Street, and Florence and DJ in Cwmdonkin Drive. She saw Dylan in Swansea when he was a year old, but did not see him again, she told Edwards, until he was staying at Blaencwm when "he was grown up."[71]

Pencelly Uchaf (93 acres): Florence's first cousin, Annie, daughter of Evan and Anne Williams of Llwyngwyn, lived here with her husband, William Evans, and his sister Elizabeth. William took over the running of the farm from his father, and is shown here on the 1910 land values survey as the owner of the farm. They lived here for most of Dylan's life, until their deaths in 1951.

Maesgwyn (two kitchens, living room, five bedrooms, 132 acres): Thomas and Sarah Evans farmed Maesgwyn. Sarah was the daughter of Evan and Anne Williams of Llwyngwyn, and was Florence's eldest first cousin. Sarah moved in with her relatives in Llwyngwyn in 1939, but she continued to own Maesgwyn, and died a year after Dylan.[72]

Llwyngwyn (kitchen, three living rooms, six bedrooms, 190 acres):

41. Thomas and Sarah Evans of Maesgwyn, on the right.

Florence's uncle, Evan Williams, and his wife, Anne, lived here from about 1886. After Evan's death in 1897, Anne stayed on with four of her children: Hannah, Jane, William and Thomas John, all first cousins of Florence. Anne Williams died in 1924, and Hannah a year later. William inherited Llwyngwyn and continued to live here, together with Thomas John and his wife, Mary Ann.

When William died in 1942, Llwyngwyn was left to Thomas John, who lived here with Mary Ann and their daughter, Haulwen, and Sarah Evans, formerly of Maesgwyn. Sarah was "the matriarch" that John Malcolm Brinnin met on his visit to Llwyngwyn in the summer of 1953, "her shrivelled little body entirely covered in a Spanish profusion of rich black silks ... " Brinnin also admired

42. Anne Williams of Llwyngwyn, seated, with her daughter Hannah

the bare, scrubbed kitchen, with its fire-place big enough for five men to stand abreast in, its hanging sides of bacon, great black iron pots and witches' brooms ... we were given large cups of warm milk out of a pail brought in by a red-faced milkmaid. We drank it, bravely, and were surprised to find we liked it.

Brinnin took less pleasure when he and Dylan were taken round Llwyngwyn's fields by Thomas John; Brinnin sank to his ankles in mud and "could not understand a word of our guide's English."[73]

Dylan's second cousin, Haulwen Williams (later Morris) inherited Llwyngwyn and Maesgwyn, and her children – who are the great-great-grandchildren of Thomas and Anne Williams of Waunfwlchan – help her to run the two farms today.

43. Thomas John and his daughter, Haulwen, with unknown child

44. Mary Ann Williams, Haulwen's mother, outside Llwyngwyn

1, Blaencwm (kitchen, living room, three bedrooms): Owned by Dr Dan, son of Waunfwlchan and then by Florence's brother, Bob, who moved here from St. Thomas in the spring of 1927 and lived in the cottage until his last illness in 1960, when he moved into Llwyngwyn, where he died in 1962. Bob's sister, Polly, joined him at Blaencwm in the autumn of 1928, and was here until her death in 1946.[74]

2, Blaencwm (kitchen, bedroom): Owned by John Williams, son of Waunfwlchan, and then by Florence's sister, Theodosia, and her husband David Rees, who retired here in early 1933. The cottage was bequeathed to Idris Jones on Theodosia's death in 1941. Florence and DJ moved in after Theodosia had died, and stayed until April 1948. Idris Jones then lived here until his death in 1959.[75]

Waunffort (31 acres): This farm is almost opposite Blaencwm. Florence's half-sister, Anne, married Robert Williams of Waunffort, though they do not appear to have lived here. In the 1940s and 1950s, Waunffort was occupied by Samuel and Gwenllian Thomas, and their daughter, Gladys, who is mentioned in Dylan's July 1945 letter to Oscar Williams. Dylan refers to her "black bloomered bottom" being slyly observed by an Italian POW. Dylan also mentions Waunffort in his letter of June 5 1947 to his parents, asking about furniture they had in store at the farm.

The Caravan: Dylan and Caitlin had access to a caravan. Paul Ferris' notes of his interview with Annie Lewis of Llettyrneuadd record the use of a caravan somewhere along the Blaencwm lane. Sarah Ann Evans of Llanybri also mentions in her interview with Colin Edwards that Caitlin used the caravan to meet her Laugharne lovers. We don't know where the caravan was, but Rees Davies told Edwards that Dylan and Caitlin stayed for a while at Trefach, Llansteffan, a farm about two miles along the lane from Blaencwm. Perhaps the caravan was at Trefach.

Rose Cottage, Llansteffan: Florence's half-sister, Anne, lived here with her husband, Robert Williams of Waunffort farm, and their children, William and Doris. Dylan stayed with them for holidays from about 1919 to 1922.[76]

There were, of course, other relations in the area, including some of the eleven children of Richard Jones of Pentrewyman, father of Jim Jones and Rachel Jones. These children, described in Note 46 have been difficult to trace, but the following two farms are of interest:

Dolaumeinion (kitchen, two living rooms, five bedrooms, 111 acres): David and Margaret Francis, relations of Florence, were here until about 1896 – see Note 71. Jim and Rachel's half-brother, David Jones (b.1879, d.1943*g*) lived here with his wife, Lettice Maud (b.1889, d.1978*g*), from 1919 to 1930, as the *Registers of Electors* show, before moving to Ffynnonfair, a smallholding in the village of Llansteffan.

Pwntan-bach (14 acres): Jim Jones' and Rachel's half-sister, Mary, lived here with her husband, Henry Davies, 'a cowkeeper' and eventually a labourer in the milk factory. They had two children, Olwen and Les, cousins-in-law to Dylan. The young Dylan walked across the fields from Fernhill, passing through Dolaumeinion, to play with Les, who was the same age. Olwen has passed on many memories of Dylan, including one of Les teaching him to swear in Welsh, as they sat amongst the horses in the Pwntan stables.[77]

The list of mourners at Annie Jones' funeral in 1933 tells us about some of the other relations that the young Dylan had around him when he visited Fernhill and Blaencwm. The people named in the funeral report as Annie's cousins include Mr and Mrs John Francis of Lacques Newydd and his sisters, Dosi, Mary Ann and Sarah Anna Francis of Down Farm (see Note 71 about the Francis family); John and Margaret Jones of Trehyrne farm; Miss Mary Lloyd of Llwyn-du; Mrs Anna Evans of Pentowyn; Mrs Roseanna Thomas of Dyffryn Tawel; and Mr and Mrs Lewis of Meini. No doubt "cousins" would have included cousins-in-law and second cousins, as well as those (such as Roseanna Thomas of Dyffryn Tawel) who were not cousins at all but close family friends.[78]

Another important set of relations in the area were the other children of Sarah and Evan Davies of Pen-y-coed. Besides Mary Ann Williams at Llwyngwyn and Russell at Pen-y-coed, there were their siblings John Hywel Davies (m. Phyllis Lewis) at Plas Isaf farm in the village of Llanybri; Margaret Davies (m. Jack Jones) at Llwynon, Llanybri; Olwen Davies (m. Daniel Evans) at Brook Forge; and Gwyn Davies (m. Amy) at Ffald, Llangynog. This family group of Davieses and their spouses was only fully present on these farms from 1940 onwards, though John Davies was at Plas Isaf during the 1920s and 1930s (as was Daniel Evans at Brook Forge, with his father, Henry.)

Relative Insanity

From the above, we can work out the identity of the 'mad' and 'inbred' relations who lived in the "hill-lane" that ran along from Blaencwm, to whom Dylan referred in his July 1945 letter to Oscar Williams. They were uncle Bob and aunt Polly, of course, in 1, Blaencwm, Idris Jones in Mount Pleasant, and, in Llwyngwyn, Sarah Evans, Thomas John and Mary Ann Williams and their daughter Haulwen, together with farm worker Emrys Morris, whom Haulwen was later to marry.

Needless to say, there was no insanity and little inbreeding, and the families continued to prosper, as they had done since the early days of Waunfwlchan and Llwyngwyn, though Tirbach eventually became derelict.

3. Aunts and Uncles:
Some Thumbnail Sketches

Brinley Edwards put together brief descriptions of the Williams family, and of their Llangain relations. In this chapter, I reproduce his notes on Florence's siblings, together with material I have gathered from other sources, though information on their occupations and finances is given in Chapter 4. Where Brinley has provided a description, I place it first in quotation marks.

Thomas Williams: Brinley contacted several of Thomas' parishioners, including Miss Anna Jones, Fairfield Farm, Knelston, Reynoldston, who wrote:

> The Rev. Thomas Williams was a Congregational minister for a time at least in Lancashire. He married and I think his wife must have had considerable private means as he retired when comparatively young. They came to live at Nicholaston Hall where he had a few fields and one or two cows. This proved an expensive hobby, and after a while, they sold the Hall, and moved to a very pleasant double thatched house at Penmaen ... He preached for us at Knelston Baptist Church several times and his sermons were always extremely thoughtful and interesting. He was a very cultured man and was very fond of poetry – especially Browning. I remember him showing me a book of photographs, mainly of Gower seascapes and each was illustrated by an apt quotation from Browning. He left Penmaen to live at Clyne ... I believe he and Mrs Williams died there ... by the way, they had no children. I do not think he was strong and his back was bent – a slight hump. Perhaps that was why he retired early. His wife was very refined and pleasant.

Brinley's notes also contain the following account of their time after Nicholaston Hall:

> Mr and Mrs Williams lived in a house in Blackpill known as Brook Villa. It was a fairly large house and is now made into two houses

... Mr and Mrs Williams lived very quietly – did not entertain – visitors were very few ... Mr Williams had a great deal of trouble in trying to stop people walking past the side of his house to Clyne Valley ... Mrs Williams was a Miss Davies. Mr Williams was in Swansea when he had a seizure in Rutland Street ... I understand that Mrs Williams née Davies is from a well known Swansea family. Sister to Rev Dd. Davies, also related to The Ross of Swansea – Rev. Dd. Hughes and Jones Hughes.

In his interview with Colin Edwards, Harry Leyshon, a family friend of Florence, described Thomas Williams as "rather a peculiar character – he was a bit eccentric, I think, something after Dylan's own type – bohemian, in a way."

Annie Williams: "Very short, stocky type – dark curly hair, fair skin – strong, healthy, not pretty – quite educated, jovial, talkative, slow moving – did not make a go on the farm – would pay nobody – probably poor – kind, nicely spoken, gave plenty of welcome, always a cup of tea – English and Welsh."

45. Annie Jones, née Williams, Fernhill

Annie's husband, Jim Jones, was "Tall and dark. Big in his ways – no work in him – left Fernhill farm to ruins – they were in a poor way – received £1 per week compensation – but there was nothing wrong with him." Even at Pentowyn, Jim was a lazy farmer, so Mary Ann Williams told Colin Edwards:

> Jim Jones was too much of a gentleman there to work ... he was taking his shoes off the horses then, to have a message to go to the blacksmiths in Llansteffan. For to go down to have a drink.

Nevertheless, Jim's nephew, the author John Llewellyn Jones, notes that although Jim was "certainly a bit idle, had a roving eye and liked his pint, [he] was far from being the domestic tyrant and drunken womaniser of Dylan's story ['The Peaches'].[79]

Jim and Annie's son, Idris, was "Fairly tall – dark curly hair – long fingers – thought a lot of himself – not interested in Dylan, did not talk about him – heavy smoker – often ill – spoke Welsh English accent – spent freely."

In 'The Peaches', Idris is Gwilym, "a tall young man ... with a thin stick of a body and spade-shaped face. You could dig the garden with him." Local man Gwilym Evans described Jim and Idris to Colin Edwards:

> Rusty, you know, reddish. And the same type of hair as Idris, rough, curly, dark ... not too heavy. Medium. But he was – like Idris – about five foot ten ... the same old thing was in Idris, you see. Swagger, like ... Idris was very kind of effeminate in a way ... he could speak Welsh alright ... 'Jaico' we used to call Idris ... 'Oh, Jaico,' he used to say. And Jaico they used to call him.

FitzGibbon met Idris in London in 1945; from Dylan's description, he had expected to meet "at least a Welsh Heathcliff" but found Idris to be "a rather quiet, shy countryman" (1965, p.31). John Llewellyn Jones, first cousin to both Idris and Dylan, also remembers Idris as a "mild young man".

Idris was as uninterested in farming as his father. He worked as an apprentice in the Richard Lewis draper's shop in Swansea High Street, and spent his weekends with Theodosia and David Rees at Paraclete manse.[80] He served in the First World War in the artillery. Afterwards, he was a postman in Llansteffan, but was knocked off his bike by an American army jeep, and received substantial compensation. He lived

46. and 47. Idris Jones as a young boy and a young man

with his parents at Fernhill and Mount Pleasant; Gwilym Evans also mentions in his Edwards interview that for a time Idris lived with David and Theodosia Rees at 2, Blaencwm.

Idris benefited from inheriting Mount Pleasant from his father, as well as 2, Blaencwm from Theodosia. The 1945 *Rural Housing Report* describes him as a 'casual labourer', though according to William Phillips in his interview with Colin Edwards, Idris "never took on a job anywhere. And nobody ever tried to employ him. Although there was a great shortage of agricultural workers down there ... "

In her interview, Sarah Ann Evans, who ran the Farmers' Arms in Llanybri, recalled Idris' generosity and vulnerability:

> Oh, it was a pity for him ... his father and mother died. I was sorry for him. You know, the people were frighting on a person ... sometimes I would tell them "For God's sake," I said, "leave Idris alone. You're only pinching money from him to have beer, that's all you are doing." He was so kind, he'd give a shilling or half a crown to them ... last days, he didn't have nothing, poor thing.

Appropriately enough, it was Idris who was called upon to deliver the vote of thanks when Smyrna chapel held a debate on the subject '*Mai gwell un rhoddi na derbyn*' ('That it is better to give than to receive').[81]

Both Colin Edwards' interview with Gwilym Evans, and Brinley's notes, contain a number of stories about Idris, including his affected and imperfect English, his efforts at 'preaching', and his participation in a mock murder trial and bizarre hair-cutting sessions in the stables of Smyrna chapel, which the police on one occasion unsuccessfully raided. Thompson (1965) also notes Idris' eccentricity when escorting Sir William Jenkins' pony and trap through Llangain, alternating shouts of encouragement to the pony with snatches of a hymn 'Praise be to Jesus'.

John Williams: "Very much like his sister Polly – English speaking but could speak Welsh – always well dressed ... expensive taste – jovial but rather quiet – energetic – occasional drink – not a heavy smoker."

There is little biographical information on John, apart from his occupations. This paucity is probably due to the fact that he died in 1911, and few memories of him would have survived to the 1960s when Colin and Brinley Edwards were doing their researches.

When John married Elizabeth Ann Evans, a St. Thomas woman from a poor family,[82] the wedding took place in the leafy suburb of Newton – in Paraclete chapel with David Rees as the officiating minister. This suggests a concern with the niceties of social position, and probably reflects the growing income of George Williams and his family.

Paul Ferris notes John's financial help to members of the family, including DJ and Florence, and Harry Leyshon described him as a "very good friend of Canaan Chapel and I know he presented a Bible and hymnbook for the pulpit".

Polly Williams: "Short, thin, frail – dark hair which she put in a few coils at the back of her head. Fair skin – smartly dressed – very fit personality, talkative but a lovely person – very cool and pleasant. Good vocabulary – and very musical ... more English than Welsh."

Polly was probably a vain person and conscious of appearances, lying in her census returns about her age. In the 1901 return for Pentowyn, she gave it as twenty-five, and fancifully described herself as 'Living on own means'. Perhaps she wanted to give the impression that she was living the life of a country gentlewoman. Caitlin was particularly scathing about her at Blaencwm:

...Aunt Polly was a terrible nuisance, always asking questions and chattering. She was a tiny little shrivelled-up creature, and she used to spend her days looking at Vogue and imagining herself in velvet

48. A note on this photograph makes the following identification:
Back row, from the left: John Williams, Rev. David Rees, Thomas Williams, Bob Williams.
Front: Florence, Theodosia and Polly Williams

gowns, which was a grotesque fantasy. (1986, p.87)

Polly was a kind and loving aunt to Dylan and Nancy, protecting them at Blaencwm from the worst of their father's anger.

Theodosia Williams: "Medium height – average build – fair, curly hair raised to the top of her head and made to resemble a bun. Nicely dressed – jovial – energetic – nicely spoken – preferred English to Welsh – health was good though she died of a stroke."

There is little biographical information on Theodosia, save her obituary in the *Carmarthen Journal* of April 18 1941. Of her time at Blaencwm, the *Journal* said:

> Mrs Rees was highly esteemed in the district. Of a very kindly and genial nature, she was a lady of much charm, and had endeared herself to a large circle of friends. She will be long remembered for her charitable disposition and good deeds.

Theodosia's husband, David Rees, was "short average built – skin pale – dark hair – small dainty moustache ... very jovial – energetic – very nicely spoken. Good vocabulary in Welsh and English ... very fond of children's names – he knew the meaning of children's names. Smoked cigarettes in company – very fluent in both languages. Hobby: gardening – fond of collecting names of plants."

Rees was the "son of a Llanelly assayer", according to the *Mumbles Press*, and Thompson (1965) says his first job was as a steelworker in Llanelli. After a distinguished student career as a classical scholar, Rees became the minister, first, at Canaan chapel, and then in 1898 at Paraclete, Newton. He was a lover of music, a botanist, archaeologist and a keen member of the Langland Bay Golf Club for twenty years. His time at Paraclete can be charted through the pages of the *Mumbles Press*: he was a hardworking minister, instigating the extension of the chapel and its schoolroom (twice), as well as the introduction of a new pipe organ and electric lighting, all paid for by a series of concerts, whist drives and other events. Thompson (1965) notes that Rees organised weekly 'Penny Pop' concerts of local musicians, and also put on improving readings and lectures for the community. Dylan wrote an article about Rees on his retirement from Paraclete, which appeared in the *Herald of Wales*, November 5 1932, the day before Rees preached his last sermon.

Rees took Dylan on rambles throughout the Gower, says Harry Leyshon in his interview with Colin Edwards, building up Dylan's

49. Theodosia Rees, left, with Jane Harris, seated, at Dishley Court, Leominster, 1932. See Note 44. Unknown woman on right.

knowledge of the local flora and fauna: "I think David had a great influence on his knowledge of flowers and plants all through the district, and he took an interest right through his life in it." Relations between the two later soured, as Ferris has described (1999, pp.12, 13, 68).

Theodosia and David Rees played an active part in the life of Smyrna chapel, Llangain, where he was a deacon. Rees' death was front page news (with photograph) in the *Carmarthen Journal*. The chapel was packed for his funeral, with five ministers (one a professor) taking part in the service. The death and funeral reports noted that Rees was

> a man of great charm and had a natural gift for friendship ... he coupled a wide knowledge and a keen intellectual capacity with a kindly disposition and an ardent desire to help his fellows. He was extremely popular among all sections of the community, irrespective of creed or party, although he was a man of strong convictions.[83]

William Robert Williams: "Medium built – curly hair – the average of the family – reddish round features – very shy – looked miserable –

lazy, slow moving – rather odd type – did not like gossip. Later on in years white whiskers and moustache – thought a lot of himself – they say he looked like Jesus Christ."

Ferris describes Bob as "a mental defective of sorts ... . He was the simple one, shy and slow-witted, who could be seen shuffling over the bridge from St. Thomas with a shopping bag, wearing an overcoat green with age that came down to his ankles" (1999, p.13). Yet there must have been far more to him than this. He was, for example, one of the executors of his father's Will, and of that of his sister Theodosia, and he looked after his property interests in St. Thomas right to the end.

Thompson's informants told him that Bob had "gained something of a local reputation as an 'odd sort', a man who did not trust banks, giving out the intimation that he had lost a great deal of money through some sort of financial manipulation" (1965, p.98).

Caitlin was as disparaging about Bob as she was of Polly: "There was Uncle Bob, who never said anything: he used to sit on a chair all day, and then sometimes he would get up, stretch his legs, walk out of the front door and sit on a wall, always with his hat on ... " (1986, p.50).

Pamela Hansford Johnson met Bob on a couple of visits to Blaencwm, and she was altogether more sympathetic to "poor old" Bob, describing how he "could hear threatening voices coming to him over the wireless even when it was turned off" (1974). Like his brother John, Bob helped his siblings with money, including loans to Annie and Jim Jones at Fernhill to pay the rent (Ferris 1999, p.17). In his Will, he was even-handed and generous to the friends and relatives around him at Blaencwm, also remembering Dylan and Caitlin's children, as well as his niece, Theodosia, in far-off New Quay.

4. The Family Finances

George and Anna Williams left Carmarthenshire for Swansea about 1865, accompanied by their three young children, and probably in flight from the family scandal described in Chapter 1. Their circumstances when they first arrived at 29, Delhi Street, St. Thomas, must have been very difficult. The 1871 census return shows them living there with five children. Another child, Sarah Jane, was born the following year. There was also another family in the house, a widower and his three adult children.

George and Anna did not let the grass grow under their feet. George appears to have been a porter on the Great Western Railway when he first arrived in Swansea. But at the 1871 census, he was a guard, and by 1881 an Inspector, finally becoming Chief Shipping Inspector, his rank on retirement. George bought 29, Delhi Street in 1881 with a mortgage from the Swansea Imperial Permanent Building Society.[84] By the time of the census that year, the widower and his children had gone and the Williamses occupied the whole house. George also acquired 30, Delhi Street, and property in Pontypridd, which provided some rental income, as well as the status of deacon at Canaan chapel, and superintendent of the Sunday School there.

George retired in 1905. He was presented with "a marble clock and a purse of money" and his colleagues wished him a long and happy retirement.[85] But a few months later he died. His Will gave his wife, Anna, a life interest in his property, and the income from it. After Anna's death, Polly was to inherit 29, Delhi Street and all its effects and furniture; Thomas, John and Robert were to have equal shares in 30, Delhi Street; and Annie, Polly, Theodosia and Florence were to have equal shares in the two shops George owned at 25 and 26 Richard Street, Cilfynydd, Pontypridd. Polly was to receive the residue of the estate. Value at probate: £867.

The drive towards self-improvement may have come as much from Anna as from George. Her father and elder brother had done the same in Llangain, improving their lot by moving into larger holdings, and

50. George Williams, Dylan's grandfather

linking up with neighbouring families through marriage. Both in Llangain and St. Thomas, the various Williamses were, financially at least, a cut above their neighbours. Most of George and Anna's children showed themselves equally capable of improvement, as the following notes describe.

Thomas became a minister and, as we saw in the previous chapter, married a wealthy Swansea woman. He tried to live the life of a well-read country gentleman. I could find no Will or grant of Probate. (Probate is not generally required if the estate of the deceased is small, or if the majority of assets were held jointly with, for example, a spouse or next-of-kin.)

Annie was a dressmaker in Swansea and then a housekeeper at Tirbach. In her interview with Colin Edwards, Doris Fulleylove says that she believed Jim and Annie's moves to Pentowyn and Fernhill were financed by "Auntie Florrie's people", though Jim was always a tenant farmer. The move to the fifteen acres of Fernhill must have been a major disappointment after Pentowyn's two hundred acres and its retinue of domestic staff and farm workers. Annie was helped later in life by her cousin, Annie of Pencelly Uchaf, who bought Mount Pleasant for them. Her relations continued to support Jim after Annie's death: William Williams, another cousin, gave Jim work on the nearby Llwyngwyn farm, "for him to have something to have food."[86] I could find no Will or grant of Probate.

John worked his way up on the docks from coal weigher (1881) to railway foreman (1891) to foreman coal trimmer (1903) to stevedore (1911) – the dates mark his progress on census returns, his marriage certificate, and his death certificate. He was able to buy at least two properties in St. Thomas, probably through building up his savings by living at home with his parents – which he did until he married in 1903 at the age of thirty-nine.[87] Harry Leyshon told Colin Edwards that John "was a foreman on the docks, I think connected with coal shipping and he was really well-off". Neither the Swansea trade directories nor the Edwards interviews yield any information to confirm Ferris' suggestion that John may have owned a small cargo handling company – though in this enterprising family it cannot be completely ruled out. John left 6, Kilvey Terrace and 1, Bay View Terrace, St. Thomas, to his wife Elizabeth Ann, together with all his estate. He left nothing to any of his siblings. Value of estate: £599.

Polly was a Pupil Teacher at the time of the 1881 census. She became a music teacher and chapel organist, and was greatly helped through inheritance. At the age of thirty-eight, she was the child who did best from her father's Will, inheriting the family home in 1913. She also had money from the sale, or renting, of the two shops in Pontypridd, in which she had inherited a share from her father. Polly also had the income from renting out 29, Delhi Street after she moved to Blaencwm in 1928. In her Will, she left number 29 to her brother Bob (as well as her furniture at Blaencwm) for his lifetime only, after which it was to go to Florence. Florence also inherited the remainder of the estate. Value of estate: £908.

We know very little about Theodosia's financial affairs. She left her house, 2, Blaencwm, to her nephew Idris Jones of Mount Pleasant. Her furniture and the remainder of her estate was to be divided equally between her siblings Polly, Bob and Florence. Value of estate: £2,348.

Bob worked as a coal trimmer in the holds of ships, a job considered as dirty, exhausting and dangerous as mining itself. But by 1905, his father's Will described him as a coal shipper. Theodosia's Will in 1941 has him as a coal shipping foreman, though he had long retired by then. He had inherited nothing from his brother John but, nevertheless,

Bob had sufficient capital to buy 1, Blaencwm and to retire there in 1927, when he was just fifty. Presumably he, too, had been able to build up his savings from his wages by living at home with Polly. After his mother's death in 1913, he also had a half share of the rental income from 30, Delhi Street with his brother, Thomas. By 1930, he owned 30, Delhi Street outright, and took the whole of the rent from it.[88]

Bob's capital was augmented further in 1941, after Theodosia's bequest, and, when Polly died in 1946, he drew the rental income from 29, Delhi Street until his death. Certainly, he appears to have been amongst the most well-off of George and Anna's children, though he lived a simple life.

Bob bequeathed all his furniture, domestic articles and ornaments to Mrs Haulwen Morris, daughter of Mary Ann Williams of Llwyngwyn. The proceeds from the sale of his 'real estate' and his 'ready money' were to be distributed as follows: £300 to Mary Ann Williams and £150 to three neighbours, including Gladys of Waunffort and Gerwyn Thomas of Dyffryn Tawel. The residue was to be divided equally in three shares between Theodosia, the daughter of his brother, John; Mary Ann Williams; and "the children of my late nephew Dylan Thomas Playwright and Author", who were to receive one third between them. Value of estate: £3,100.

And finally, Dylan's mother, Florence. It may have seemed as if she had made the best catch of all – D.J. Thomas was a Carmarthenshire boy with a first class degree from Aberystwyth, and a promising career in front of him. And for his part, the nephew of landlord-fighting Gwilym Marles found himself in a family of small-scale, but clearly astute, urban landlords.

Florence certainly got social status and, eventually, a new house in the Uplands, but they were short of money for most of their married life. They stayed in rented accommodation for their first ten years together, until in February 1914, they bought 5, Cwmdonkin Drive on a ninety-nine year lease. To pay for the house, DJ and Florence borrowed £350 from Elizabeth Ann Beor, the eldest daughter of Swansea solicitor Richard White Beor, at a rate of interest of 5% p.a. They were required to insure the house for £500, and, most unusually for the time, it was put in their joint names.[89]

We do not know what they paid for the house but it was probably about £500 – it is reasonable to suppose that, at that time, the purchase price of a newly-built house would have been close to its insurance value i.e. its re-building costs.

On February 18 1933, DJ and Florence borrowed a further £150 from Beor – perhaps to pay for Nancy's wedding in May – again with the house as collateral, and at the same rate of interest. As the house documents make clear, DJ and Florence repaid only the interest to Beor when making their regular repayments on both loans.

Biographers have already noted that DJ and Florence's financial circumstances were often difficult. Money and gifts from Florence's siblings, as well from DJ's brother Arthur, kept the family going during their "financial pickles", as Ferris has put it. It's said that DJ had to give Welsh lessons to bring in extra cash, and on at least one occasion there was a lodger in 5, Cwmdonkin Drive.[90] DJ's tastes were simple but expensive: beer, whiskey, good books and fashionable clothes. His colleague, John Morgan Williams, suggested to Colin Edwards that DJ's salary as senior English master was about £500 per annum, and his pension half that:

> I don't think he quite completed the forty years, but he wasn't far short I should say. Well, then, of course, he'd get ... less than half pay ... the cost of living was going up and, of course, your pension remained stationary ... and his pension would be ... just over two hundred and fifty pound a year ... it took you seventeen years to reach your maximum. From two hundred and forty to four hundred and eighty, it took seventeen years. Fifteen pound a year your increment was ... It was all right during the Twenties, with the Depression period. And then, as things began to get more expensive, these people like D.J. Thomas suffered great hardship, because their pensions remained as they were with the cost of living soaring.

If Morgan Williams is correct, then DJ would have reached the top of the scale by the 1920s, and his salary would have remained constant, apart perhaps from extra allowances, until his retirement. Morgan Williams also notes that DJ had been reluctant to take on the role of Senior Master, because its administrative duties brought no extra cash.

The £500 owed to Elizabeth Beor would have been a particular source of anxiety during the depressed years of the 1920s and 1930s, when the value of the house may have fallen. Since DJ and Florence were repaying only the interest each month, their ability to repay the capital would have largely depended on the house maintaining or increasing its value.[91] Certainly, the 1930s was a period of tension, anger and rows over money, as Nancy's letters (quoted in Ferris, 1999, pp.65-68) help to illustrate.

DJ retired from teaching in December 1936, and in March the following year, he and Florence moved to Bishopston, renting a smaller house which Dylan describes in his letter of March 29 1937 to Emily Holmes Coleman. The lack of space forced DJ to sell "sacks of unwanted books", as Ferris (p.147) has noted, but the sale brought in much-needed cash. They rented 5, Cwmdonkin Drive to schoolteacher Emlyn Davies.

The move to Bishopston probably reflected DJ's wish to live in the country, something that Dylan had written about in 1934 in a letter to Hansford Johnson of May 2. Some of the Edwards interviews refer to DJ's love of the countryside, and his colleague, John Morgan Williams, also talks about DJ's weekend image as a tweed-suited country gentleman. Bill Green said the same about DJ's year at South Leigh in Oxfordshire – "He looked more like an old country squire ... ."

But going to Bishopston also brought DJ and Florence a little financial relief: the rent from Emlyn Davies was probably about £4 to £5 a month, with Davies also paying the rates. The rent they paid out at Bishopston would have been a good deal less. Although they still had to pay Elizabeth Beor the interest on the money borrowed from her, the decision to go to Bishopston made economic sense.[92]

Emlyn Davies has hinted at the economic reasons for the move to Bishopston, when Colin Edwards interviewed him at 5, Cwmdonkin Drive:

> Dylan's father died a very poor man ... he had a house here, which he couldn't look after; his salary was too small, as a schoolmaster, and he was a poor man. It was the kind of poverty that the teaching profession experienced.

Dylan visited his parents at Bishopston in July 1939; they were, he told Henry Treece, "forced, by silliness and an almost hysterical greed for safety, to be so penny-cautious ... " The February 1941 bombing of Swansea compelled DJ and Florence to think of moving again, and Theodosia's death in April that year presented an opportunity of going to Blaencwm. But for these 'penny-cautious' people, the dispute with their landlady over manure and money (described in Note 92) was more important than the threat of German bombs, and they delayed the move for a month.

DJ and Florence probably left for 2, Blaencwm in June 1941. Florence had inherited a share of Theodosia's estate, and perhaps it was this money that helped repay the £500 they owed Elizabeth Beor, which they did on April 8 1943. A few weeks later, they sold 5, Cwmdonkin Drive to Jacob Plosker for £730. If they had bought the house in 1914 for £500, then they had made a profit of £230, minus the £150 they had borrowed from Beor in 1933 i.e. just £80. This, of course, was no profit at all, given the interest they had been paying Beor since 1914. Thereafter, DJ and Florence lived in rented accommodation.[93]

There have been many speculations about the causes of D.J. Thomas' bouts of ill-temper – his failure as a poet and his fate as a provincial schoolmaster are the most common – but to these we might add anxiety about money, and envy at the success of some of Florence's siblings. Any fall in the value of 5, Cwmdonkin Drive during the Depression would have been a particular source of worry, adding to the resentment he may have felt at having to borrow and accept gifts from the Williams family. Whilst DJ stood still, Florence's siblings, with one exception, made good either through hard work, marriage or acquiring property. It may have been especially galling for DJ that Bob, the coal trimmer, was able to retire so early to the countryside. Thomas Williams, too, was leading the life of a country gentleman, whilst Theodosia was comfortably off as a minister's wife, before retiring, with money in the bank, to Blaencwm. Retirement for DJ brought poverty; German bombs also brought evacuation to the real country-side of the "cows and clots" of Blaencwm, followed by exile to Oxfordshire, and then dependence in Laugharne, where Nancy and Gordon Summersby helped to pay the rent, and Billy Guts and Dai Thomas were taken in as lodgers.[94]

DJ died intestate, and his estate, valued at £165, went to Florence. In her Will, Florence made nine specific bequests identifying those who were to receive her personal possessions and items of furniture: her grandchildren Aeron, Llewelyn and Colm; her friends Mary Davies, Rachel Evans, Hettie and Kenneth Owen; her son-in-law Gordon Summersby; and her daughter-in-law Caitlin ("my fur coat and fur cape and my bed linen and table linen and chest of drawers in my upstairs bedroom, my Hoover and my carpet sweeper ... ")

As for money, Florence distributed £150 between Hettie Owen, Rachel Evans, Mary Davies and the sons of her executor, Alun Thomas, with anything remaining going to Aeron. Florence also directed that on the death of her brother Bob, 29, Delhi Street was to be sold and the proceeds given to Gordon Summersby. Value of estate: £891.

Part Three: Stories and Facts

Introduction

The following four chapters show, in their different ways, how it is possible to build upon fragments of material gathered by Colin and Brinley Edwards to provide a fuller account of a particular aspect of Dylan's life.

A note by Brinley that Llangynog church had a memorial tablet for the wife of Robert Ricketts Evans, the Fernhill hangman, was an important step forward in discovering more about this remarkable family. The tablet provided names and dates, so the hunt proceeded through birth and marriage certificates, solicitors' papers and love poems, leading eventually to an introduction to Ricketts Evans' great-grandson. Then later I discovered Ricketts Evans' diaries in the National Library of Wales, as well as those of his eloping daughter's solicitor. The full story is found in Chapter 5.

In Chapter 6, I have taken material about Blaencwm from Colin Edwards' interviews and placed it alongside information gleaned from archival sources and Dylan's letters – I hope this gives a better understanding of Dylan's time at Blaencwm, and the importance of Llanybri and Llansteffan.

Chapter 7 brings together data from a number of sources to demonstrate how deeply involved Dylan was in the theatre, as an actor, script writer and producer. The theatre was a major part of the teenage Dylan's life, a phase in his development that has been greatly underestimated.

A clue provided in the Bill Latham interview enabled me to search for two of the news stories that Dylan had written as cub reporter on the *South Wales Daily Post*. These are reproduced in Chapter 8.

5. The Fernhill Hangman and the Flower Mountains of Lancashire

Wales has lost one of the most eccentric of her sons, one around whose memory will ever hang a veil of weird, creepy sensationalism. (Robert Ricketts Anderson's obituary in the *Western Mail*, August 28 1901.)

Robert Ricketts Evans – who later changed his name to Anderson – lived at Fernhill before Annie and Jim Jones, and there are many stories that he had once been a hangman. Paul Ferris (1999, p.340) notes Dylan's knowledge of the hangman story, and its influence on some early poems. FitzGibbon (1965, p.29) suggests the hangman tales contributed to Dylan's sense of the macabre, and influenced his early stories, including those in *The Map of Love*.

The account that emerges from Brinley Edwards' notes and Colin Edwards' interview with Rees Davies is as follows. Fernhill was built by *Davies yr Halen* (Davies the Salt); his daughter (who is not named) inherited her father's wealth, and subsequently married Robert Ricketts Evans. When Mrs Ricketts Evans died, she left her estate to their daughter (also not named), who later fell in love with a man called Bloomer. Ricketts Evans objected to a marriage unless his daughter signed over the deeds of Fernhill to him. She refused, so he barred the windows of the house to stop her running away with her lover. But she managed to escape, married Bloomer and went to live in Liverpool.

FitzGibbon tells much the same story but provides no names; in his account, the daughter ran off with a "gentleman from Carmarthen". FitzGibbon also adds another detail from the local story – that on discovering that his daughter had fled, the hangman hanged himself in the house. FitzGibbon includes Dylan's elaboration that the hangman dispatched his victims not only in Carmarthen prison but also at Fernhill. Brinnin recalls Dylan's embellishment that the hangman killed himself not because his daughter had eloped but because he was "overcome with remorse for his long career as master of the gallows" (1965, p.198).

Ferris' account is broadly similar, based on research shared with him by the owner of Fernhill. Ferris does not give any names other than Robert Ricketts Evans; nor does he mention the suicide. In the story given to Ferris, Ricketts Evans was the assistant to the Carmarthen hangman. Ferris also provides one significant detail – that the daughter ran off with a German. This proved very useful to me in researching the story – when I had no success in tracing the name 'Bloomer', I wondered if it could be a Welsh-whispered version of a German name.

To be let
And Entered upon at Lady-day next
For a term of years or yearly

Fern Hill Mansion-house, (now in the occupation of Charles Morse, Esq., who is going to leave the Principality) delightfully and romantically situated within five minutes' walk of the good turnpike road leading from the well-supplied, cheap market, and post town of Carmarthen, to the picturesque and much admired sea-bathing village of Llanstephan, distant about four miles from the former, and three miles from the latter; consisting on the ground floor of a breakfast and dining room, kitchen, pantry, scullery, and large underground cellar. On the second floor, a drawing room, four bed rooms and closet.

Two-stalled stable, coach house, spacious yard, with a constant supply of water in it.

Hot-house, two excellent gardens well supplied with choice fruit trees.

About 15 Acres of well-cultivated and valuable meadow and pasture land, with a fine plantation and pleasant walks ornamented by a cascade thereto adjoining.

An out-kitchen, laundry, several additional bed rooms, and other offices will be forthwith erected, and annexed to the Mansion-house, should the incoming tenant require it.

For further particulars, apply (if by letter, post paid) to Capt. Davies of Myrtle Hill near Carmarthen; or to John Rees, Esq. of Water-street, Carmarthen.[95]

The Hangman's Diaries

Robert Ricketts Evans kept a daily diary, and those for the years 1853 to 1865 are held in the National Library of Wales.[96] They provide a fascinating account of the life of a gentleman farmer of the time. The diaries record Ricketts Evans' household expenditure, his mounting debts and his social activities. The early diaries also detail his building work on the property, as well as his planting programmes including, in March 1853, the firs that were later to cast so much shadow on the house.

The diaries describe Ricketts Evans' trips to London (for the theatre, tea parties, boxing and hangings) and Tenby (for the races); they also indicate the warmth of his feelings for his young daughter, Frances (or Fanny, as he called her), and the attention he gave her by way of letters, presents, money and visits when she went away to boarding school. The diaries are of particular interest because they cover the period leading up to Frances' departure from Fernhill in 1865.

Like Mother, Like Daughter: A Double Elopement

Robert Ricketts Evans was born on November 17, 1818 in Carmarthen. He was the son of Evan Evans, an attorney in the town, and Frances Ricketts Anderson, whose father was an officer in the Dragoons, and amongst whose forebears were colonial judges serving in India and Jamaica. This information is contained in a National Library of Wales (NLW) archive document, which also informs us that his mother died when Ricketts Evans was only five years old. Evan, his father, died eight years later in 1831.[97]

Ricketts Evans spent his early years at Glanrhydw Farm, Llangendeirne. It is sometimes said that he studied medicine at Guy's Hospital, though there is no evidence for this apart from the medical and anatomical knowledge he displayed in his writings on hanging. This, however, could have come from his attending surgical operations, as his diary noted: "At St. Bartholomew's Hospital saw several operations performed" (November 26 1853). Little else is known about Ricketts Evans' childhood and boyhood years, and the rest of his life, says his obituary, was "entwined in the doings of hangmen, prizefighters and gentleman of that ilk".

In 1841, Ricketts Evans married Maria Hodge Davies, who had been born on July 28 1824 at St Peter's, Carmarthen. The entry in the parish register for her birth notes that she was the "illegitimate daughter" of John Davies, Esquire, of Glogddu in the parish of Llangynog, and Frances Hodge, spinster, of Priory Street.

John Davies also owned Fernhill and other properties. He died in 1828, and in his Will he passed on all his personal and real-estate to Maria, placing it in trust for her, but also further entailing it to her

51. Robert Ricketts Evans in his trap, with driver.

children. After Davies' death, Maria was made a Ward in Chancery. The NLW archive document says that Maria was placed as a "ward under the guardianship of Captain Harding of Myrtle Hill and afterwards Captain John Davies."[98]

The guardianship was poorly exercised, as Ricketts Evans' obituary noted:

> He wooed clandestinely a Miss Maria Davies, a ward in Chancery, living with the late Captain Bankes-Davies of Myrtle Hill, near Carmarthen, whose descendants now live at Llwyndu, near Llanstephan. The courtship culminated in an elopement in the dead of night, a hurried flight, and a marriage known only to his own intimate friends. The wonder expressed at the time was that the then Lord Chancellor did not step in to exercise his official prerogative over his ward.

The 'hurried flight' took them to London, where they were married on August 30 1841 in St George's, Hanover Square. Maria had only just turned seventeen. The Lord Chancellor had not stepped in because Maria's guardian, John Davies, had given his consent – he was present at the wedding and witnessed the wedding certificate.

233

Sometime after the marriage, the couple returned to live at Fernhill where Ricketts Evans devoted himself, says the NLW document, to "pugilistics and dog-fights". In March 1843, Maria and Ricketts Evans entered into a postnuptial agreement, confirming the entailment of John Davies' property to any children Maria might have, i.e. Ricketts Evans would not inherit Davies' estate on Maria's death. The following year, Maria gave birth to a daughter, named Frances Maria, who was born, as her birth certificate shows, at Fernhill on August 5 1844.[99]

Just three years later, on November 22 1847, her mother Maria died "by disease of the heart", at 24, Brompton Square, London. Her remains are deposited in Holy Trinity Church, Brompton. Maria's probate grant of administration shows that she left a personal estate of "Goods Chattels and Credits" valued at three hundred pounds. Maria died intestate, so this money passed to Ricketts Evans, but her estate that had come from John Davies, including Fernhill, was already settled on her baby daughter, Frances.[100]

The NLW document notes that after Maria had died her friends made Frances "a Chancery ward". On July 29 1858, the Court of Chancery appointed Ricketts Evans "receiver of the rents and profits of the freehold estates of the said John Davies" until Frances reached the age of twenty-one.[101] For the next few years, Ricketts Evans was to be embroiled in a number of legal battles, or "Chancery suits" as he called them in his diaries, presumably because he was being challenged over the way he was using the rental income from the properties being held in trust for the young Frances. There were also problems over his tenancy at Fernhill, and on at least one occasion he was given notice to quit (1858 diary, March 14).

Ricketts Evans was an aggressive litigant, but after Maria's death he also sought comfort in other things, as his obituary tells us:

> There was now not a prize-fight in the Kingdom which Evans did not attend, nor an execution which took place in which he did not act as ... assistant.

In the 1851 census, Ricketts Evans, age 38, is described as a Widower and a Gentleman. With him at Fernhill are seven-year-old Frances, her Governess – a Miss Reynolds – and three servants. His life continued to be 'adventurous', as it was put by his obituary writer, who went on candidly to admit that the deceased must have been a man with a most pronounced penchant for the fair sex, and one of his proudest boasts, oft-expressed, was the long list of conquests he had made during his life amongst 'the Fancy' in the Metropolis.

But it was a local girl who took his fancy – on July 11 1854 he "saw Mary Ann for the first time." The diary entry for the next day reads "Mary Ann slept here this night." Mary Ann Gravel, the daughter of a farmer called Richard Gravel, stayed on as housekeeper, and within a year she gave birth to the first of three sons.[102]

By the summer of 1854 when Frances was ten years old, Ricketts Evans resolved that she would go away to school, and for the next few years she led an unsettled life. In July, his diary notes that Frances and Miss Reynolds went to Bristol and Chepstow, and stayed there until September. But perhaps Frances didn't like what she saw, because on October 24 Ricketts Evans noted "Fanny went to school this morning for the first time". The school was in Tenby, where Frances stayed for the next year.

In February 1856, Ricketts Evans decided that Frances would, after all, go to school at Chepstow, where he had relations and some property interests. Father and daughter left for that town on February 25. The following day he took her for a drive "to see the late Mrs Anderson's grave". That night, "Fanny slept at Miss Penn's for the first time", and started the next day at Ann Penn's Ladies School at Tidenham, Chepstow.

There seem eventually to have been difficulties with Miss Penn over the payment of fees and, in August 1859, Ricketts Evans and Frances travelled to Waterloo, just outside Liverpool, and "called to see Miss Richards respecting her school". They agreed terms of "£49 a year and £4 for accomplishments", and Frances started school on September 2. Nine months later, in May 1860, Ricketts Evans hurried to Liverpool to visit her. She was seriously ill, and he remained with her for most of the summer. She eventually recovered; it appears that Ricketts Evans blamed the school for Frances' ill health for, on August 16, they travelled to Southport where Frances started school in Birkdale, on the outskirts of the town.

Later that month, Ricketts Evans took the sixteen year old Frances to see Dr Henry Blumberg, who attended to her ears. Blumberg had been born in Hungary in 1829, the son of a professor of oriental languages. He was a well-qualified doctor, with two post-graduate

52. Henry Blumberg, about 1877

qualifications, including an M.D., but he was also a homoeopathist. Blumberg – "a tall sparely built man, with long black hair luminous eyes and sallow complexion" – was a poet, linguist (six modern languages), philosopher and a man of letters. He was also a man of some substance – the 1861 census tells us he lived at 8, Higher Bold Street, Southport, together with a cook, housemaid, and groom. A few years later, the staff found themselves looking after a very special guest when Frances arrived with him hotfoot from Carmarthen.[103]

For most of 1861, Frances alternated between Southport and Fernhill until in November Ricketts Evans went to Southport, settled his bill with Blumberg and took Frances down to London. He arranged insurance on her life, and went sightseeing with her, including a tour of Newgate prison. On December 18, they left London by train for Vienna and then went on to Pest in Hungary. We do not know the reasons for the trip, though diary entries note that a relation, Captain Roberts Anderson, was attached to the Hungarian royal household. Frances and her father had dinner with him in Pest.

There is no diary for 1862, and that for 1863, and the two following years, shows a remarkable change of handwriting. Frances took over writing the diary, but the content was read out to her by her father – it was still his diary.[104]

The 1863 diary tells us that Ricketts Evans and Frances arrived back in London from Hungary on January 9 1862. They did not return home and there is no clue as to where they went, though they could well have been in Llangollen where they appear to have owned a house. They were certainly at Llangollen in January 1863, and did not return to Fernhill until April, where Frances spent the rest of the year.

And Henry Blumberg? In 1862, he took up the post of "travelling physician to the Russian Prince Sangonski Csartoryski". He returned to Bournemouth for a year and "then went abroad again as physician to Lady Harriet Prosser".[105] He was also busy writing poetry which he published in 1864. The collection contains poems on political issues, including one condemning slavery in America. There are also many poems about his love for Frances, and the pain of being separated from her. As poetry, it has little value – English was Blumberg's third language, after German (his first), and Hungarian – but the poems do provide some clues to the development of their romance. In 'Madrigal', Blumberg tells us that "It is a year, nay, 'tis above, / Since I was near thee," a lament that he continues in another poem, 'Absence'. In 'Waltz', he chides her for being a dutiful daughter:

> Speak not to me of duty, Miss,
> Of parents, friends, or of your home;
> The duty which you owe, – it is
> To follow me where'er I roam.
> Did you not swear, in moonlit walk,
> To be my wife, to love but me?
> And now, Miss Clara, now you talk
> Of what to others you must be!

Blumberg also reproaches "stern duty" in 'Parting', and in 'To Mary' he hints that Ricketts Evans may have been wanting her to marry someone else: "Speak, Mary, can it be? It is not well! / I love thee! shall another call thee wife?"

I found no photograph of Frances Maria but that of her daughter, Rosalia, may provide some idea of what her mother looked like. Blumberg's poem, 'Fragment of Description', also tells us something about the young Frances – "In shape and figure she was slight and

53. Rosalia, daughter of Henry and Frances Blumberg

small". Her voice "was sweet, and womanish, and low", her "tongue was eloquent" and her speech the "plumage of a gorgeous bird". Blumberg gives a whole stanza to his lover's hair:

> I cannot tell the colour of her hair,
> It was not dark, nor was it very light;
> Most people, I dare say, would call it fair, -
> A word which ranges from a reddish bright
> To a bright red, – but it was tingéd right;
> With golden rings of summer setting sun
> It fell in massive locks, and curléd slight;
> That is, when all its fetters were undone,
> And she stood like Madonna, but without the son."

Blumberg appears to have returned to Britain sometime in late 1864 or early 1865, after attending to the health of Lady Prosser. As her father's diaries show, Frances was at Fernhill throughout 1864, as well as in the spring and early summer of 1865, passing her time walking and riding, usually with her younger brother Johnny.

August 5 1865 was Frances' twenty-first birthday, the day she would inherit the property that had been destined for her.[106] As usual, she went out riding, a piece of information given in her father's diary that confounds the story that she was locked up in Fernhill behind barred windows. Ricketts Evans celebrated with "some Hungarian wine as it was her birthday", a lovely irony on the very evening that Frances would flee with her Hungarian lover. All this was recorded in the diary, with Frances writing and her father dictating. Then Ricketts Evans' handwriting appears on the page. He writes that Frances has a severe cold and has "absented herself", presumably going upstairs to her room. She was, of course, preparing her flight from the house, as her father described in two further entries on the page: "This night Fanny unfortunately left us ... when Fanny wrote this diary I never expected this from one I so dearly loved."

But why did Frances depart so late from Fernhill – she had been at liberty to leave at any time that day, or during the previous days. There seems to be a clue in the back of Ricketts Evans' 1863 diary when he notes that Frances had been born at "10 minutes past nine at night". It's possible she wanted to leave only when she had fully reached the age of twenty-one, and perhaps her powerful sense of duty to her father compelled her to stay with him to the very last minutes of her minority, eating dinner together as normal, and even staying long enough to write up the diary with him.

What happened after her departure is described in the NLW archive document:

> ...she fled from Fern Hill to the Parade, Carmarthen, where she had refuge from the inevitable pursuit, at Mr and Mrs Thomas Rogers' house. By this exodus she avoided signing already prepared legal deeds transferring her property to her father. In a fortnight afterwards she left for the English town where she had last been educated, and married a spectacled German Homoeopathist Practitioner named Blaumberg.

There was hardly much of a pursuit – "great grief" overwhelmed Ricketts Evans and he was confined to bed for the next few days. He sent friends and neighbours to look for Frances, and some went as far afield as Tenby and Pembroke. On August 10, word was sent that Frances had been seen on the Parade, and Ricketts Evans records in his diary that he "sent Fanny some clothes & boots, also a bottle of Wine for Mrs Rogers and Fanny." Two days later a Dr Williams was sent "to see Fanny ... & was with her sometime but got no satisfaction from her".

It may seem strange that Frances stayed in Carmarthen for so long after leaving Fernhill but she needed time to take control of her business affairs. Her attorney, John Barker of Quay Street, was on holiday until August 15, as his diaries show. Frances must then have instructed him to look after her property and its rental income because the very next day she left Carmarthen "with some man". Her father did not hear about her departure for another three days.[107]

Frances and Henry Blumberg travelled to his home in North Meols, Southport, which is given as her place of residence on their marriage certificate. It was not until the beginning of September that Ricketts Evans learnt that she was there. He despatched a friend to speak with her but she refused to see him. Later in the month, Ricketts Evans met with John Barker, and then received a letter from Frances on October 10, "which letter was dictated by Barker". Its contents sent Ricketts Evans to bed where he stayed all day. Barker's diary for October 14 1865 shows that he, Barker, was already collecting rents on behalf of Frances.

On January 15 1866, Ricketts Evans left for Southport, but Frances refused to see him unless Barker was present. A meeting was arranged at the end of the month with Barker, Frances and Ricketts Evans, but "nothing settled". Ricketts Evans left Southport on February 12 to travel to Brecon prison, presumably for an execution. He complained bitterly that Frances had refused to see him since their meeting with Barker, though she had sent him money to cover his expenses in Southport.

Barker agreed to a further meeting in Carmarthen on May 10, having previously warned Ricketts Evans about paying the rent he owed Frances for Fernhill. Barker's diary notes that at the meeting Ricketts Evans' requests for money were refused. There was a discussion about the sale of a property in Kidwelly: would "Miss Evans allow her Father the disposition of the money?" Barker told him that Miss Evans "wants no penny herself but makes the condition that the proceeds go towards liquidation of her Father's debts". On May 26, Barker rubbed salt in the family wounds when he visited Fernhill to carry out a rent review.

Although Frances and Henry Blumberg had eloped, they did not rush into marriage. Perhaps they wanted a period of engagement – after all, they hardly knew each other. They had first met just a few days after her sixteenth birthday in August 1860 – and he was fifteen years older than her. The only time they had together to develop their relationship were the months in 1861 when Frances was attending school in Southport and, perhaps, during the mystery year of 1862 when we know little of her whereabouts.[108] She was at Fernhill for most of 1863, 1864 and the first half of 1865. This is an extraordinary story of a young girl's love surviving long periods of separation from her lover, a love defying time, as Henry noted in his poem 'To my Lute', written during their years of separation:

We walked upon the velvet lawn,
Amid the shade of oak and lime;
We watched the day's resplendent dawn;
We talked of love, defying time.
The roses guessed what was to come,
They blushed, but blushing still would peep,
And all the flowers woke from sleep.
Some laughed, some sighed, but there were some
Who knew the future...

Frances and Henry were married on September 13 1866 in the parish church at Chepstow – or, to put it more colourfully, Miss Fern Hill married Mr Flower Mountain. The certificate shows that the marriage was done by licence, the means for ensuring a quick and quiet wedding with the minimum of publicity. It appears, too, to have been a small affair. No family on either side are mentioned as witnesses, one of whom was a solicitor from Tidenham, and the other the daughter of the landlady of the lodging house where bride or groom, or perhaps both, stayed the night before the wedding.[109]

Frances and Henry had five children, only one of whom was in employment at the 1901 census. The others were living on their own means or being supported by their mother, even though one was thirty years old, and the other two were over twenty-five. It is curious that children whose parents and grandparents had fled their homes to marry their lovers, should themselves have remained, at the time of the 1901 census, unmarried, and ensconced at home with their widowed mother. All but one were to remain unmarried.[110]

Frances' coming of age, and her marriage, meant considerable change in Ricketts Evans' life. There are no diaries for the years after 1865 but we know from his obituary that his financial affairs began to worsen, partly because he no longer had access to Frances' rents. In May 1869 (and again in May 1874), he legally made over his furniture and other personal possessions at Fernhill to Mary Ann Gravel, as a way of protecting them from his creditors – "of whom he had many, as he would not, if he could help it, pay any one for goods, labour, which he had ordered". Sometime after 1872, Ricketts Evans adopted his mother's maiden name, and became Robert Ricketts Anderson. On October 18 1877, he married Mary Ann, aged 42, at a ceremony in Camberwell, London.[111]

During the first few years of his new marriage, Ricketts Anderson was involved in a protracted legal dispute. In December 1876, John Barker, acting on instructions from Henry and Frances Blumberg, had issued him with a notice to quit Fernhill. Over the next three years, father and daughter were engaged in High Court claims and counter-claims over the property, though Ricketts Evans' main concern was to gain £7,579 in compensation for the improvement works carried out whilst Frances was a minor.[112]

Ricketts Anderson died, aged eighty-three, on August 26 1901, some thirty-six years after his daughter had left Fernhill – he had not killed himself on discovering her elopement. Neither had he hanged himself – his death certificate records "Senile Decay. Enlarged Prostate. Exhaustion". He had wished to be cremated but he was buried, like his son William, at Llangynog church, as the parish registers confirm. This was done in accordance with the wishes of his daughter, who had travelled down from Southport to supervise the funeral arrangements. It was Frances' first return journey to Fernhill since she had eloped – "the news of the old gentleman's illness," says the obituary, "overcame all scruples."

Ricketts Anderson left a Will, but at probate the value of his effects was £105.4s – he died a poor man. Henry Blumberg had died on June 5 1893, with his effects valued at £13,406. His Will distributed his estate amongst his children, mostly to his eldest son, Henry, who also inherited his father's medical practice. Blumberg left his books, papers and paintings to various friends, as well as two shillings to every child in the Childrens' Sanatorium in Southport, to be given to them on the day of his funeral. He left nothing to Frances, save a life interest in the household furniture and plate, because she was "entitled to sufficient separate estate".

Frances Maria Blumberg died on October 24 1911, with effects of £8,927. She left Fernhill and her other Carmarthenshire properties in trust to her children Samuel, Gustav, Rosalia and Edith.[113]

Hangman or Not?

Ricketts Anderson's grandson, Fred Evans of Llansteffan, wrote to Brinley Edwards in 1966 to say "It was true that my grandfather was a well known character, known as Evans the Hangman of Fernhill, it's understood he took part in the executions in various prisons during his days ... " Rees Davies says in his interview with Colin Edwards that Evans was sacked from a post of assistant hangman because the prison chaplain complained "he didn't do his job civil ... he caught to his feet or his legs ... and hanged by them – to make sure he was dead! To have the weight!"

There is no evidence that Ricketts Evans/Anderson held the post of hangman or assistant hangman at Carmarthen prison or any other.[114] But we do know, from his obituary and writings, that for most of his life he took a great interest in capital punishment, and was a close friend of most of the executioners who worked in British prisons. He certainly attended many executions, though not, it seems, in any official capacity but rather as a friend of the executioners who valued his medical and technical advice on "the proper, expeditious fulfilment of capital punishment". For example, on May 11 1874, the Governor of Newgate prison invited Ricketts Anderson to participate in a hanging:

> The Sheriffs are very desirous that Calcraft should have some assistance at an execution fixed for the 25th Inst. and Calcraft named you as the person he wished to be with him, and unless I hear to the contrary I shall expect to see you here on Saturday 23rd Inst. by 10 a.m.[115]

Ricketts Anderson was a prolific letter writer, and was never slow to send his advice to executioners and Home Secretaries – one of these letters is at the end of this book. He often wrote to the newspapers, as he did to *The Times* on December 21 1875, when he says he has "attended nearly all the principal [executions] that have taken place in this kingdom" since the 1850s. He mentions, too, that he has "occasionally acted alone", sometimes in triple executions such as those at Liverpool and Gloucester. Ricketts Anderson goes on to protest that he had never sought any appointment as an executioner, that his interest in executions "was on purely humane grounds" and that "I am opposed to the infliction of the death penalty, and after the considerable experience I have had I claim the right to speak with some authority on the subject".

But his interest in executions went a little further than this; it had a 'creepy' side, a word much used by his obituary writer, who wrote:

> He was a privileged spectator at almost every public execution in

England and Wales, making special journeys to witness them, and amongst the curios which he had collected were the rope that hanged Butt, the young gentleman farmer who shot his sweetheart, as well as the scarf and pin which Butt wore on the morning of his execution; the 'traces' used at the execution of the notorious Mrs Cotton; and one of the gloves of Edward Oxford, the young man who attempted to assassinate the late Queen Victoria ...

Ricketts Anderson became a public figure, and was variously dubbed by the press as 'the Amateur', 'the Doctor', and 'the Medical Executioner'.

A Common Interest in the Bizarre

Rees Davies told Colin Edwards about the friendship between Ricketts Evans and Dr William Price of Llantrisant. It was the story of Price's attempt to cremate his son that inspired Dylan to write 'The Burning Baby'. Rees Davies describes a visit by Price to Fernhill:

> I saw him there one time ... we were going to school in the morning and we saw a brake with two pairs of horses and we knew him then as Jac yr Falcon. He was the driver, and Dr Price Llantrisant, he was standing on his feet and Evans, the two standing up in this, not a big brake, but two pairs of horses, and Jac yr Falcon driving up ... it was great for us to see something like that ... I think they were some party, Dr Price, I don't know whether Evans the hangman belonged to them ... it was a rumour that he [Evans] knew something about medicine and I don't know whether it's right or not.

There is more in Ricketts Anderson's obituary about his friendship with Dr Price; they were "bosom friends" and besides their advocacy of cremation, "many are the tales of the eccentricities they held in common". According to Nicholas (1940, p.44), it was Ricketts Anderson who set light to the pyre on which Price was publicly cremated on Llantrisant mountain.

An Ordinary Fellow for All That

Besides dog-fights, cock-fights, bull-baiting, bare-knuckle boxing and mock hangings, Ricketts Anderson enjoyed a number of harmless

54. Ricketts Anderson with Dr William Price, left, about 1891

pastimes. He was an inveterate practical joker, liked to watch men running, and challenged locals to cycle races – he rode on a penny farthing – and is said to have made a cycle track at Fernhill. He did have the reputation for being fierce and aggressive but Rees Davies noted

> ...he was very kind but some people thought of the hangman as a dangerous man, but we didn't think so as schoolchildren. We went larking about to see if we could see him, to take his attention. He was bringing us sweets, apples and anything, and he had a son ... and very often he wanted us to come into the garden and have a little play on the way home, and the little boy playing with us. He liked children, and children liked him, once they came to know about him.

To the poor, Ricketts Anderson was "most considerate and compassionate" – his diaries record regular donations "to Charity". Working men, his obituary also tells us, "hailed with pleasure a job at Fern Hill as the place always afforded so much amusement and plenty of good cheer". The obituary took up a good part of a page in the *Western Mail,* but the writer lamented that it was only a "cursory biographical sketch" of a man with a "remarkable love of the weird".

6. Life at Blaencwm

This chapter is largely about Dylan's time at Blaencwm, but it also provides an opportunity to see how important Llansteffan was to him. From early childhood, there was hardly a year of his life when he didn't visit the village, either on holiday, or when he was staying at Blaencwm, or crossing on the ferry from Laugharne.

For most of the 1920s, the Blaencwm cottages had various tenants, none of whom appear to have been relations. It is highly unlikely, therefore, that Dylan stayed at Blaencwm before early 1927, when his uncle Bob moved into number 1, followed a year later by Polly.

Dylan's childhood holidays at Fernhill came to an end when Jim and Annie Jones moved to Mount Pleasant. By the beginning of 1930, when Dylan was fifteen, Blaencwm had become his Carmarthenshire base, an escape from the rages of his father, where he and Nancy were looked after by Polly:

> When he [DJ] put his foot down, they went to stay with aunts ...
> they would disappear to stay with auntie Polly in Carmarthen. And
> return when all was well ... and, of course, Dylan used to disappear
> every holidays ... I don't know about the parents staying, but I think
> the uncles would come up and collect them, and take them down.
> I don't think Mr and Mrs Thomas went down there to stay very
> much ... auntie Polly was very kind, very good to them ... I always
> heard a lot about her.[116]

By 1933, Annie Jones' illness meant more family visits to Blaencwm, staying with Bob and Polly and walking up the lane to see Annie at Mount Pleasant – presumably the purpose of the visit by Florence and Nancy in January 1933.[117] Annie died on February 7; the burial on February 11 was, said the *Carmarthen Journal*, "large and representative", with three ministers officiating – two non-conformists and the vicar of Llangain. But Dylan does not appear to have been there: his name is not on the full and detailed list of family mourners in the *Carmarthen Journal*, or on that in *The Welshman*, of February 17. And if Dylan was accurate in his Notebook dating of 'After the funeral' to "Feb 10. '33", then he must have written the first version of the poem the day before the funeral.[118]

In Dylan's September 1933 letter to Hansford Johnson, Blaencwm was "a highly poetical cottage where I sometimes spend weekends". A month later he wrote to her again, this time revealing rather more jaundiced attitudes:

> I am staying, as you see, in a country cottage, eight miles from a town and a hundred miles from anyone to whom I can speak to on any subjects but the prospect of rain and the quickest way to snare rabbits. It is raining as I write, a thin, purposeless rain hiding the long miles of desolate fields and scattered farmhouses. I can smell the river, and hear the beastly little brook that goes gurgle-gurgle past this room.

By November, he was writing from Swansea, recalling "the despondency" of Blaencwm, and his three mile walk to Llansteffan to buy cigarettes. The road was "bounded by trees and farmers' boys pressed amorously upon the udders of their dairymaids ... . There was, of course, no cigarette machine in Llanstephan". Dylan's favourite Llansteffan pub was the Edwinsford, which was kept until 1937 by Thomas and Catherine Thomas, one of whom was related to Dylan's mother. Thomas and Catherine's daughter, Florence, was named after 'Auntie Florrie Swansea', as she was known in the family.[119]

Whatever Dylan's feelings about Blaencwm, he was there again in Whitsun 1934, and he and Glyn Jones (whose great-grandfather farmed Cwm Celyn, near Llanybri) walked from Llansteffan over Parc yr Arglwydd to the estuary and crossed to Laugharne. Dylan was back in November, complaining in a letter to Geoffrey Grigson that he was living on just carrots and onions.

Dylan continued to visit Blaencwm even after he had moved to London. He was planning to be there in early April 1935, with the intention of crossing the estuary with Glyn Jones to visit Richard Hughes. It seems that Dylan also took Pamela Hansford Johnson to see the Blaencwm relations – her diary notes that she was there on April 22, and thought David Rees an "old brute"; even so, she returned to the cottages – 'Ruritania' as she noted DJ called Blaencwm – with Florence Thomas at the end of August 1935.[120]

In January 1937, Dylan wrote to Emily Holmes Coleman from Blaencwm, telling her he 'often' stayed at the cottages. Hansford

55. An early postcard of Llansteffan

Johnson also returned to Blaencwm in 1937, though not with Dylan. Whilst he had written of the "beastly little brook", she, forty years on, remembered that

> It was idyllic: the purest and sweetest and floweriest countryside. Through the cottage garden ran a little stream edged with rushes and primroses ... a wayside bank so thick with violets and primroses that no green was visible. (1974)

Dylan and Caitlin married in July 1937, and they lived mainly in Hampshire and Laugharne. But they still found time for Blaencwm, and they spent Easter there in 1938.[121] Local man Rees Davies told Colin Edwards that "they were coming down there back and forth on their holidays and staying there much more than holidays, much longer than holidays ... before the War". His daughter, Mrs Gwyn Williams, also remembers Caitlin staying in Blaencwm on her own before the War, presumably 1939, the year that Llewelyn was born:

> Llewelyn in those days was in a carry cot, and very tiny ... Caitlin was living there for a while. When the baby was small, and I was in her company for a little while on occasions ... she was an extremely nice person, and she was very devoted to animals, and she was very taken with dogs and puppies and sows with a litter. She'd rave over them.

56. Pamela Hansford Johnson, left, with Polly, Florence, David Rees, Theodosia, and Bob at Blaencwm

In May 1939, Keidrych Rhys and Lynette Roberts "took the pastoral way to Laugharne. Down a narrow winding lane thick with blackberry bushes and budding wild roses, down past the Pentowyn fields" to the ferry Bell House at Black Scar point (Roberts, 1983). Dylan often made the journey the other way, pulled by the attractions of the Farmers' Arms in Llanybri. After leaving the ferry, the quick and pleasantest route from Pentowyn, in summer at least, was the footpath across the fields to Mwche farm, from where he would have continued along the country lane to Llanybri. If his business had been in Llansteffan, Dylan would have walked along the bottom road from Pentowyn, often calling with Edgeworth Williams at Llys Hendy. Williams, a gentleman farmer whose parents had farmed Cwrtmawr, Llanybri, was a good deal older than Dylan, and had been friendly with Florence and her siblings when they had holidayed in the area in their younger days. He was a well-read man, and on good terms with a number of 'literary people' who lived in, or visited, Llansteffan.[122]

There were also meetings in 1939 with Glyn Jones, who was spending the summer in Llansteffan, and visits by 'snailing' Aunt Polly to Sea View. Other visitors included Vera Phillips, Dylan's friend from early childhood, and her parents. They had, as Evelyn Milton describes, come across from Llansteffan, where Vera's father had been born and brought up.

Dylan and Caitlin were back in Llansteffan in October 1939 for the wedding of Keidrych Rhys and Lynette Roberts. They stayed the night before in Underhill, a guest house run by Tom and Annie Johns. Dylan, who was the best man, had borrowed a suit from Vernon Watkins for the occasion, but Ocky Owen reprimanded groom and best man for being poorly dressed, and sent them both off to buy buttonholes. After the wedding in the church, there were "some sandwiches and a drop in the Castle pub here", before the bride and groom left in the Post Office van to catch the honeymoon train at Carmarthen. Dylan and Caitlin were driven to Pentowyn to take the ferry back to Laugharne. They arrived safely home, though Dylan had lost a shoe floundering around in the mud waiting for the ferry.[123]

There were also visits across the estuary in 1940 – Rupert Shephard photographed one return trip, as Dylan was carried ashore by Booda the ferryman. The next year, DJ and Florence Thomas moved to 2, Blaencwm, after Theodosia's death. For the next couple of years, Dylan lived a nomadic existence as he travelled the country making wartime documentaries. Caitlin was based largely in Talsarn and Laugharne, where she was able to keep an eye on her parents-in-law. In July 1944, Dylan, Caitlin, Aeronwy and their dog moved in with DJ and Florence. The same month, Dylan wrote to Vernon Watkins that Llangain is "a mean place", where dogs piss on the back doors, unwanted babies are shoved up chimneys, and condoms are put in offertory boxes.

They were soon on their way to New Quay, but, after nine months, they were back in Blaencwm in July 1945, where they remained throughout the summer. Dylan wasn't slow to reveal his "fond loathing", as Ferris puts it, for the Llangain farms and his country cousins, writing to Oscar Williams in July 1945:

> Up the hill-lane behind this house too full of Thomases, a cottage row of the undeniably mad unpossessed peasantry of the inbred crooked county, my cousins, uncles, aunts, the woman with the gooseberry birthmark who lies with dogs, the farm labourer who told me that the stream that runs by his cottage side is Jordan water ... the woman who cries out 'Cancer!' as you pass her open door.

Indeed, Dylan had once told Hansford Johnson that "Wales is like cancer; it's something you don't like having but it can't be cut out."

57. A 1930s postcard of the countryside at Blaencwm, just out of shot on the right

Dylan was able to escape to London but Caitlin remained with his parents "in a hutch in a field ... with two neurotics & a baby and a dog, bound to Daddy-likes-his-dinner and eternal afternoon walks". Sometimes the country cousins would come to London: Emrys Morris of Llwyngwyn, Idris Jones and Robert Hobbs went there, and Dylan took them to 'the pictures' and on a round of pubs.[124]

But what was life really like in Blaencwm? We can get an idea of the living conditions, and the tensions they aggravated, from the Carmarthenshire *Rural Housing Inspection Report* (RHIR) of 1945. The report describes 1, Blaencwm as a 'fairly old' semi-detached cottage, comprising a kitchen and living room and, up the 'rather steep' stair-case, three bedrooms. The rooms were relatively small: the living room was only three yards by four, as was the largest bedroom. Cooking and lighting were by paraffin, and food was stored in safes outside, there being no internal larder. Water was carried in a pail from a spring at Dyffryn Tawel, the next cottage. The toilet was an earth closet in the garden. The RHIR notes that there was "extensive rising and penetrating dampness in all rooms".

As for number 2 next door, DJ and Florence had a monthly tenancy; according to the RHIR, they paid £18.4s rent per year to Idris Jones for what the report describes as a 'new' semi-detached 'house', tucked onto the end of number 1. It had probably been built in the early 1900s, if not before. It comprised only two rooms: a kitchen downstairs, and up above, a bedroom, both some four yards by four. There was no living room. Like next door, cooking and lighting were by paraffin, water came from the well, but the toilet was a more inferior pail closet outside.

What are we to make of the rent of £18.4s pa? We can see from the RHIR, which gives the annual rent for each tenanted property, that the going rate for a two-roomed house or cottage in the Llansteffan area was £4 to £6 a year. DJ and Florence could have rented a four bedroom house in Llansteffan for £12 a year. Either there was a gross typing error or DJ and Florence were being fleeced by their nephew.

It is not easy to work out the living arrangements at the cottages. Caitlin has written that "We had a tiny little room at the top of the house..." (1986). Since there was only one bedroom at number 2, DJ and Florence must have slept downstairs or next door in Bob and Polly's spare bedroom. Or perhaps Caitlin, Dylan and the children were sleeping in number 1. During the day, Polly and Bob's living room may have become their base. Perhaps it is this room that Dylan described in an October 1933 letter to Hansford Johnson:

> I am facing an uncomfortable fire, a row of china dogs and a bureau bearing the photograph of myself aged seven – thick-lipped, Fauntleroy-haired, wide-eyed, and empty as the bureau itself. There are a few books on the floor beside me – an anthology of poetry from Jonson to Dryden, the prose of Donne, a *Psychology of Insanity*. There are a few books in the case behind me – a Bible, *From Jest to Earnest*, a *History of Welsh Castles*.

It may also have been from this living room, or "parlour with a preserved sheepdog", as Dylan put it, that he wrote, "on a cardtable holding up a jamjar of cigarette-ends", to Oscar Williams in July 1945. The letter hints at the difficult living conditions in the "breeding-box" cottage. Llewelyn is outside in the "frog-filled" rain destroying one of Aeron's dolls. Inside

> I can hear, from far off, my Uncle Bob drinking tea and methylated spirits through eighty years of nicotine-brown fern. My father, opposite, is reading about Hannibal through a magnifying glass so small he can see only one word at a time. I could lie down and live with Hannibals. And my wife is washing an old opera.

No doubt the cramped conditions exacerbated DJ's irritability –

58. The Harries children of Pilroath farm, 1940. Ben, Arthur, Tomos (standing), Eluned, Henri, Mair.

"he's one bald nerve" wrote Dylan. DJ had no room of his own to escape to, as he used to have at Cwmdonkin Drive. As Ferris describes (1999, p.176), Polly the chatterbox got on his nerves. He was starved of intelligent conversation: "There's nothing here but cows and clots," he once said. Things were different for Florence – she had her many relations around Blaencwm and she already knew most of the farming families in the area. She was on close terms with Waunffort and Dyffryn Tawel, and with Sarah Harries at Pilroath farm, whose son Arthur was a student vet, and treated the Thomas dog when it was poorly.

In fine weather, Dylan and Caitlin escaped to the countryside, often walking across to Fernhill, and calling in with Rees Davies at Creigiau-bach farm for tea – a footpath runs from Brook Forge near Blaencwm across to the farm. There were also daily walks to Pilroath for milk, and for strolling across the marsh so that Caitlin could swim in the estuary. Caitlin, as several Edwards interviews describe, worked hard on bringing in the harvests at Llwyngwyn. In the evening, Dylan would walk or cycle to Llansteffan, which had three pubs – the Castle, the Union Hall and, of course, the Edwinsford Arms, which his letter to Oscar Williams in July 1945 described as "a sabbath-dark bar with a stag's head over the Gents and a stuffed salmon caught by Shem and a mildewed advertisement for pre-1914 tobacco ... "

Sidney Evans, talking with Colin Edwards, recalled Dylan's visits to the Edwinsford:

> Dylan used to come in the evenings, regular. And he'd call a pint, it was always a pint and a pint with a handle to it ... he used to be a man that didn't have a lot to say, but he listened to everything that was going on and occasionally would put a word in here and there ... it was only occasionally he dropped a yarn ... his mind was occupied. He'd be looking by here – I don't think he saw anybody but just, as if he was in a dream ... his wife spent a lot of her time here ... she used to come down pretty regular in the evening ... on her own. You didn't see them much together.

Harry Jones of the general stores remembers that Dylan liked to sit on the settle in the kitchen, not in the bar. He was, he told me, often summoned to come across to the Edwinsford to help put Dylan on the 9.25pm bus back to Blaencwm:

> I used to go in and say "Come on Dylan, the last bus is here." Then he'd start saying poetry in quotations, and then he'd bang his head on the settle and say to himself "In the morning, Dylan, in the morning." The grate there used to be full of his cigarette packets with his poetry on.

The Farmers' Arms in Llanybri also continued to be a favourite pub. It was run by Sarah Ann Evans, who told Colin Edwards:

> When he was living in Llangain ... they were there about half eleven o'clock in the morning with me ... but then he'd go for a walk and he'd come back that evening again, it may be nine o'clock on him now ... one or two drinks – not much ... no, no lunch. Only when he was bringing his wife, walking. They were having lunch then, bringing the basket like a gypsy. You could see they were gypsies – fair! I was ashamed to see them, having their food by there, sitting down like gypsies, and I was putting a cloth on the floor for them! Cloth on the floor, and eat their bread and cheese, and I think they had an onion with them once here!
>
> ...it was about three or four authors, they were coming very often to see Dylan ... Keidrych Rhys was with him sometimes in there ... he was coming to the house, sitting on a chair, sleeping. 'Mr Rhys, you want to sleep?' I used to tell him. 'No, I'm alright.' – and I was

59. Sarah Ann Evans,
photographed in the 1960s

getting tired, seeing him sleeping on the chair for two hours.

Brown ale was [Dylan's] drink, mostly ... oh, drink quietly. I never saw him – he was a nice man ... I liked Dylan ... oh, Dylan was a proper gentleman. He was real farmer in his way, you know, talking to you ... he used to like to have Llangain people there. Some of the boys from Llangain, and talking to those always.[125]

Illness dogged Dylan's parents through the post-war years. His mother was "very very ill" in the spring of 1946, about the time that her sister Polly died. Dylan stayed with them at Blaencwm for ten days in August, on his way back from Ireland. Florence was still unwell, and Dylan was despondent, writing to Donald Taylor that

I'm here for a week or so, and, in this tremendous quietness, feel lost, worried about the future, uncertain even of now. In London, it doesn't seem to matter, one lives from day to day. But here, the future's endless and my position in it unpleasant and precarious ... I've reached a dead spell in my hack freelancing, am broke, and depressed.

When Dylan was in Italy the following year, it was his father who was poorly, and Dylan seems to have wondered whether cold and damp Blaencwm was the cause, or at least an impediment to recovery: "It seems all wrong, us here in the great sun, on the Riviera, & Dad ill, who

60. The Farmers' Arms, Llanybri

would, I'm sure, feel so much better for a complete change of climate."

In early 1948, Florence was in hospital with a broken leg after falling down the stairs at Blaencwm, which three years earlier the RHIR had noted were unlit. Dylan travelled down to 'Misery Cottage', as he called it. Nancy was also there helping to look after her parents. Dylan wrote despairingly to Caitlin:

> Here it is snowbound, dead, dull, damned; there's hockey-voiced Nancy being jolly over pans and primuses in the kitchen, and my father trembling and moaning all over the place ... Oh, this Blaencwm room. Fire, pipe, whining, nerves, Sunday joint, wireless, no beer until one in the morning, death.

In April, DJ and Florence came to live in a cottage in South Leigh, Oxfordshire, close to Dylan's new home. Idris Jones moved into 2, Blaencwm, and uncle Bob continued to live in number 1 until 1960.

After moving to Laugharne in May 1949, Dylan and Caitlin kept up their visits to the Llansteffan area, as Emrys Morris of Llwyngwyn recalls in his interview – "they walked down from living in Laugharne for a long time, and then walking up on the riverside". Laugharne resident Jane Dark told Edwards that "they were very fond of the countryside. They did a lot of picnicking – ever such a lot of picnicking. They used to get in the boat across the river estuary and picnic on the other side." Dylan and Caitlin also came often to the Farmers' Arms at Llanybri, as Sarah Ann Evans remembers:

> He was coming very often to see me ... walking he was ... with a walking stick ... it's about four miles from Laugharne to St Clears and from Newchurch then to Llanybri, that's six miles ... him and his wife, walking always ...

In the summer, Caitlin would put the children on the ferry and send them across to Pentowyn, where they would be met and driven back to Pilroath – Llewelyn, and occasionally Aeron, would sometimes stay the whole summer holiday on the farm. When Florence and DJ went to live in Laugharne, it was Mair Harries of Pilroath who went across on the ferry to help them move into Pelican. In August 1949, Mair took Llewelyn out to Lundy Island to visit Nancy and Gordon Summersby.[126]

In September 1953, just two months before his death, Dylan went with John Malcolm Brinnin and Rollie McKenna on a tour around Llansteffan. They called at Capel Newydd, Llanybri:

> The sun was low in the sea now, and the music of the hymns from the evening service floated over the windless hill-top. This was the burial place of all of Dylan's maternal ancestors. When we left the car and walked toward the crowded gravestones, Dylan and his mother went ahead. Proceeding slowly on her canes, she paid respects to one grave after another, pointing out to Dylan names he had probably forgotten ... Mrs Thomas moved staunchly yet laboriously, her eyes wet as she now and then looked away from a grave into the yellowing distance, her words to Dylan merely informative, betraying little of what we could tell she was feeling. In the cool evening sun, each with his own thoughts, we stood in a glassy silence. (Brinnin, 1965, p201)

Dylan also took Brinnin and McKenna to Fernhill, Llwyngwyn and finally to uncle Bob at Blaencwm, though Brinnin thought he was called Tom, "a smiling old man in an unblocked felt hat that made him seem taller than he was by a whole foot ... " Although it was Dylan's last known visit to the family cottages, it was not quite his last visit to the Williams square mile – the day before he left for London to make his final journey to America, he and Florence took tea with the Rev. Hopkin Evans of Capel Newydd, Llanybri.[127]

61. Florence Thomas and Mary Davies at Blaencwm

Parlour Poems

Despite its privations, Blaencwm was a place where Dylan could write. Some Notebook poems were written at the cottages in September and October 1933 e.g. 'Before I knocked', 'Not forever shall the lord', 'Before we mothernaked fall', 'The sun burns the morning', 'My hero bares his nerves', 'In the beginning', and 'Here lie the beasts of man'. Many of these were in *18 Poems*. Perhaps others had been written in the time Dylan had spent here since 1927 – when Florence was clearing out cupboards at Blaencwm after his death, she found seven poems written by her young son, juvenilia, says Ferris, "fair copies in a childish hand".

Dylan worked on 'Vision and Prayer' and 'Poem in October' in August 1944 at Blaencwm, though both had been started much earlier. In August and September 1945 at the cottages, he revised 'Unluckily for a death', and completed 'Fern Hill', 'In my craft or sullen art', and the radio talk, 'Memories of Christmas'. He also worked on the proofs of *Deaths and Entrances*.

A Secure Sense of Place

In the many changes of address and other disruptions in Dylan's life, Blaencwm provided a fixed point from the spring of 1927, when he was twelve years old. The return of his uncles, aunts and parents to the cottages would have helped to confirm his ties to Fernhill and Pentrewyman, where he had spent his childhood holidays. All the significant family farms and cottages were within easy walking distance of Blaencwm, except Pentowyn on the estuary, though it was only four miles away.

Here, around Blaencwm, was a rich concentration of family history, memories and relations, which may have helped to provide Dylan with what Tremlett has called a "secure sense of place". Yet this particular place was rooted in the wider family experience: Florence had come here on holiday as a young girl and, after her marriage, she and DJ were frequent visitors to Carmarthenshire. There was also a flow of relatives and friends who came to visit in St. Thomas and Cwmdonkin Drive and, as Addie Elliott describes, contact with Carmarthenshire relations was also maintained through their visits to Swansea Market. It was to Carmarthenshire that the family retired, and it was the grave-yard at Llanybri that George and Anna Williams, and most of their children, chose for their final return journey.

7. Dylan on the Stage

Much of my time is taken up with rehearsals.
> Dylan to Trevor Hughes, 1932

I've been really busy – what with my damnable walks ... rehearsals for a play (I don't know why I keep on doing this), drawing the drawings for the play ...
> Dylan to Pamela Hansford Johnson, 1934

One of the most helpful aspects of Edwards' interviews, and of his own unpublished biography, is that they give an account of Dylan's involvement in amateur dramatics. They indicate just how deeply the teenage Dylan was involved with the theatre, as well as the skills he brought to the stage. This was to prove valuable experience in his later radio broadcasts and poetry readings.

The stage was a major part of Dylan's life from 1930 to 1934, primarily as an actor, but also as writer, producer, set painter and occasional theatre reporter for the *Evening Post*. The learning of lines, rehearsals and performances took up a large part of Dylan's time. In his interview, Thomas Taig describes the amount of work involved for the Little Theatre actors, both as a resident company and one that toured south Wales. Malcolm Graham notes that each play would take a month's rehearsal, several evenings each week. Taig also comments on weekend rehearsals. Most of the productions ran for several nights, often a week.

In this context, it is of interest that Dylan's most intense period of involvement in the theatre – 1933 – was also the time when he was working hardest at his poetry – he wrote some ninety-four poems between February 1933 and the beginning of May 1934.

The theatre was a Thomas family affair: Edwards' interview with Addie Elliott mentions Dylan's parents' outings to the Empire theatre; and Joyce Terrett notes his mother going to the Grand. Dylan's sister Nancy was very active in school productions and at the Little Theatre, and once considered a career on the stage. Dylan's talent as an actor is mentioned in several interviews; interviewees note not just DJ's readings of Shakespeare as an influence on the young Dylan, but also Florence's keen sense of the dramatic, her powerful voice and her skills as a storyteller. We should bear in mind, too, the possible influence of Dylan's elocution teacher, Gwen James, who had been trained in drama, as well as speech and elocution.

The following is a list of plays in which Dylan appeared. I have compiled it from Edwards' interviews and notes, the Little Theatre collection at the City of Swansea Archives, the D.R. Davies deposit at the National Library of Wales, a search of the *Western Mail*, the *Evening Post* and *Mumbles Press*, and the reviews documented in *Dylan Thomas in Print* by Ralph Maud (1970), which are denoted by an asterisk. The plays are listed by title, the part that Dylan took and the date of production, where known.

Mirador Dame School
Dylan's earliest known acting performance was in a Christmas play, when he was given the part of a colonel (Thompson, 1965).

Swansea Grammar School

1. *Abraham Lincoln*	Edward Stanton	May 1929 *
2. *Oliver Cromwell*	Oliver Cromwell	February 1930 *
3. *Strife*	Roberts	December 1930 *

In early 1931, Dylan wrote to Percy Smart and said he was producing two plays for the school, and acting in them. George Body gave Colin Edwards a detailed description of a play, for which Body was a stage hand, that the school put on at the Llewellyn Hall, in which Dylan had a "very small part" as a young sentry. This was the first occasion on which Body had seen Dylan act, and "a short while after" Dylan joined the YMCA Junior Players. Body could not recall the name of the play. Dylan, says Body, "was on about five minutes in the whole production, but the acting that that lad gave...it really used to grip me...every night I saw Dylan do that part, it brought a lump to my throat, the sheer sincerity of the acting ... "

Dylan helped to found a Reading Circle, as a branch of the school's Dramatic Society. Twenty-five pupils took part in a reading of Galsworthy's *Escape* in early 1931. Ross (n.d.) notes that Dylan also wrote two sketches – 'Desert Idyll' and 'Mussolini at Breakfast' – whilst at school.

YMCA Junior Players

According to the interview with Frances Morgan, Dylan first made contact with the YMCA Junior Players when he was fifteen – perhaps in the summer or early autumn of 1930. Hedley Auckland confirms that Dylan was still at school when he joined. The Junior Players gave Dylan another opportunity to meet girls, and also increased his contact with boys from outside the Grammar School, such as George Body who took part in *Man at Six*. Dylan acted in the following plays:

1.	*Man at Six*	Sir Joseph Pine	February 1931 *
2.	*Captain X*	Amos Rigg	April 1931 *
3.	*The Fourth Wall*	Edward Laverick	December 1931 *
4.	*The Monkey's Paw*	A Sailor	
5.	*Capgar/Capguard*	A Poet	

The information on Dylan's time with the Junior Players comes from Edwards' interviews with Hedley Auckland, Frances Matthews, Glynn Hopkins and George Body, and from Edwards' unpublished biography. Ross (n.d.) provides a quote on "the extraordinary strength of Dylan's acting" in *The Monkey's Paw*. The Auckland interview gives details of *Capgar*. The Edwards archive contains photocopies of the programmes of *Captain X*, a three-act comedy, and *The Man at Six*, a three-act thriller. The leader of the Junior Orchestra at both plays was Solly Plosker, the son of Jacob Plosker, who bought 5, Cwmdonkin Drive in 1943 – see Chapter 4. Solly was a pupil at Swansea Grammar at the same time as Dylan, and was taught by D.J. Thomas.

Dylan appeared in at least one other production for the YMCA Players about "two men in the world, and all the rest of the world were women" – the title is not known but George Body describes it in his interview. The Junior Players occasionally performed away from the YMCA e.g. the Matthews/Body interview notes a performance for the Hafod Brotherhood in Landore in which Dylan took part. Body also conjectures that Dylan may have appeared in a one-act play called *A Little Fowl Play*, performed at a garden party, but there is no confirmation.

In his interview with Edwards, Hedley Auckland notes that Dylan also wrote plays for the YMCA Players, including *Capgar*, and also appeared in comedy sketches. He mentions, too, that Dylan produced *The Fourth Wall*, as well as "shorter plays for our club nights." In his interview, Glynn Hopkins remembers the seventeen-year old Dylan as an "excellent producer" and "a very loveable sort of chap".

Swansea Dramatic Club

In his letter of July 1931 to Percy Smart, Dylan writes that he is "busily rehearsing" for two plays being produced by this Club:

1.	*Captain X*	Amos Rigg
2.	*Waterloo*	An elderly soldier

I have not been able to find confirmation of these productions.

The Little Theatre (Swansea Stage Society)

> I've been acting on and off – mostly off – both as an amateur and a vague professional since I was the size of your thumb ... My speciality is the playing of madmen, neurotics, nasty 'modern' young men and low comedians – quite straight acting.
>
> Dylan to Hansford Johnson, 1933

Thomas Taig describes in his interview how Dylan came to him with a script when he was still at grammar school. Both Eileen Llewellyn Jones and Colin Edwards had been independently told that Dylan's first performance for the Little Theatre was alongside his sister, who was playing Viola in *Twelfth Night*, when he was fourteen. The programme for the performance does not contain a cast list, and the review in the *Post* on January 8 1929 mentions only that Viola and Sebastian "were competent".

1.	*The Merchant of Venice*	A Messenger	November 1931
2.	*Hay Fever*	Simon Bliss	February 1932 *
3.	*The Witch*	Johannes	March 1932
4.	*Beaux Stratagem*	Count Bellair	April 1932 *
5.	*The Merry Wives of Windsor*	Host of the Garter	February 1933 *
6.	*Peter and Paul*	Peter	March 1933 *
7.	*Faith*	Faith Healer	July 1933
8.	*Upstream*	Henry Hooker	October 1933
9.	*Strange Orchestra*	Val	December 1933 *
10.	*The Way of the World*	Witwoud	January 1934 *
11.	*Martine*	Julien	February 1934 *
12.	*Richard II*	King's Groom	March 1934 *
13.	*Hay Fever*	Simon Bliss	April 1934 *

Wynford Vaughan Thomas told Fryer (1993, p.40) that Dylan had acted in *The Merchant of Venice* and "had the minuscule part of a messenger from Belmont." It was also performed in January 1932 in Trecynon, and in Ammanford in February. Vaughan Thomas played Lorenzo in all three performances, though we cannot be certain that Dylan was in the Trecynon and Ammanford productions – it was such a small part that anyone could have done it.[128]

Eileen Llewellyn Jones played alongside Dylan in *The Witch* and describes his performance in her interview with Edwards. The Mumbles Press review of *The Witch* lists Dylan as D.O. Thomas. *Faith*, a one-act play, is reviewed in the *Mumbles Press*, July 13 1933.[129] Dylan rehearsed *Martine* but did not take part in the performance.

There are two reports of Dylan in other plays: first, Ruby Graham told Colin Edwards that Dylan had appeared as Sir Toby Belch in *Twelfth Night*; Jeffrey Milton also told Edwards that he had heard of this performance. Eileen Llewellyn Jones could recall no such event, and no programme notes or reviews have been unearthed. Second, Joyce Terrett informed Edwards that Dylan "played this quite important part" in *The March of the Singer*, sometime after the performance of *Hay Fever* in 1932, but I have not been able to find confirmation.

Dylan's involvement with the Little Theatre went a good deal further than the week-long performances at its Mumbles base; it was also a touring company that took part in drama festivals and competitions, the prizes for which were essential in keeping the Little Theatre solvent. These "valleys productions" include:

Upstream	Pontypridd Drama Competition	October 9 1933
Upstream	Cwmdare Drama Festival	October 12 1933
Upstream	Llandeilo Drama Competition	October 30 1933
Upstream	Trecynon Drama Festival	November 1933
Upstream	Llandybie Drama Competition	November 22 1933
Upstream	Gwaun-cae-Gurwen Drama Comp.	November 27 1933
The Way of the World	Llandybie	January 25 1934
The Way of the World	Gorseinon	
The Way of the World	Pembrey Drama Festival	March 1934

The sources of information for these productions are given below. (DT) means that the review mentions Dylan.

The Pontypridd and Cwmdare performances of *Upstream* are reviewed in the *Evening Post* of October 10 (DT) and the *Western Mail*

October 13 1933 (DT) respectively. The other performances of *Upstream* were as follows: Llandeilo, *Evening Post* October 30 1933 (DT); Trecynon, *Evening Post* November 13 1933; Llandybie, *Western Mail* November 23 1933 (DT); Gwaun-cae-Gurwen, *Evening Post* November 28 1933 (DT). The Llandybie performance of *The Way of the World* is in the *Evening Post* of January 26 1934 (DT) and the Pembrey performance in the *Western Mail* of March 26 1934 – the adjudicator mentions the "astonishing artistry" of the production. The Pembrey, Gorseinon, Llandybie and Trecynon performances, and the prizes they won, are also described by Eileen Llewellyn Jones in her interview with Edwards, and by Ross (n.d.), who confirms the Gorseinon production and Dylan's part. Some of the valley productions e.g Gwaun-cae-Gurwen, are also referred to in Dylan's November and December 1933 letters to Hansford Johnson. He also told her that

> I've just started rehearsals for the *Way of the World*, a play to be carted around the Welsh valleys where they won't understand one bawdy word from the beginning to the end ... I'm playing Witwoud, the second consecutive effeminate part. Much more of this type of playing, and I shall be becoming decidedly girlish.

Dylan was not exaggerating; when they took *The Way of the World* to Llandybie

> none of the audience understood the play at all and the first few rows were occupied by young children sucking sweets and throwing the papers about and they decided they couldn't follow the play, so they just talked all through it. And the next few rows by courting couples, who were too absorbed in each other to listen to the play. Dylan was on the stage, I think, at the beginning, but he and somebody else shouted their way through it. (Eileen Llewellyn Jones)

The listing of the plays reveals how hard Dylan, and his fellow actors, worked on the Little Theatre productions – in the six months between October 1933 and March 1934 they learnt, rehearsed and put on five productions in the theatre at Mumbles, each running for several nights, and at least nine touring performances of *Upstream* and *The Way of the World*.

The Little Theatre was as much about friendship as performance:

265

Wynford Vaughan Thomas and Vera and Evelyn Phillips were also members, Fred Janes sometimes helped with painting the sets, and Tom Warner with the music. Kenneth Hancock became involved after his return from the Royal College of Art in 1933, and, in July 1934, the *Mumbles Press* reported that "the rising Mumbles artist is adorning the proscenium of the Little Theatre ... with panels of his own designing." The Little Theatre also had a range of social activities, including bridge evenings, informal parties, Saturday evening club nights and a Winter Social Season which, in 1933, opened with a dance, when The Blue Havanas Band "played some of the newest dance music".

FitzGibbon also suggests that Dylan may have occasionally worked as an extra at the Grand Theatre, and that, in the spring of 1934, he considered applying for a job with the Coventry Repertory Company – though FitzGibbon may just have taken this from Dylan's letter to Hansford Johnson of May 2 1934.

Laugharne

On November 30 1939, Dylan wrote to Vernon Watkins from Sea View that "I've been asked to do a one-act play here for something or other, & can't think of a play – I want Taig's advice." On December 18, Dylan produced, and also took part in, a one-act farce by Ernest Goodwin called *The Devil Among The Skins*. The other actors were Richard and Frances Hughes, and the local butcher, T.J. Davies. The farce was part of a 'Laugharne Entertainment' organised by Frances Hughes for the Red Cross. It is mentioned in the *Carmarthen Journal* of December 22 1939.

London

Thomas Taig (1968) refers to his plan to take over the Mercury theatre in London in August 1939 for a season of Welsh plays:

> Dylan was keen to join the company, provided that he did not have to act; his job was to compere the show and read poems – his own and others – between the plays.

The proposal is also described in Dylan's letters to W.T. Davies of July 5 1939, Thomas Taig of August 23 1939 and other letters in the days thereafter. The event did not happen because of the outbreak of war.

Dylan participated in dramatic productions on the radio, mostly in the 1945-53 period; most of these are listed by FitzGibbon (1965), and include the parts of Satan in *Paradise Lost*, Second Brother in *Comus*,

Aristophanes in *Enemy of Cant* and Private Dai Evans in *In Parenthesis*. Dylan also worked on the stage, including the following:

1.	*Desire Caught by the Tail*	February 1950
2.	*Island in the Moon*	Mr Obtuse Angle February 1950

Both these performances were on one programme, produced by Eric Capon, on February 16. The programme notes for *Desire Caught by the Tail* describe Dylan as the stage manager.

Dylan appeared in Humphrey Searle's adaptation of Edith Sitwell's *The Shadow of Cain* at the Palace Theatre, London, on November 16 1952, and again in the Royal Albert Hall on January 13 1953.

Llareggub
Dylan took part in the following readings of *Under Milk Wood*:

1. The Institute of Contemporary Arts, London, May 1952
2. The English Society, University College, Cardiff, March 10 1953
3. The Fogg Museum, Harvard University, Cambridge, Mass., May 3
4. The Poetry Center, New York, May 14
5. The Poetry Center, May 28
6. Summer Drama School, Porthcawl, August 5
7. Tenby and District Arts Club, October 2
8. The Poetry Center, New York, October 24
9. The Poetry Center, October 25 1953

Reading 1 of the unfinished play was done with Bill McAlpine and Harry Locke[130]; readings 2 and 3 were solo performances of the unfinished play; the Porthcawl and Tenby readings were solo performances; Dylan participated with a cast of actors for readings 4, 5, 8 and 9.

8. The Cub Reporter

Dylan started work for the *South Wales Daily Post*, later the *Evening Post*, in the early summer of 1931. His experiences there have been described in Part 1 by some of those who worked with him. Dylan's first piece for the paper was on July 15 1931 about the actress Nellie Wallace, and his last was on January 14 1933, an article called 'Genius and Madness Akin in World of Art'. He also wrote articles for the *Post*'s sister paper, *The Herald of Wales*, and these have been documented by Maud (1970). In his interview with Edwards, Hedley Auckland notes that it was part of Dylan's job "to go along to the theatre shows and the cinema shows and report on them, on a Monday night."

We still know virtually nothing about what Dylan wrote as a junior reporter covering the everyday news stories of Swansea, though we get a flavour of it in *Return Journey*. So Bill Latham's comment in his interview with Colin Edwards is particularly welcome:

> he [Dylan] began to be given assignments completely on his own ... it was at that time when Britain went off the Gold Standard and almost every day we ran a series of articles describing how people had been hoarding golden sovereigns or golden half-sovereigns in their homes, were digging them out and taking them to jewellery shops, and realising three or four times their face value, and I well remember that Dylan wrote some brilliant news stories describing some of the remarkable incidents which were then occurring in every jeweller's shop in Swansea.

Britain suspended the Gold Standard on September 20 1931. The decision was soon followed by a General Election and months of economic instability. It led to a panic in selling gold, and Swansea was no exception. The *Post*'s lead front page story on February 26 1932 started:

> A *Daily Post* representative who made enquiries in Swansea today found that the gold rush in the town has begun in earnest. From

268

the early hours of the morning until the shops close, jewellers are busy dealing with a steady flow of sovereigns, half-sovereigns and old gold. One prominent Swansea jeweller states his average purchases of sovereigns to be well over 1,600 a week ...

The piece then went on to describe what was happening across the country, and the effects on gold prices and the economy. It seems unlikely that Dylan wrote all of this himself, and he probably collaborated with a more experienced journalist. The next two articles, according to Latham, would have been Dylan's. The first appeared, again on the front page, on February 29:

The Swansea gold rush continues unabated. Friday and Saturday were record days for the Swansea jewellers, whose shops were full from morning til [*sic*] night.

One well-known local jeweller purchased over 1,000 sovereigns in two days, and a quantity of broken gold, which, at the end of Saturday night, filled six boot boxes to the brim.

A man brought the same firm of jewellers 15 £5 gold pieces on Saturday morning, and another man, later in the same day, brought well over 50 golden medallions to be sold. Some articles that find their way into the hands of the gold buyers are beautiful examples of the goldsmith's art.

One brooch purchased contained a lock of Madame Patti's hair, and another had inscribed across it: "From the Society for the Promotion of Speaking Welsh in Wales", and was dated 1802.

If the jewellers of Swansea could only keep some of the medallions and trinkets and brooches they purchased instead of sending them to London to be melted down, a museum of great interest could be founded in the town.

A reporter stayed in the jeweller's shop to-day for just over half an hour. During that time quite 50 sovereigns were handed over the counter.

Sovereigns are now fetching 26s. 8d, a penny decrease since Friday.

The story continued to run – another article appeared on the front page on March 7, and this time Dylan brought in a number of references to social conditions in Swansea:

Where all the gold comes from in Swansea is a mystery. The gold rush shows no signs of abating, although it has continued over a period of nearly four weeks.

In one week a firm of local jewellers has bought over 1,800 sovereigns and between 500 and 600 ounces of scrap gold.

The new week has opened in a manner which promises the busiest time of all since the rush started. In 15 minutes this morning one jeweller bought 50 sovereigns, mainly in twos and threes, and a pile of gold that filled a card-board box.

Curios continue to pour in. A Swansea dealer has bought a collection of old-fashioned ladies' lucky charms, including the tiniest gold fiddles, hearts, watering-cans, and rabbits.

A man who came to sell some sovereigns, told a jeweller that his sister had paid £450 in gold as deposit on a house just before the gold rush started. He was thinking of how much that gold would mean today.

One woman took what she thought were 16 half-sovereigns to be sold on Saturday. She was told, to her bewilderment, that they were sovereigns.

A woman was forced, in order to pay her rent, to sell a gold medal presented to her in memory of her husband who was killed in a colliery accident.

Another woman, in order to pay for the week's food, sold a golden bar, on which five hearts were engraved, one for each of her five children.

The price of the sovereign remains at 27s., but the price per ounce paid for scrap gold has gone down 2s. 6d. since Saturday.

In his interview, Bill Latham told Edwards of his intention to return to Swansea and to go through back copies of the *Post* to identify Dylan's news stories. If he did this, I have not been able to trace it.

Appendices

A letter from Robert Ricketts Anderson of Fern Hill to the Home Secretary, May 23 1876

To the Home Secretary,

Whitehall.

Sir,

I again trouble you upon this subject, which, it will be admitted, is difficult and delicate to deal with. The taking away individual life is, as the law now stands, a painful necessity, and one we may not at present wish to discuss. It is, I presume, granted the dreadful ordeal should be carried through with humanity; and justice (apart from the humane question) demands that nothing be done that can add to the pain of the operation, and certainly it will be conceded that justice and not vengeance is the object to be obtained. I suggest the appointment of an expert, possessing the required knowledge of surgery to carry out the sentence, and that his first object, and the object of all legislation in the matter, should be to eliminate all unnecessary suffering when earthly hope has passed. Most men meet death firmly and resignedly; few turn a deaf ear to the exhortation to repent when addressed by a kind and considerate man, whose religion is the religion of sincerity, and the condemned, invariably, admit the justice of the sentence, placing their hopes in one above. The doomed one should be addressed firmly, and, as far as can be, cheerfully assured that he will not be hurried into eternity without being allowed proper time and means to prepare himself, and he should be made to feel confident that no unnecessary punishment be inflicted upon him.

Stimulants may be carefully administered whenever need for them appears to exist. The calls of nature should be particularly attended to. This is too often forgotten or painfully neglected. The drop should not exceed eighteen (18) inches, to enable the rope to be properly adjusted as low as possible with the knot under the ear, and the body steadied by the executioner so as to prevent catching and twisting by a long fall. Few necks are thus dislocated. The drop should be on a dead level with the floor, and held firmly by concealed bolts worked by an upright lever, on which the executioner places one hand while he steadies the body with the other. Straps firm, but not pressing. A knowledge of surgery and experience in details will assist to adjust the apparatus according to the weight and height of the culprit. Palmer, who was a surgeon, adjusted his own rope. There are seldom denials of guilt at the very last, and even Müller made a sort of admission with the words last escaping him, which might have been completed had a short interval been allowed. Everything should be tested previously to the execution. Any misadventure or failure upsets the equilibrium, renders the operator nervous, and produces unnecessary pain. Some men do not appear to dread death, and will

272

even eat heartily to the very last. Some will have particular fancies, which in moderation may be permitted.

Spare diet is more conducive to a quick death. Formerly no consideration was given to these and other matters I might name, nor was bodily or mental ailments considered. The culprit was tied by ropes, and hurried off into eternity regardless of all feeling for his position. A sort of brutal ignorance of the proper appliances often added to the pain of the unfortunate condemned.

Some years ago a case occurred in Wales where the ring of a scaffold gave way, and the body fell upon the platform, the victim of this bungle vigorously asserting that he had been hanged and the law vindicated, but he was again forced to his doom. This is not the only case that has happened. A competent and duly authorized man should be appointed to preside and carry out the law at each execution, whose dictum should be absolute in all matters of detail. Twelve o'clock is a convenient time to carry out the sentence, at which time the Governor, Sheriff, Chaplain, Surgeon, Visiting Magistrates, Warders, &c., should attend as a satisfaction to the public, (now that executions are private,) that the law has been carried out. The body should be taken down as soon as life is extinct, which, in quick deaths, does not exceed a few seconds. Custom gives an hour before removing it, when an inquest is held. During this interval, I believe, a breakfast is provided, to which the officials are invited. Nothing can be more indecorous than bargaining for the *price* to be paid for the execution. A certain sum should be fixed, sufficient to insure the duty being properly performed by a *competent* and duly qualified authority. Disagreeable as this office may be, it should not be left to chance, lest the unfortunate being doomed to die such a death should suffer more than is absolutely necessary. In the event of there being more than one prisoner to be executed, each trap should be kept distinct. I may lastly observe that the deep drop is objectionable from many points of view, and the insertion of the ring in the neck end of the rope, must be an additional source of pain.

Believe me,

Your humble Servant,

Fern Hill,   R. R. ANDERSON.

Carmarthen,
23rd May, 1876.

P.S.—As I am now staying in town, I will avail myself of the opportunity of calling for your reply, with which I hope to be favored. Should you desire further information, I shall be at your service.

A List of Those Interviewed
by Colin Edwards

I have added keywords after each name as a rough guide to the content of each interview. Interviews that have keywords such as 'Llansteffan', 'Llangain' and 'Llanybri' indicate that the interview will contain information relating to Fernhill and other farms, and to Blaencwm.

Carmarthenshire (excluding Laugharne)
May Edwards Bowen – Fernhill and Pentrewyman
Bill Davies – Llansteffan
Mary Davies – Johnstown
Rees Davies – Fernhill
Watt Davies – Llangain, Fernhill and Pentrewyman
Wynford Davies – Carmarthen
Gwilym Ivor Evans – Llangain and Fernhill
Sarah Ann Evans – Llangain and Llanybri
Sidney Evans – Llansteffan
Doris and Randolph Fulleylove – Llansteffan, Llangain and family life
M.A. Jones – Llangain and Fernhill
E.J. Harding – Llangain and Fernhill
Annie Lewis – a relative of Florence
Emrys Morris – Llansteffan, 1950s
Ocky Owen – Llansteffan and Llangain
William Phillips – Fernhill and Pentrewyman
Gwilym Price – grammar school pupil and Fernhill
Tudor Price – Fernhill and Pentrewyman
M.A. Rogers – Llangain and Fernhill
A.E. Savage – at school with Dylan's father
D.J. Thomas – on D.J. Thomas' parents (interviewee is not Dylan's father)
Mrs Gwyn Williams – Llangain
Mary Ann Williams – cousin-in-law of Florence Thomas, Llangain
Tom Williams – Llangain and Fernhill

Swansea
Rev. Leon Atkin – politics, religion
Hedley Auckland – dame school, grammar school, YMCA Junior Players
Freda Strawbourne Bassett – *Evening Post*, the Bassett family and Swansea haunts
Gwyneth Bell – Paraclete, Newton
Gilbert Bennett – grammar school pupil, Swansea memories
George P. Body – YMCA Junior Players
Waldo Clarke – grammar school pupil, author
Ronald Cour – grammar school pupil, friend, sculptor
Gwen Bevan Courtney – teenage friend

W. Emlyn Davies – 5, Cwmdonkin Drive, Florence Thomas
Gwyneth Edwards – Jackie Bassett
Addie Elliot – Dylan's nurse
Dr Gwilym Evans – lodger at 5, Cwmdonkin Drive
Avril Fisher – Paraclete, Newton
Charles Fisher – grammar school pupil and *Evening Post*
William Francis – Superintendent, Swansea Police – Swansea haunts
Ruby and Malcolm Graham – Little Theatre
John Griffith – BBC
George Guy – grammar school pupil and D.J. Thomas at Bishopston
Guido Heller – grammar school pupil
Glynn Hopkins –YMCA Junior Players
Eric Hughes – Little Theatre
Esther James – Dylan's elocution lessons
Fred Janes – friend, painter, material on Dylan in London
Eileen Llewellyn Jones – Little Theatre
Bill Latham – *Evening Post* and Swansea haunts
Jack Latham –YMCA Junior Players
Eluned Leyshon – friend of the family, St. Thomas
Harry Leyshon – friend of Florence, St. Thomas
Thomas Alban Leyshon – friend
Frances Morgan Matthews –YMCA Junior Players
Charles McKelvie – grammar school pupil
Edward McInerney – grammar school pupil
Geoffrey Milton – husband of Sarah Evelyn
Sarah Evelyn Milton (née Phillips, sister of Vera Killick) – the young Dylan,
    Mewslade, the Little Theatre and Talsarn
John Cole Morgan – grammar school pupil
Benjamin J. Morse – Swansea acquaintance and translator
Trevor Ogbourne – *Evening Post*
Mably Owen – friend
R.T. Pelzer – Swansea haunts
Idwal Rees – grammar school pupil
Leslie Rees – grammar school pupil, Swansea haunts and people
Rose Walters Roberts – Little Theatre
Ethel Ross – Little Theatre, Swansea, and Laugharne
Dilys Rowe – Swansea and London
Percy Eynon Smart –dame school, grammar school, school magazine
Thomas Taig – Little Theatre
Joyce Terrett – Little Theatre
Ronald B. Thomas – grammar school pupil
Ronnie Thomas – *Evening Post*
R.M. Glyn Thomas – grammar school pupil and camping at Mewslade
Barbara Treacher (née Auckland) – grand-daughter of D.J. Thomas' first cousin –
    family reminiscing

Bert Trick– friend, political mentor (with Nell Trick on two tapes)
Tom Warner – friend, musician
Gwen Watkins – author and teacher, widow of Vernon Watkins
Vernon Watkins – friend, poet
Gillian Williams – Florence Thomas' midwife
J. Morgan Williams – grammar school teacher
John Morys Williams – grammar school teacher
Richard Bell Williams – landlord of the Mermaid, Mumbles
W.G. Willis – *Evening Post*
Ralph Wishart – friend, bookseller

Cardiganshire
Mrs Walker Darling – New Quay
John Patrick Evans – New Quay, landlord of the Black Lion
Edward Evans – Lampeter, landlord of the Castle Hotel
Griff Jenkins – New Quay
Olive Jones – New Quay

Oxfordshire
Lionel Drinkwater – South Leigh
Bill Green – South Leigh
E.A. Gunn – South Leigh
Harry and Joan Locke – South Leigh and London
Bill Mitchell – South Leigh
Mrs D.H. Murray – South Leigh
Enid Starkie – Oxford

Czechoslovakia
Ian Grossman, theatre director
Jirina Haukova, poet and translator
Jiri Mucha, poet
Josef Nezvadba, writer
Aloys Skoumal, diplomat
Zdenek Urbanek, writer
Viola Zinkova, actor

London
Gaston Berlemont – the French House
Philip Burton – BBC, friend
Lawrence Gilliam – BBC
Rayner Heppenstall – BBC, writer, friend
Trevor Hughes – friend, writer
John Laurie – actor
Robert Pocock – BBC, friend
Elizabeth Ruby Beaufoy Milton – friend, dancer

Ruthven Todd – poet, artist, friend
Sean Treacy – the Kings Arms

Laugharne
Sally Brace – home help for D.J. and Florence Thomas
Jane Dark – resident
Rachel Evans – D.J. Thomas' first cousin
Dr and Mrs David M. Hughes – family doctor
Frances Hughes – friend
Richard Hughes – friend, author
Nellie Keele Jenkins – district nurse
Mr and Mrs John Morgan – friends
Leslie Parsons – resident
Phil Richards and his daughter Romaine – Cross House Inn
Billy Williams – friend
Ebie and Ivy Williams – Brown's Hotel, Laugharne

Italy
Piero Bigongiari – poet, academic and translator of Dylan's work
Augusto Livi – writer
Mario Luzi – poet and Nobel Prize candidate
Eugenio Montale – poet, winner of the 1975 Nobel Prize for Literature

Iran
A.H.S. Raffari – British Petroleum
Olive Suratgar – University of Tehran

America
Ruth Witt Diamant – English lecturer
Rollie McKenna – photographer
Sheriff Bill Steele – Arizona
Oscar Williams – poet, unofficial agent

General
Aneirin Talfan Davies – BBC, friend
W.T. (Pennar) Davies – Principal, Swansea Congregational College
W.B. Edwards – Loughor Mill
Aeronwy Thomas Ellis – Dylan's daughter
Gwynfor Evans – Plaid Cymru, Dylan's conscientious objector status
Constantine FitzGibbon – friend, biographer
Glyn Jones – friend, author
Bridgit Marnier – Dylan's sister-in-law
John Ormond – friend, author
Jack G. Wallis – Mousehole, Cornwall

References

J. Ackerman (1998) *Welsh Dylan*, Seren

J. Bland (1984) *The Common Hangman*, Ian Henry Publishing

H. Blumberg (1864) *Poems: English and German*, Williams and Norgate

H. & G. Blumberg (1934) *Poetry and Prose*, Williams and Norgate

J. M. Brinnin (1965) *Dylan Thomas in America*, Arlington

D. Cleverdon (1969) *The Growth of Milk Wood*, Dent

E. J. T. Collins, ed. (2000) *The Agrarian History of England and Wales*, vol. vii 1850-1914, Cambridge University Press

A. Curnow (1982) 'Images of Dylan' in the *NZ Listener*, December 18

C. Davies (2002) 'A Nest of Singing Birds' in *The Carmarthenshire Antiquary*, 39

J.A. Davies (2000) *Dylan Thomas's Swansea, Gower and Laugharne*, University of Wales Press

C. Edwards (1968) *Dylan Remembered* (an unfinished biography, National Library of Wales)

J. Edwards (1999) 'Gwilym Marles: Dylan Thomas's Illustrious Forebear', *New Welsh Review*, Winter

O. M. Edwards (1905) *Gwilym Marles.*

G. E. E. (1934) 'Gwilym Marles 1834-1879: Centenary of a Notable Personality', *Carmarthen Journal*, April 27

P. Ferris (1993) *Caitlin: The Life of Caitlin Thomas*, Hutchinson

P. Ferris (1999) *Dylan Thomas*, Dent

P. Ferris, ed., (2000) *Dylan Thomas: The Collected Letters*, Dent

C. FitzGibbon (1965) *The Life of Dylan Thomas*, Little, Brown

J. Fryer (1993) *Dylan: The Nine Lives of Dylan Thomas*, Kyle Cathie

P. Hansford Johnson (1974) *Important to Me*, Macmillan

B. Hughes (1998) *The Cat's Whiskers*, Hughes

W. Johnson (1995) *Streets Apart*, Johnson

References

N. Martin (1986) *Gwilym Marles*, Gomer

R. Maud (1970) *Dylan Thomas in Print*, Dent

T. I. Nicholas (1940) *A Welsh Heretic: Dr William Price, Llantrisant*,
Foyle's Welsh Co.

A. Road (1963) 'Portrait of the poet as a young reporter' in the *South
Wales Evening Post*, November 8

L. Roberts (1983) 'Parts of an Autobiography', in *Poetry Wales*, 19.2.

E. Ross (1958) 'Dylan Thomas and the Amateur Theatre' in
The Swan, March

E. Ross (n.d.) *Dylan Thomas and the Amateur Theatre*,
Swansea Little Theatre

T. Taig (1968) 'Swansea Between the Wars', in *The Anglo-Welsh Review*,
Summer

C. Thomas with G. Tremlett (1986) *Caitlin: Life with Dylan Thomas*,
Secker and Warburg

D. M. Thomas (1995) *Under Milk Wood*, ed. Walford Davies and
Ralph Maud, Everyman

D. N. Thomas (2000) *Dylan Thomas: A Farm, Two Mansions and a
Bungalow*, Seren

D. N. Thomas (2001) 'Under Milk Wood's Birth-in-Exile' in *New Welsh
Review*, Spring

D. N. Thomas (2002) *The Dylan Thomas Trail*, Y Lolfa

D. N. Thomas (2002) 'Dylan's New Quay: More Bombay Potato than
Boiled Cabbage', in *New Welsh Review*, Summer

K. Thompson (1965) *Dylan Thomas in Swansea*, Ph.D,
University of Wales

G. Tremlett (1993) *Dylan Thomas: In the Mercy of his Means*, Constable

K. Trick (2002) 'Bert Trick – the Original Marx Brother', in *New Welsh
Review*, Autumn

J. Towns (1995) *Dylan Thomas: Word and Image*, Swansea

Acknowledgements

Mary Edwards did everything possible to facilitate the preparation of this publication, and in providing biographical material on Colin Edwards. I am grateful for Mrs Edwards' support, confidence and hard work throughout the project, and indebted to her for the flow of material from Colin Edwards' papers in California.

Michael Williams, Edwards' step-brother, also provided biographical material, and shared information about his mother, Doris Seys Pryce. Thanks, too, to Olwen Morse Edwards.

Many thanks to the National Library of Wales, including Rhidian Griffiths, Director of the Department of Public Affairs, and particularly staff in the National Screen and Sound Archive of Wales, including its Head, Iestyn Hughes, Dafydd Pritchard, Assistant Curator and Paul Johnson, former Assistant Curator. I am also grateful to Huw Owen, former Keeper of Pictures and Maps at the Library, Richard E. Huws, Head of Reader Services, and Dr Ceridwen Lloyd-Morgan, Head of the Manuscripts Unit. Thanks also to Brian Dafis, Mark Davey and Scott Wayby. I owe much to the help and encouragement of other National Library staff in the Reading Room, Manuscripts, Maps and Photographs, and especially Linda Davies and Sarah Humphreys in Photocopying. The National Library bore the cost of transferring the Edwards interviews to mini-discs, and of making the transcriptions; it also contributed a good deal more in staff time in the preparation of materials for this book.

Working on the Edwards archive has been very much a team effort. Joan Miller has been an excellent partner in preparing the transcriptions, and this book would not have been possible without her dedicated and painstaking work on Colin Edwards' interviews.

Thanks to Griff Jenkins of New Quay and California who first told me of the existence of the Edwards archive, and to Seren, particularly Mick Felton. The Arts Council of Wales and the Society of Authors provided grants that allowed me to work on the project, and I am grateful for their help.

Acknowledgements

I am indebted to a number of people who provided information and advice, particularly Paul Ferris, Jeff Towns and James A. Davies, who also generously contributed material from their files. And to Walford Davies, John Edwards, Victor Golightly, John Harris, Beryl Hughes, Richard Ireland, Maralyn and Derek John, Kevin Lane, Ralph Maud, Sol Plosker, Illtyd Protheroe, Alan Road, Kerith Trick, Peter Wihl and Robert Williams.

I am grateful to Eiluned Rees for introducing me to Llansteffan friends and neighbours, and for help on archival and photographic sources. Robert and Liz Evans were extremely generous in sharing their material on Robert Ricketts Evans. Thanks also to others in Llansteffan, including Michael Lowndes, Kusha Petts, Huw Johns, Haydn Evans, Mary Phillips, Mair Lewis, Harry Jones, James Owen, David Evans and Dorian Evans. Special thanks to Edna Dale-Jones for her help in finding a number of important documents in the Carmarthen Archives relating to Robert Ricketts Evans and Fernhill.

Richard E. Huws, Elwyn and Mair Thomas, Eleri Bearne, Gareth Evans, Betty Jones and Mary Tucker helped enthusiastically in putting together the Brechfa branches of Dylan's family tree, and I am very grateful for their assistance and hospitality.

I received valuable help from Susan Deacon in putting together the Llangain branch of the tree. I am especially grateful to Haulwen Morris of Llwyngwyn and Sara Morris of Maesgwyn, and with special thanks to Kimberley Morris for letting me into the secrets of Llwyngwyn cake making. Austin Davies of Plas Isaf, Llanybri, also provided helpful details on the children of Sarah and Evan Davies of Pen-y-coed; and Dora and Glenys Lewis provided information on the Llettyrneuadd family and their ancestors. Thanks to Margaret Barton and Doug Roberts of the Pontarddulais Paraffin Gang, and my godmother Muriel Grey Williams, who all helped with various queries about Cross Hands and Pontarddulais. My son, Dan Thomas, went truffling for me amongst records in London, Cardiff and the 1901 census website.

A number of people in Southport helped me to unearth material on Frances and Henry Blumberg, including Dave Gregson of the North Meols Family History Society, Gill Hamilton, Sandy Cribb, Christine Beard, Walter Johnson, Nicola Kenyon of the *Southport Visiter* (sic), and Andrew Farthing at the Southport Public Library who greatly facilitated my work in the Library on the Blumberg family.

I have happily spent a good deal of time in various archives and libraries. Many thanks to the excellent Carmarthenshire Archive Service, most especially Terry Wells, who was never short of good humour, patience and new leads, and did much to push forward my research. I am especially grateful to Sharon Richards, Superintendent Registrar at the Carmarthen Register Office, and her colleagues Gaynor Davies and Lorraine Eastwood, who have played an important part in assembling information on Dylan's family tree. Staff at the Swansea Register Office also helped in this task, and I am grateful for their flexible and prompt responses to my queries. Thanks, too, to Richard Elvin at the Family Records Centre in London and Kim Collis at the City of Swansea Archive, and staff at the Glamorgan Record Office, the Lancashire Record Office, the Monmouthshire Register Office, the Probate Registries in Carmarthen and York, and at Ceredigion Libraries.

I am indebted to John and Jean Jones for their continuing help, and for chicken-sitting when I went away to work on this book; and to my other neighbours in Ciliau Aeron through whose fields I daily tramp looking for inspiration, which I usually find, and mushrooms, which I seldom do: thanks to Glyn and Anne Davies of Tynbedw, and Rhiannon Jones of Maes y Felin.

Thanks to David Waterman and Sheila Lucas, and Annie and Paul Hewett, whose kindness allowed me to reflect on Dylan's Carmarthenshire roots from the olive groves of Provence.

And as always, Stevie Krayer, without whose love, advice and indexing this book would not have been completed.

Photographs and Maps

I am grateful to Robert Williams for his kind permission to use Oloff de Wet's 1951 sketch of Dylan for the cover of the book. Thanks to Jacky Piqué for the sketch maps of the family farms and family trees, and to the following for their photographs:

Colin Edwards Archive, NLW: Thomas and Anne Williams; George Williams; Florence's brothers and sisters; Idris Jones; the young Florence; Nancy Thomas; Annie Jones, Fernhill; Bert Trick's bungalow and the interviewees.
Carmarthenshire Cultural Services: Dylan as a young man.
Southport Public Library: the Blumberg photographs.
Jeff Towns/Dylan's Bookstore Collection: Dylan as a baby.
Pamela Hansford Johnson Estate: the Blaencwm relations.

Acknowledgements

Western Mail: William Price and Robert Ricketts Anderson.
The Evening Post: Hay Fever.
Mary Edwards: Colin Edwards
Paul Ferris: The Thomas family outside the Poplars.
Haulwen Morris: Thomas and Sarah Evans, Anne Williams, Thomas John and Mary Ann Williams.
Glyn Howells: Views of Llansteffan and the Thomas bus
Mair Lewis: The Pilroath siblings
Nancy Davies: The Farmers' Arms, Llanybri
Liz and Robert Evans: Robert Ricketts Evans in his carriage
Eleri Bearne: John and Margaret Evans and their children
James Owen: Ocky Owen
Richard E. Huws: John and Margaret Thomas and their children.
Susan Deacon: Dylan as a boy; Nancy and Dosie Harris; Theodosia Rees and Jane Harris

While every effort has been made to trace copyright holders of quoted text and photographs, this has in some cases proved impossible, but we will make appropriate acknowledgement in any reissue or reprint.

Notes

Introduction

1. *Evening Post* July 21 1972, radio script 'Dylan as a Youth', and Edwards' unpublished biography. Tilly Roberts (née Evans) ran the Post Office in Kingsbridge, Gorseinon.

2. Letter, May 29 1966. There is a detailed description of the Mill and its garden in the Edwards archive at the National Library of Wales (NLW).

3. Interview, NET, Colin Edwards archive, interviewer not known but could have been Edwards. Elsewhere, Hansford Johnson describes Florence's "delightful sense of the ridiculous." (1974).

4. Information provided by Carmarthen bank manager, J.P. Lewis, who was at the Model School with DJ – see Colin Edwards' Notebook A-M in the Edwards archive, National Library of Wales. Thompson (1965) has noted that DJ was secretary of the Musical Society in 1897-98 when he was a student at Aberystwyth.

5. Colin Edwards' notebook, 'Dylan's Drinking Spots', also mentions The Plough, Glanamman, the White Lion, Ferryside and the Cennen Arms, Trap, Llandeilo. (NLW)

6. Letter to Pamela Hansford Johnson, October 1933. A double-decker United Welsh bus went from Swansea to Pontarddulais via Fforestfach, Penllergaer and Pontlliw. A single decker went via Waunarlwydd, Gorseinon and Grovesend. All these villages had more than one pub, of course, and only Gorseinon and Pontarddulais had a cinema. The next town after Pontarddulais on the road to Carmarthen was Cross Hands, where Dylan had cousins – see Chapter 1. A Western Welsh single decker ran from Carmarthen to Llansteffan, stopping at the lane that led to Blaencwm. Besides the information on Pontarddulais provided by Hughes, we should note that DJ's niece, Minnie Greville Bowen, lived there in the late 1940s and early 1950s, as the *Register of Electors* shows, before moving to Weston Super Mare. Amongst the mourners at the funeral of Dylan's uncle, David Rees, was a Pontarddulais cousin called Mrs Williams. (*Carmarthen Journal*, March 3 1939.)

7. July 1926: 1st in the Mile under 15. July 1928: 1st in the Mile under 15. July 1929: 1st in the Quarter Mile under 15, and 1st in the Mile

under 15. December 1930: 2nd in the Cross Country, Senior. (As reported in the school magazine, taken from Maud, 1970.)

8.   Letter from Edwards to Ralph Maud, May 27 1966.

9.   The interview with Freda Strawbourne Bassett adds further details about the reporters' watering holes. Francis also tells us about the names of some of the characters in 'Return Journey', and other writings; 'Half Hook', for example, was the *nom de plume* of reporter Freddie Farr. The interview with Ralph Wishart provides a little detail on the Grand Hotel, and about 'Sod of a Day Doris', the barmaid in the cocktail lounge.

10. Sarah Ann Evans of the Farmers' Arms in Llanybri, who knew Dylan from his times in Llangain and Laugharne, told Edwards: "He talked about his mother, very often about his mother ... he would be saying 'I wouldn't be where I am now only because of my mother.'"

11. NFT interview, interviewer not known but could have been Edwards. Levy's comment recalls the Edwards interview with Joyce Terrett where she talks about Dylan's interest in a book she had called *Cleanliness and Godliness*, by Reginald Reynolds, "a very witty but very erudite history of sanitation ... "

12. Edwards subsequently made three more visits to Trick without FitzGibbon. He recorded some seven hours of conversation with Trick between April 1964 and December 1965.

13. Letter to Ralph Maud, November 14 1966, the Maud archive, National Library of Wales.

14. Letter, Edwards to Ralph Maud, February 3 1965, the Edwards archive, National Library of Wales. Interestingly, Aneirin Talfan Davies recalled FitzGibbon's interview with him: "I managed to save FitzGibbon from some mistakes. Yes, 'cavalier' is the word. He came rushing down to Cardiff, saw us for an hour or two over dinner + managed to get the facts wrong! – as one would expect." (Letter to Ralph Maud, October 2 1966, the Maud archive, National Library of Wales)

15. It's of interest here that much of FitzGibbon's account of Dylan's time at the *Evening Post* is taken unattributed and unacknowledged from Road (1963). Nor does FitzGibbon acknowledge that the account he reproduces of Dylan learning shorthand from F.V. Jeffrey was first published by Jeffrey in the *Evening Post* of November 19 1963.

16. Letter to David Thomas, December 27 2001

Part One:
The Memories 1914-1930

17. Gillian Williams told Edwards the time of birth was early morning. After consulting his mother, Dylan told Rayner Heppenstall that "I was born about 11p.m." (Letter, November 27 1939).

18. In her discussions with Edwards, Florence says: "We used to read to him. But really he taught himself to read. He used to buy *Rainbow* and *Puck* and the other children's papers and, as I couldn't read to him all the time, he eventually got to read himself." At about four years old, says Florence, DJ started reading Shakespeare to Dylan. (*Image of the Early Dylan Thomas*, by Colin Edwards, the Colin Edwards archive, National Library of Wales.)

19. Gwen James (1888-1960) was an Associate of the Royal Academy of Music and a Licentiate of the Royal Academy of Music (drama and elocution). She also gained a Diploma at Elsie Fogarty's Central School of Speech Training and Dramatic Art (and a First Class Certificate in Drama.) At the Royal Academy, she was awarded the Albert Hunt Shakespearean Price and the Charlotte Walters Prize, and won silver and bronze medals in drama and elocution. From her home in 23, Bryn-y-Mor Crescent, Swansea, she offered training in 'Dramatic Art, Elocution, Voice Production, and Speech Defects'.

20. Owen ran a barber's shop, the Llansteffan Shaving Saloon, that was also a general store. "It was the Parliament of the village...with incredibly good talk ... if John went there at lunch time for a haircut, I would have to go along and drag him out." (Kusha Petts, conversation with David Thomas.)

21. Tudor was the son of Mr and Mrs Tom Price, and the maternal grandson of Thomas and Elizabeth Williams, who ran the Factory.

22. Besides Smyrna and the church, there was a post office, elementary school, blacksmith and *Siop Newydd* with its Refreshment Rooms (*Kelly's Directories of South Wales*).

23. Rev. James John, minister from 1908 to 1930. Succeeded by the Rev. Hopkin Evans in 1933 until 1972.

24. At the 1921 census, 14% (33 people) of Llangain parish spoke only Welsh. 84% spoke Welsh and English.

25. The family daily paper seems to have been *The Daily Telegraph*. See Dylan's letters to Hansford Johnson, May 2 1934, and to Oswell Blakeston, January 27 1937; and other references.

26. In his interview with Edwards, Bert Trick says of Dylan's visits to the cinema: "Eynon's got this shop in the Uplands Square, and Dylan and his contemporaries, they used to go into Eynon's and they could buy what they called a "tuppenny bag of stales"...and if the picture wasn't

to their liking they used to pelt the pianist."

27. Dylan refers to having a beard ("a curly ginger growth, neatly irregular, sweetly disorderly.") in a letter to Bert Trick from Ireland summer, 1935.

28. In his unpublished biography, Edwards writes *Capgar* as 'Cap Guard'.

The Memories 1931-1934

29. One of Colin Edwards' notebooks has the following entry under the Singleton Hotel: "Dylan fond of a Jewish barmaid called Gwen there."

30. An actor and friend of Dylan's. See his letters in 1948 to him.

31. A teacher and sister-in-law of Fred Janes.

32. Alban Leyshon paints a different picture in his interview.

33. Professor Benjamin Farrington was a Classics professor in Swansea.

34. Fisher's *nom de plume* was 'Blue Dun'.

35. A school teacher, WEA tutor and illustrator of Dylan's poems. He first met Dylan in 1931, and, when Dylan's parents moved to Bishopston, he lived in 5, Cwmdonkin Drive from 1937/38 to 1973, first renting the house and then later buying it.

36. Possibly the Heather referred to in Dylan's letter of December 1935 to Hansford Johnson – *Collected Letters*, p.233.

37. In a note in the Edwards archive, Trick also mentions Meurig Thomas and Leslie Lewis. Trick's grocery shop was at 69, Glanbrydan Avenue. He had previously lived at no. 44, whilst working for the Inland Revenue. Kerith Trick (2002) has written about his father and Dylan.

38. A clear example of this device is "once below a time" in 'Fern Hill', and also the 1939 poem of that name.

39. Dylan describes the meeting in his October 1934 letter to Hansford Johnson. Kerith told me that he later met Leslie Lewis who confirmed that there was little, if any, exaggeration in the accounts of the meeting. Dylan refers to the meeting in his February 1935 letter to Trick.

40. The letter is in *Collected Letters*, sent about July 3 1934. The rally at the Plaza was on July 1. On May 14, W.T. Mainwaring Hughes, vice-chairman of Swansea Conservatives, had resigned to join the British Union of Fascists. The Union's new office in Swansea was opened on May 18 at 10, Walter Road. On May 21, Louis Armstrong and his Harlem Hot Rhythm Band opened for a week at the Empire – "one of the most overwhelming turns Swansea Empire patrons have seen." (*Evening Post* reports, May 1934).

41. Clarke was at Swansea Grammar School from 1918 to 1925, and lived at 3, Cwmdonkin Drive. He was a teacher in London for most of his life, and worked for seven years for the Egyptian Education Service. He wrote westerns and thrillers.

Part Two

Chapter 1: Dylan's Family Tree

42. The best collection of *Registers of Electors* for Llansteffan and Llangain is in the Carmarthenshire Archives, but there are large gaps at particularly relevant periods – from 1887 to 1904, and 1907 to 1917. Funeral notices are a useful way of identifying family members. They are also helpful in identifying neighbours in a period for which there are no *Registers of Electors* available.

43. George's birth certificate gives his parents' names, and a birth date of August 16 1838. The Llwyngwyn family bible gives a birth date of August 16 1840. In the 1851 census, George, age 12, is at 'Alltyknap', Llanllwch, with his parents, and his brother John, aged 7, who died in 1895 and is buried in Capel Newydd, Llanybri, with other Williamses. The 1871 and 1881 census returns for George at 29 Dehli Street, Swansea, give his birthplace as Alltycnap and Llanllwch respectively. George and Anna's marriage certificate gives the name of George's father as George Williams. I labour this point because Brinley Edwards' notes say that George's parents were Benjamin and Elizabeth Williams of Morfa bach, and that he was born on December 23 1839, and I have obtained a certificate of such a birth. I believe this was another George Williams. (I am grateful to Susan Deacon for drawing this to my attention.)

44. John (1784-1846) and Anna (1774-1860) Williams of Pen-y-coed farm, who married at Llangynog on November 7 1814, were Dylan's great-great-grandparents. Anna had previously been married to William Williams, and they had two children: Mary (1809- *circa* 1860) who married Thomas Williams, the minister at Ebenezer chapel, Llangynog; and Daniel (1812-1898) who farmed at Waunffort, and whose descendent, Robert Williams, married Anne, grand-daughter of Waunfwlchan (Doris Fulleylove's mother). Besides Thomas who went on to farm Waunfwlchan, John and Anna had a daughter, Sarah (1818*b*-1882). Sarah had an illegitimate child by Theophilus Daniel – Jane (1842-1932), who married John Harries, and they farmed at Mydrim until his death in 1894. Jane and her three sons then moved to The Sherrifs, Lyonshall, Herefordshire and Dishley Court, Ivington, Leominster, but remained in touch with the family, particularly Nancy Thomas and Theodosia Rees. On November 18 1851, Sarah married William Thomas (1824-1886) of Plas Isaf, Llangynog. They had two daughters – Anne who married her cousin Evan Williams of Llwyngwyn; and Hannah (1855-1922) who married Joseph Thomas. Hannah and Joseph, who had four sons, farmed Pen-y-coed from

about 1886 and then in the 1890s moved to Pantyrhuad, Eglwys-Cummin (SN235.118), some five miles west of Laugharne, and they are buried at Capel Newydd, Llanybri. (Thanks to Susan Deacon for this information, which she took from the Pen-y-coed family bible.)

45. No father's details are given on Thomas' birth certificate. George finally did the decent thing and married Anna in the autumn of 1860. George, Anna and Thomas were still at Waunfwlchan at the 1861 census.

46. The 1891 census confirms that Richard Jones and his second wife, Margaret, lived at Pentrewyman with eleven children. Richard married, first, Rachel, and had James (Jim), Ann, Rachel (b.1874*b*) and Richard (b.1872*b*, d. September 1901*g*). He married, second, Margaret (b.1842, d.1911*g*), and had David (b.1878*b*, d.1943*g*), Mary (b.1879*b*), John (b.1881*b*), Margaret, Elizabeth (b.1884*b*, d. December 1937*g*), Jane (d. November 1914*g*) and Sarah. The author, John Llewellyn Jones, was a grandson of Pentrewyman.

47. She is buried alongside David George, her brother; John Williams, d. November 1 1895*g*, her paternal uncle; and "Anna Williams – Swansea", d. April 24 1892*g*, who may have been John Williams' wife, or Polly's paternal aunt.

48. The family Bible incorrectly gives David George's birth date as 1877. The birth date of 1875 provided by both the census and his death certificate is also wrong. David's death certificate notes that the person who registered his death was an uncle, W. Lewis of 2, Victors Terrace, St. Thomas. Presumably this was David's second uncle, i.e. the brother of his maternal grandmother, Elizabeth.

49. Amy's age is given as four on the 1851 census. She is shown as a publican's widow on the 1881 census return. Brinley notes her marriage to David Jones, and the 1881 census return describes Amy's five year old son as 'William Jones'. David and Amy seem to have lived at Alpha House, Ferryside. The 1901 census return gives the names and ages of Elizabeth, Mary, Sarah and David. Tom and William come from a letter from Alun Thomas (see next note).

50. This information about Mary, and about her sister Theodosia, was provided by Theodosia's grandson, Alun Thomas, a Carmarthen solicitor, who wrote to Brinley Edwards in August and September 1967 – the letters are in the Edwards archive. Mary is shown in the 1861 and 1871 census returns for Waunfwlchan. By the 1881 census, she is shown living with her husband Gwilym Rees at Cyganfach, Llandyfaelog, with Elinor, William and Thomas. But in the graveyard at Capel Newydd, Llanybri, there is a grave for 'Mary Williams of

Waunfwlchan', who died June 25 1890, aged 38. These birth and death dates are virtually the same as those of the Mary who married Gwilym Rees. Those wishing to pursue this branch need to resolve this puzzle about Mary Williams. From the 1901 census, it appears that Gwilym Rees re-married, and had four more children. (I am grateful to Susan Deacon for the birth dates of Amy's, Mary's and Theodosia's children.)

51. Robert's death is noted on a fragment of gravestone to the left of the path that runs from the gate at Capel Newydd, Llanybri, to the chapel door. The fragment also lists the death of his mother, Anne, and brother, John.

52. In her interview with Colin Edwards, Anne's daughter, Doris Fulleylove, said: "Dylan was my cousin, mother and Dylan's mother Auntie Florrie being sisters". Off tape she told Edwards that George Williams, Florence's father, was also the father of her mother Anne. This untaped information about George Williams is in Edwards' Notebook 'Dylan's Relations A-S', in the Edwards archive, National Library of Wales. Anne's birth certificate does not name the father. Since Doris, who lived at 5, Cwmdonkin Drive for most of the 1920s, knew the full story then it is highly likely that Dylan did as well.

53. William's siblings were David b. July 1 1802*c*; Ann, b. December 7 1806; John, b. May 1 1809; Thomas b. August 12 1814*c* and Benjamin b. February 25 1820*c*. Brinley's notes contain no information on David and Hannah Thomas and their six children. I have taken the data from the International Genealogical Index, which confirms Gelli Grîn as the place of birth of all six children. Various census returns also give the birth years of three of the children, though they are a year out. Gelli Grîn is at SN 517.318, Landranger 146. After the death of his parents, the eldest son David Thomas and his wife Margaret ran Gelli Grîn, and were there at the time of the 1861 census. The 1851 census says Gelli Grîn was 40 acres.

54. I have taken Evan and Anne's birth dates from their marriage certificate, which describes Evan as a miner, his father as a farmer, and William Lewis as a gardener. Evan and Anne were married in St. David's Parish Church, Carmarthen. Brinley notes that the inscription on Evan and Anne's gravestone at Llanllwch was composed by Evan.

55. The names of Jane Ann's daughters came from Brinley's research, and I have taken the data on residence from *Registers of Electors*. The 1901 census tells us that William and Jane Greville and their children spoke Welsh and English. All of Jane Ann's daughters survived Dylan. Brinley provides the Weston Super Mare address and made contact with the sisters there. The information on Evan and Anne's three

children who died in infancy came from Evan and Anne's gravestone at Llanllwch.

56. Dylan's letter to his parents of January 12 1947 refers to DJ and Arthur travelling to London to see "about poor Will." This may indicate that Will was dead or dying at that date.

57. Evan and Anne may have had another son, Thomas, whom Ferris mentions in a caption to a photograph (1999, p.136ff). There is no Thomas shown in the 1881 and 1891 census returns for Evan and Anne's family, nor is a Thomas mentioned by Kent Thompson and Brinley Edwards. He may have been born much earlier, or there may have been an error in captioning. Brinley's letter of January 4 1967 to Colin Edwards refers to one of DJ's brothers as a 'mystery man', about whom DJ's Weston Super Mare nieces were reluctant to talk. Could this have been Thomas? The information on Arthur's jobs is in Colin Edwards' Notebook A-T in the Edwards archive, National Library of Wales.

58. I am grateful to Martin (1986) and to John Edwards for this information. After Marles' death, Mary Williams opened her own school for young ladies in Carmarthen. She was also Secretary of the British Women's Liberal Association, and was an "eloquent speaker". (Funeral notice, *Carmarthen Journal*, June 19 1903.)

59. Brinley missed Hannah and Simon. I am grateful to Hannah's great-grandchildren, Tom Elwyn Thomas, Eleri Bearne (née Evans), Gareth Evans, Betty Jones (Elizabeth Esther Thomas) and Mary Tucker (née Thomas) for providing information after I had placed a letter in the *Carmarthen Journal* asking for help. Elwyn Thomas has a written record of the family made from information provided by his father and grandfather. Baby Hannah is shown on the 1851 census living with her parents and elder brother at Glan-rhyd-y-gwiail (NLW Reel 68, Llanybydder). By 1861, the family were at Nantpoth [Nantpoeth], which they had presumably taken over from a relative, Simon Lewis, a shoemaker, who had brought up the young Gwilym Marles (NLW 1861 Reel 55, Llanfihangel ar Arth; Simon Lewis is shown at Nantpoeth in the 1841 return - Reel 10, Llanfihangel ar Arth. Nantpoeth is a few hundred yards from Gelli Grîn). Hannah is at Nantpoeth in 1871 with her mother and her young baby, Anne (Reel 76, Llanfihangel ar Arth) and in the 1881 return. By 1891, Hannah is lodging at Pant-maenog [meinog] farm, Llanfihangel Rhos-y-corn, with her children William and Margaret, living on her own means (Fiche 603.1, Llanybydder). Whilst her great-grandchildren say that some of Hannah's children were love children, the 1871 and 1881

census returns show her as married to a farm labourer, but her name is given as 'Thomas' and he does not appear on the returns. The 1891 return describes her as being single. Telling the census taker that a daughter who had love children was married was a common subterfuge, as was describing such children as nieces or nephews. The grid points for farms mentioned in the text are: Glan-rhyd-y-gwiail SN 558.323; Ty'r-cwm 538.344; Glan-capel-mair 555.329; Rhiw-saith-bren 525.334; Gwargraig 513.428; Pant-maenog 547.335; Gwernogle Bach 529.345; Pentre Evan 546.346; Aberduar 525.441. Some of these farms are now derelict or lost in conifer plantations but all can be seen on the 1907 second edition OS sheets for the area around Brechfa.

60. Information that DJ had a first cousin called Annie Righton came in Colin Edwards' interview with her granddaughter Barbara Treacher. We know from the Treacher interview, and from Carrie's birth certificate, that Annie married William Righton, and that her maiden name was Thomas. We also know from the 1901 census that Annie was born in Brechfa in 1868. The Burman Street address is on Clara's birth certificate. Colin Edwards' interviewee, Hedley Auckland, was the nephew of Alford, Clara's husband. In his interview, Hedley says that Florence Thomas was the sister of Clarrie Auckland. This is incorrect.

61. See the following sources: Eliza (Lisa) – Towns (1995); Lewis – *Carmarthen Journal*, April 27 1934, in which the author also notes that only four children (daughters) were still alive, but one, Mary Emerson died later in the year on December 15. The three children who died young were Minnie, Lewis Williams (1) and Hilda.

62. The family were unable to find the photograph for this book because its owner is suffering from Alzheimer's, and she cannot remember its whereabouts. Dylan appears to have visited Brechfa in 1949: in a letter to John Davenport of October 11, he writes that "I've been getting on with my script, broadcasting from Swansea ... and being a pest up in the wilds here, Mydrim, Brechfa, & Marble Town." Brechfa also appears in one of his jokes – see the Edwards interview with Sidney Evans.

63. I am grateful to Richard E. Huws, Eynon's son, for this information. The family tree is as follows: Dylan's great-grandfather, William Thomas, had a brother called John who, in 1834, married Esther Evans. Their son John Thomas (1843-1918) married Margaret Rees (1855-1919). Their daughter Margaretta (b.1890) married David John Evans (b. 1884), and their daughter Megan (1912-2002) married Eynon Lloyd Hughes (1910-2002). This whole line from John and

Margaret Thomas settled in Abergwili, at Meini Gwynion and then Tycanol, where Eynon and Megan lived until 1955.

64. Dylan called Arthur "the pleasant uncle" (letter to Pamela Hansford Johnson, December 1935). Ferris quotes Arthur's landlady as saying he was "a kind-hearted man who liked his pint, an ordinary sort of man, not educated". According to the interview with Addie Elliott, Arthur had "a quite serious" relationship with a Miss Potts of Port Talbot. She also noted he was a frequent visitor to 5, Cwmdonkin Drive, and Ferris (1999, p.29) mentions the financial help that Arthur gave to DJ and Florence. James Shore Townsend witnessed DJ and Florence's marriage certificate and was presumably DJ's best man.

65. Doris Fulleylove notes in her Edwards interview that from 1922 to her marriage in 1928 she stayed in 5, Cwmdonkin Drive "quite a lot". Randolph Fulleylove confirms that they did their courting at number 5.

Chapter 2 The Insanitary Farms

66. Thomas and Anne are shown on the 1841 census return for the farm. They moved here sometime after the birth of their daughter Anna in March 1840, and before the census of 1841.

67. The information about Sarah and Evan Davies and their children came from Haulwen Morris of Llwyngwyn and Susan Deacon. The 1918 *Register of Electors* shows the Davies family at Pen-y-coed.

68. This information about Evan Williams, John Williams, Dr Dan and Annie came from the Colin Edwards interview with Rees Davies, Brinley Edwards' notes, the minutes of the Llansteffan Parochial Church Council, and details of the public auction of the Lacques Estate on September 2 1882 (the last two of which are in the Carmartheshire Archives). In their interviews with Colin Edwards, Rees Davies and Mary Ann Williams of Llwyngwyn confirm that Annie and Jim started off in Tirbach, before moving to Pentowyn. Idris' birth certificate confirms he was born at Tirbach. (Pentowyn often appears in sources as Pentowin or Pentewyn and Tirbach as Tyrbach). Annie was still living with her parents in St. Thomas at the time of the 1891 Census.

69. In a statement made in 1934 about a boundary dispute, Jim said he had lived at Fernhill for about twenty years – i.e. from about 1909 (Bishop 88/8, Carmarthenshire Archives). We can tell from the *Registers of Electors* that Jim and Annie were at Fernhill in late 1928, but were not there in early 1930. Brinley's notes say that they left Fernhill in 1928.

70 John's ownership: 1910 land values survey; Idris' ownership is noted in the RHIR.

71. The exact relationship of Annie Lewis to the Williamses is not clear but it was confirmed for me by Annie's daughters, Glenys and Dora Lewis. The line is traced back to David Francis (1820-1855*g*) and his wife Margaret (1850-1893*g*) of Dolaumeinion farm. Their children included Mary (1850-1893), Amy of Down farm, Theodosia (1856-1933*g*), Sarah (1860-1944*g*), Jane (1862-1941*g*) and John (1858-1942*g*) who bought Boksberg Hall, Llanllwch, and lived there with his siblings, Theodosia and Jane. Sarah Francis married, first, William Lewis and, second, David Rees of Wernddu farm. David and Sarah (who was first cousin to Anna Evans of Pentowyn), lived at Llettyrneuadd from at least 1910. There were four children from the two marriages: Margaret Jane Lewis (1888-1972*g*) who married William Jones and lived from about 1930 at Pentrewyman farm and from 1953 in Peniel; Annie Rees (1895-1981*g*); Gwen Rees (1898-1908*g*); and Theodosia Rees. These four children were, of course, first cousins of their aunt Amy's six children who lived at Down farm and Laques Newydd, some of whom are mentioned in the report of the funeral of Annie Jones Fernhill as her cousins. About 1917, Annie Rees married Tom George Lewis (1889-1968*g*) of the Ffordd, Llansteffan. They lived at Llettyrneuadd all their married life, and had Colin (1917-1993*g*); Dora (1918-) who inherited Boksberg Hall; Glenys (1920-); Meriel (1923-2000*g*) and Elena (1930-2002*g*). None of these five children married. Most of this family from David and Margaret Francis onwards is buried in Smyrna, Llangain. (Information given to me by Dora and Glenys Lewis, and from Smyrna gravestones.)

72. The farm is sometimes spelled Maesgwynne. There is no consistency in spelling over time or from one archive to another. The same is true of nearby Maesgwynne Mansion, lived in by the Carver family.

73. Brinnin, 1965, p.199. Sarah's age at the time was eighty-two, not the ninety-six reported by Brinnin.

74. Bob's ownership is confirmed by the RHIR, and the date of his arrival, and Polly's, at Blaencwm by the *Registers of Electors*. Dan's ownership: 1910 land values survey.

75. DJ and Florence are on the *Register of Electors* at 2, Blaencwm in 1948, and Idris thereafter. John's ownership: 1910 land values survey.

76. The survey for the 1910 *Duties on Land Values* shows Robert Williams as the owner of Rose Cottage. Robert and Anne were living in the cottage in the 1918 and 1919 *Register of Electors*, but not in the Registers for 1920 and 1921 – they may have moved to another house. According to the 1910 survey, Robert Williams appears also to have owned Bryngollen and Anne Williams a cottage called Brynhyfryd. See the

interviews with Doris Fulleylove and Ocky Owen on Dylan's Llansteffan holidays.

77. Brinley Edwards makes no mention of Pwntan-bach. In her interview with Colin Edwards, Mary Ann Williams of Llwyngwyn refers to the farm in relation to the Pentrewyman children. Idris Jones' funeral notice refers to a cousin, Les Davies of Pwntan-bach. Haulwen Morris of Llwyngwyn directed me to Olwen Davies, Les' sister, and to other family and friends, including Maralyn and Derek John. Olwen was born in 1912, and Les at Pwntan-bach in 1914*b*. Their father Henry died in 1944*g*, and their mother Mary in 1963*g*. Les died in 2001*g*. Pwntan-bach is today called Greenacres.

78. The *Carmarthen Journal* gave just the last names of the mourners but I have added the first names, taken from the *Register of Electors*. Dyffryn Tawel was the cottage just up the road from Blaencwm. Roseanna Thomas was married to Freddie Thomas. Gerwyn Thomas, who was probably their son, was left some money in Bob Williams' Will in 1962 – see Chapter 4.

Chapter 3 Aunts and Uncles

79. *Western Mail*, November 14 1980. Jim Jones' grand ideas of being a gentleman farmer may have come from his father, Richard, who had four servants on his Pentrewyman farm (1871 census).

80. Westgate, 'Wales and the World', in the *Western Mail*, November 25 1980. Westgate had asked for more information about Idris following the November 14 item. Brinley Edwards notes that Idris worked as a shop assistant in the Ben Evans store, Swansea, but there is no confirmation.

81. *Carmarthen Journal*, January 19 1940.

82. Though note that her cousin, D.J. Williams of 61, Windmill Terrace, St. Thomas, was a copper mill manager, and helped to finance her house in New Quay (information from John Williams' death certificate, and the title deeds of Wendawel, New Quay).

83. *Carmarthen Journal*, February 24 and March 3 1939.

Chapter 4 The Family Finances

84. I am grateful to Mr C. Jenkins for this information from the title deeds.

85. A piece in the GWR staff magazine says that George retired after forty-one years service. If this is correct, then it suggests that George started working on the railways in Carmarthen in 1864, the year his son, John, was born in Llanllwch (GWR staff magazine, PRO, Kew, researched by Susan Deacon).

86. Mary Ann Williams, interview with Colin Edwards. The information

on Annie of Pencelly Uchaf buying Mount Pleasant for the Joneses came from Haulwen Morris of Llwyngwyn.

87. Though both he and his brother Bob had to pay rent to their father – £12 p.a. each, according to the Burgesses Roll of 1903-4. John owned 1, Bay View Terrace (rented out at £12 p.a.) and 6, Kilvey Terrace. He may also have owned another house; when his widow Elizabeth Ann moved to New Quay, her address on the legal documents was 2, Bay View, but it's not clear whether she or John had bought it. It's also the address on John's death certificate in 1911.

88. Valuation Lists for Delhi Street, 1929/30, Swansea Archives. It appears Bob owned only numbers 29 and 30: Thompson (1965) talks of Bob owning two houses in St. Thomas, and Haulwen Morris of Llwyngwyn told me that "Bob had two rents in St. Thomas."

89. The house was bought from Henry Tulloch Hoskin (Gentleman of 24 Cwmdonkin Terrace) and William Henry Harding (Builder of The Grove, Uplands, Swansea). I am grateful to Kevin Lane, the present owner of 5, Cwmdonkin Drive, for supplying information about the house from the title deeds. Thanks to James A. Davies for the information about the insurance on the house.

90. Gwilym Evans, a medical student and distant relative, 1919-1921 (Colin Edwards' interviews).

91. A trawl of Swansea estate agents and the Swansea Archives brought nothing on house values in the Uplands during the 1920s and 1930s. Information in the *Evening Post* of the time is scant, but its property columns do carry some indications: a house going in Cwmdonkin Terrace in 1932 for £550, one in Sketty with four bedrooms for £550 in 1936, and another the same year in Glanmor Road for £650, this one with five bedrooms.

92. £4 to £5 a month plus the payment of rates was the going charge for renting a house in the Uplands at the time, as gleaned from the property column of the *Evening Post*. The rent at Bishopston is suggested in the following extract from Brinley Edwards' notes: Dylan's parents "stayed on one month because the woman would not pay £1.10s for a load of manure which had been delivered and dumped in the garden." The story about the manure can also be found in the Colin Edwards interview with George Guy. This interview contains some other information about the stay at Bishopston.

93. I am grateful to Kevin Lane for providing Jacob Plosker's name, and to James A. Davies for the selling price.

94. The information about the lodgers comes from Gordon Burns' article in the *Radio Times*, October 26 1972.

Chapter 5 The Fernhill Hangman

95. I am grateful to Eiluned Rees for drawing to my attention this advert from the *Carmarthen Journal*, February 24 1832.

96. Griffith E. Owen deposit, 643-654. No diary was kept for 1862.

97. National Library of Wales – MS 12357E, pp.1353 and 1358. It shows parts of Ricketts Evans' and Maria's family trees, with some narrative added. A photocopy of this document was first shown to me by Robert and Liz Evans. Robert is Ricketts Evans' great-grandson, and I am grateful to Robert and Liz for their generous help in writing this chapter. Ricketts Evans' birth was announced in the *Transactions of the Carmarthen Antiquarian Society and Field Club*, vol. 10, p.49. The birth year is confirmed by his second marriage certificate and his death certificate. Evan Evans is named in the *Transactions* report as his father, and on Ricketts Evans' first and second marriage certificates. Evan Evans was born in 1793 and his wife Frances in 1798; he died March 13 1831 and she September 1 1823. The register for St Peter's also has the following burials: Louisa Rickets Anderson, aged 4, buried May 18 1816; and Robert Anderson, aged five months, buried January 6 1816. Ricketts Evans had other relatives living in and around Carmarthen including, as his diaries note, a Miss Ricketts living in Llansteffan. (I am grateful to Terry Wells and Edna Dale-Jones for this information about Evan and Frances and the two children.)

98. The information on John Davies' ownership of Fernhill, and the details about his Will, is found in the NLW archive document and in a number of legal documents in the Carmarthenshire Archives – Trant 457. One document in Trant 457 gives the date of Davies' death as May 31 1828, and another as June 7 1828. I am very grateful to Edna Dale-Jones for drawing the Trant documents to my attention.

99. The postnuptial settlement was made on March 9 1843 – see Trant 457 in the Carmarthenshire Archives.

100. Details of Maria's death, together with her marriage to "Roberts Ricketts Evans of Fern Hill", are on a tablet in the parish church of Llangynog. The church tablet incorrectly gives Maria's age as 24; she was 23. I am grateful to the Rev. Illtyd Protheroe for supplying the details from the tablet. Maria's death certificate gives the cause of death as "disease of the heart after an attack of Rheumatism". Ricketts Evans' first name is sometimes given in sources as 'Robert' and sometimes as 'Roberts'. The information on Maria's intestacy and the grant of administration was given to me by the Family Records Centre, London.

101. Trant 457.

102. Johnny (b. August 11 1855); William Edward Gravel Evans (b.

September 7 1856, d. March 1884), who was in the Metropolitan Fire Brigade, and died unmarried; and Robert (b. 1868), a seaman. Johnny's and William's births are noted in the diaries. Robert married a May Griffiths; their son, Fred, married Megan Phillips; and their son, Robert, married Elizabeth Morgan. Robert and Liz live in Llansteffan today.

103. Henry Blumberg was born on April 12 1829 in the town of Kaschan into "a distinguished Hungarian family, his great-grandfather having been Hungarian Ambassador to St Petersburg." He studied medicine at Vienna university and when the uprising took place in 1848 against Austrian rule, Blumberg took command, with the rank of captain, of student volunteer soldiers, and was present at the siege of Vienna. When the uprising was quelled, he was forced to leave Hungary and eventually arrived in England in 1856. Two years later he became an Extraordinary Licentiate of the Royal College of Physicians. In 1860, he founded the North of England Children's Sanatorium in Southport, "the first seaside hospital for convalescent children in this country", and one that used homoeopathic treatments. Blumberg helped found the town's Literary and Philosophical Society in 1880, to which he contributed a number of papers, including 'Medicine of the Future', 'Three Poets of Despair – Heine, Alfred de Masset and Swinburne', 'Is Life Worth Living?' 'Emerson and Schopenhauer, or, Optimism and Pessimism' and 'A Sketch of the History of Philosophy'. He published two books of poems in German, and one with poems in both English and German. Blumberg also delivered the Hahnemann Lecture at the London Homoeopathic Hospital in October 1883. He opposed animal vivisection and compulsory vaccination. He played chess and was once chosen for the North of England team. He was a borough magistrate from 1880 onwards. (Taken from Blumberg's obituary, *Southport Visiter* (*sic*), June 6 1893). The description of Blumberg's appearance is taken from a patient's tribute in the *Stockport Journal*, March 19 1926.

104. We know it is Frances' writing because it matches her signature on legal documents e.g. NLW/W.C.C/ECE/EL/SD 116.

105. Taken from Blumberg's obituary.

106. What property did Frances have? Entries in Ricketts Evans' diaries show that he was collecting rents from fifteen properties in Carmarthenshire during his daughter's teenage years. The diaries of John Barker, Frances' solicitor, note that in 1867 he was collecting fourteen rents on her behalf. In the 1910 land value survey, Frances is shown as the owner of Fernhill and its fifteen acres, eighty-eight acres

at neighbouring Glogddu, land at nearby Blaentir farm, and a piece of land called Millbank, all in Llangynog parish; land of two acres called Caecud in Llangunnor parish; and land described as "Part of Dyffryn Pontyates" in Llangendeirne. Her father's obituary in the *Western Mail* notes she also owned property in Carmarthen – this included numbers 24-27 Abergwili, mentioned in the diary of her solicitor, John Barker, on October 14 1865, and a parcel of land at Abergwili mentioned in NLW/W.C.C/ECE/EL/SD116.

107. John Barker's office diaries for the years 1863 to 1899 are in the National Library of Wales – G.E. Owen deposit, 661-697.

108. It is possible Frances invited Henry to Llangollen – Ricketts Evans' diary for January 9 1863 says "Paid for lodgings at Birch Cottage as she was going to fetch B. home".

109. In 1867, Henry and Frances moved to Ventnor, and then to Southampton and Bournemouth. They lived at 4, Royal Parade, Cheltenham for three years before moving to Bonn and Kreuznach, in Germany, in 1873. They returned to Southport in 1877, to 65, Hoghton Street, and ten years later moved to Warley House, 13, Duke Street.

110. Frances and Henry's children were Henry b. December 24 1867 in Ventnor, Samuel b.1870 in Cheltenham, Gustav b.1871 in Cheltenham, Rosalia b.1873 in Germany and Edith b.1876 in Germany. *Henry* was a surgeon, linguist and an authority on aspects of Hungarian and American literature. He wrote poems, and those about the First World War, during which he was awarded the OBE (Military Division) and the *Croix de Guerre*, were published in *The Poetry Review* (September 1916 and January 1917). Like his father before him, he delivered several papers on poetry at the Southport Literary and Philosophical Society. He married Ella Frances in 1918, and died on December 24 1932. There is more about Henry in Johnson's *Streets Apart* (1995). *Samuel* was a music student in 1881, and later became a music teacher in Liverpool and then a professor of music. He died unmarried aged 40 in Glasgow in 1909. *Gustav* studied art in London at the Slade School, lived in Dusseldorf and Paris, and returned to London to work as a secretary. He published poems and short stories, one of which appeared in the suffragette paper, *Votes for Women*, in December 1909. *The Times* once attributed one of his anonymously published poems to the Poet Laureate. He also co-authored a play, *The Making of a Marriage*, which was very loosely based on his parents' elopement. A collection of his and Henry's prose and poems was published in 1934. He died unmarried in March 1932 in Kensington. *Rosalia* studied music under Sir Charles Hallé at the Royal Manchester

College of Music, and throughout her life played an active part in the cultural and civic life of Southport. She died unmarried in January 1966. I have no information on *Edith* Blumberg except that she assisted at the Children's Sanatorium and was active in the St John's Ambulance Brigade. She died unmarried in October 1926. (Taken from the Blumberg archive, Southport Public Library, and notes supplied to me by Gill Hamilton and Christine Beard.)

111. The quotation is from the NLW archive document. The legal papers are held today by Robert and Liz Evans. The 1874 document shows that he was accurately described as a Gentleman Farmer: his animals amounted to no more than "1 horse, 5 Milch cows 1 two year old heifer 1 calf 1 Bull and 2 pigs." Details of Mary Ann's marriage are taken from the marriage certificate, now in the possession of Robert and Liz Evans. A few years later, Mary Ann left Ricketts Anderson and moved into a house on The Green, Llansteffan, taking many of the contents of Fernhill that had been made over to her. Another housekeeper, Ann Thomas, was soon found. She is shown living at Fernhill in the 1881 census. By the time of the 1891 census, Ann and Ricketts Anderson had a son, Louis, aged four. Mary Ann Anderson died on November 22 1903.

112. Details of the court cases are in Trant 457. There are no documents that show the eventual outcome of the dispute, but we know, of course, that when Ricketts Evans died in 1901, he was followed about 1909 as tenant at Fernhill by Jim and Annie Jones, who paid their rent to Frances Blumberg until her death in 1911.

113. The three trustees appointed in Frances' Will included the Rev. Evan Jones of Llangain Vicarage. Fernhill appears to have been sold to a J. Williams in 1929, and Evan Jones' daughter was involved in the sale. Those wishing to pursue this should consult Bishop 88/8 in the Carmarthenshire Archives.

114. Indeed his offer to carry out the execution of David Rees in 1888 at Carmarthen prison was declined, and the job was done by Berry, with whom Anderson later became friends. See *Carmarthen Journal* March 16 1888 and Anderson's obituary.

115. Quoted in Bland 1984, p45. Robert and Liz Evans have a photocopy of the original letter. Ricketts Evans' diary notes that he had first met William Calcraft on July 16 1858. There are letters to, and meetings with, Calcraft and the Newgate governor throughout 1858 and 1859. As his diary describes, Ricketts Evans helped Calcraft on April 5 1859 at the execution of Frederick Prentice at Maidstone.

Chapter 6 Life at Blaencwm

116. Rose Walters Roberts, a school friend of Nancy's, interviewed by Colin Edwards. Dylan's first known letter is to Nancy at Blaencwm; he teases her about moving "in the gayest Llangain society". Levi Evans also describes the young Dylan being left at Llangain whilst his mother returned to Swansea (Colin Edwards archive notes).

117. See Nancy's letter to Haydn Taylor, quoted in Ferris, 1999, p.66.

118. On the day of Annie's funeral, the Little Theatre would have been doing the final rehearsals for *The Merry Wives of Windsor*, which opened on February 13. Dylan played the Host of the Garter.

119. Information provided by Mary Phillips, granddaughter of Thomas and Catherine Thomas. Thomas and Catherine were both at Annie Jones' funeral, and are shown in the list of mourners in *The Welshman*, February 17 1933.

120. I am grateful to James A. Davies for supplying this information from his notes of Hansford Johnson's diary entries.

121. Information about these visits from Whitsun 1934 is taken from Glyn Jones, *Western Mail*, April 24 1958 and Dylan's letters to Glyn Jones of March 1935, Richard Hughes of early April 1935 and George Reavey and Richard Hughes of April 1938.

122. Information given to me by Austin Davies and Michael Lowndes; and by Ocky Owen to Colin Edwards. Glyn Jones also told Edwards about Edgeworth Williams, but Williams was too ill to be interviewed. During the war, Williams moved into The Elms, Llansteffan, where he became a local 'character', seen always with his corgi, Monty, or pruning in his Vine House, the first to be built in the village.

123. The information on the wedding came from Huw Johns and Edwards' interview with Ocky Owen. Dylan writes about Keidrych Rhys' wedding in his letters to Vernon Watkins of September 29 and October 8, 1939, and Lynette Roberts (1983) has also given an account.

124. Interview with Lady Snow, NET, undated, in the Colin Edwards archive. Letter to Caitlin, August 1945. Hobbs is the carrier mentioned by Dylan in his June 5 1947 letter to his parents. The visit to London is mentioned in Emrys Morris' interview with Edwards.

125. On his trips to the Farmers' Arms, Dylan would again be walking his family tree. He would leave Blaencwm, walk down the drive to Llwyngwyn and take the track across the fields to Maesgwyn, with Tirbach off to the right. Then onto the country road to Llanybri, passing by the standing stone, Maen Melyn.

126. Information from Mair Lewis (née Harries) to David Thomas. The Lundy trip is referred to in Dylan's letter of August 5 1949.

127. They had tea at Môr Awelon, the Manse in Llansteffan. Hopkin Evans was also the minister at Smyrna, Llangain, and Bethel, Llansteffan. He was a well-read and cultured man, who ran the local drama group.

Chapter 7 Dylan on the Stage

128. The reviews of the Trecynon and Ammanford performances are in the *Evening Post*, January 21 and February 8 1932, respectively.

129. *Faith*, written by Little Theatre producer E.H. Davies, was put on as part of a playwriting competition organised by the Joint Committee for the Promotion of Educational Facilities in the South Wales and Monmouthshire Coalfields. The *Mumbles Press* reports other such competitions but the cast lists are not always given.

200. I am grateful to Robert Williams for this information.

Index

This index is replete with Williamses, Thomases and Joneses, not to mention a few Evanses and Davieses. For many, I have indicated their relationship to Dylan's mother, Florence, or to his father, DJ. I have not included very distant relations, but have noted them in the entry for parents or grandparents.

David Thomas' other books include

Organising for Social Change
Skills in Neighbourhood Work (with Paul Henderson)
The Making of Community Work
White Bolts, Black Locks: Participation in the Inner City
Oil on Troubled Waters: the Gulbenkian Foundation and Social Welfare

Dylan Thomas: A Farm, Two Mansions and a Bungalow
The Dylan Thomas Trail
The Dylan Thomas Murders